CANDIDATE

Second Edition

GW00383420

FIRST CERTIFICATE PRACTICE TESTS

5 complete exams for teaching and testing

K. Lukey-Coutsocostas and D. Dalmaris

Joyu Chan.

Prentice Hall

London   New York   Toronto   Sydney   Tokyo   Singapore
Madrid   Mexico City   Munich   Paris

Published in 1998 by
Prentice Hall Europe
A division of Simon & Schuster International
Campus 400, Spring Way
Maylands Avenue, Hemel Hempstead
Hertfordshire, HP2 7EZ

© International Book Distributors Ltd, 1996

0–13–521683–4   Without Key Edition
0–13–521659–1   With Key Edition

Designed by Derek Lee
Typeset by Fakenham Photosetting Ltd, Fakenham, Norfolk
Illustrated by 1–11 Line Art and Mike Lacey of
Simon Girling & Associates
Cassettes produced by James Richardson at Audio Workshop
Printed and bound in Malta by Interprint Limited

Library of Congress Cataloging-in-publication Data can be
obtained from the publisher on request

British Library Cataloguing-in-publication Data

A catalogue record for this book is available from the British
Library

5   4   3
1999   98

Acknowledgements

The authors wish to thank: Karen Jamieson, Bella Dietschi, Andrew
Jurascheck and Diana Bateman for their editorial assistance and
support, Jill Grimshaw and Anne Gutch of UCLES for answering
our endless questions about the FCE revised format, Ian Robertson
for his comments on the original hints section of the Speaking Paper,
Frances J. Kaltsikes, Eleni Photiou and Philippa Jecchinis for their in-
valuable 'hands on' help at the end.

To Yanni and Gigi, for their encouragement and loving support.
*To my former colleagues at the George Christopoulos School of Foreign
Languages: George, Mary, Helen, Rania, Eleni, Litsa, Stathi, Theti,
Margarita, Manoli and Yanni.*
*To the hundreds of students I taught there: thank you for sharing eight
years of my life. Remember, if you search for answers, you may find them.
Pity those who never search.*

Kathryn

*To my patient and understanding husband, Theo, and my children, Peter,
Johnny and Eleftheria.*
*To the many students I have taught over the years who have always been a
source of encouragement and shown an interest in my 'other' activities.*

Despena

**The authors and publishers would like to thank the following for
permission to reproduce copyright material:**

Jeffrey Archer for *Not a Penny More, Not a Penny Less*; Blake
Friedmann Literary, TV & Film Agency for *Pay any price* by Ted
Allbeury; British Virgin Islands Club, Redcrest © Adpartners,
Ramblers Holidays, adrift, Exodus, Ski Peak for their holiday ad-
verts; Curtis Brown on behalf of the estate of Gerald Durrell for *Two
in the Bush* © Gerald Durrell 1966; *The Daily Mail* for 'Why we are
dry-ski freaks', by David Allsop (1994) © Daily Mail/Soho; *The
European* for 'Parched Spain prays for rain' by Giles Tremlett (1995),
'At the heart of things' by Mariann Grønnestad (1995) and 'Time off
with Ballantynes' (1995) © The Financial Times; Ewan Macnaughton
Associates for 'The pies have it after a slice of part time work' by

Charlotte Beugge (1993) © The Telegraph plc, London, 1993; GEO
Australia for 'Wrapped in snakes' by Christopher Innocent (Vol 16
No. 6); *Greek News Weekly* for 'Bats are nocturnal, but not as black as
painted' by Anna Harisson, 'Bad packaging – what not to buy' by
Elizabeth Koubena and 'On Health – what do you do when you lose
your job?' by Elizabeth Koubena; *The Guardian* for 'How the west has
won' by Kimberley Leston (1994); Penguin UK for 'My Oedipus
Complex' *The stories of Frank O'Connor* by Frank O'Connor, © Frank
O'Connor (1953) Reproduced by permission of Hamish Hamilton
Ltd; Little, Brown and Company for *Triple* by Ken Follett; Nails
Magazine for 'If the shoe fits' © 1995 NAILS Magazine; Reader's
Digest (Australia) for the extract from the book *Country Australia*;
Rollerworld, Colchester for the use of their advert; Peters, Fraser and
Dunlop for *Not for glory, not for gold* by Keith Miles, published by
Century Hutchinson (1986); Piatkus Books for *A murder of crows* by
Margaret Duffy (1987); *The Sunday Times* for 'Your exclusive tickets
to the best seats' (1992) and 'Hard night for a policewoman on the
front line' by Francesca Nelson (1993) © Times Newspapers Limited
1992/1993; The Walt Disney Company for 'Disneyland, Paris';
World Wide Fund For Nature International for the animal factsheets.

The answer sheets on pages 115–118 are reproduced by permission
of the University of Cambridge Local Examinations Syndicate.

Photographic acknowledgements:
Barnaby's Picture Library: pp. 123 (TR, BL), 124 (B), 125 (T), 126 (T),
128 (B), 129 (B) and 130 (BL); Life File: p. 129 (T); Rex Features Ltd: pp.
123 (BR), 127 (B) and 130 (TL); Robert Harding Picture Library: pp.
123 (TL), 124 (T), 125 (B), 127 (T) and 130 (TR); Sally & Richard
Greenhill: pp. 126 (B), 128 (T) and 130 (BR).

Contents

Breakdown of the examination

5 papers – 200 marks

Paper 1   Reading
(1 hour 15 minutes) 40 marks – 35 questions

Part 1
6–7 multiple matching questions on a reading text or texts
Recommended time – 15 minutes

Part 2
7–8 multiple choice questions (A–D) on a reading text or texts
Recommended time – 20 minutes

Part 3
6–7 gap filling questions on a reading text or texts
Recommended time – 20 minutes

Part 4
13–15 multiple matching (and multiple choice) questions on a reading text or texts
Recommended time – 20 minutes

Possible reading texts: a factual description, a practical text, a fictional text, a personal text

Answers: on an optically scanned answer sheet

Paper 2   Writing
($1\frac{1}{2}$ hours) 40 marks – 2 tasks (each 120–180 words)

Part 1
Compulsory transactional letter (usually semi-formal)
Recommended time – 45 minutes

Part 2
Choice of 4 tasks: these could be a non-transactional letter (usually informal), article, report or composition (discursive, descriptive and/or narrative). One will be on a prescribed background reading text.
Recommended time – 45 minutes

Answers: in a question paper booklet

Paper 3   Use of English
(1 hour 15 minutes) 40 marks – 65 questions

Part 1
15 multiple choice cloze questions (A–D)
Recommended time – 15 minutes

Part 2
15 open cloze questions
Recommended time – 15 minutes

Part 3
10 'key' word transformation questions
Recommended time – 15 minutes

Part 4
15 error correction questions
   Recommended time – 15 minutes

Part 5
10 word formation questions
   Recommended time – 15 minutes

Answers: on an answer sheet

Paper 4 Listening
(approximately 40 minutes) 40 marks – 30 questions

Part 1
8 multiple choice questions (A–C) on 8 short, unrelated listening texts

Part 2
10 note taking or blank filling questions on 1 long listening text

Part 3
5 multiple matching questions on 5 short, related listening texts

Part 4
7 two or three answer questions (e.g. true/false, yes/no, who is speaking, multiple choice) on 1 long listening text

Answers: on the exam paper, then transferring to an answer sheet

Paper 5 Speaking
(approximately 15 minutes) 40 marks
two candidates, two examiners

Part 1 (4 minutes)
Questions regarding personal background of each candidate

Part 2 (4 minutes)
Questions regarding a different set of two theme-related pictures for each candidate

Part 3 (3 minutes)
Task based on a visual stimulus (e.g. photograph or line drawing) for candidates to perform together

Part 4 (4 minutes)
Questions regarding subject discussed in Part 3 for candidates to discuss together

Note: in exceptional circumstances there may be one candidate and one examiner (approximately 10 minutes)

Preparation for the exam

A week before the exam, go to the examination centre so that you do not waste time looking for the centre on the day of the exam. It is a good idea to go to bed early the night before the exam, so that you can wake up fresh and early the next day. In the morning, read a few pages in English aloud just to warm yourself up. Make sure that you arrive at the examination centre half an hour before your exam starts, so that you do not feel rushed. If you are late, your work may not be accepted.

Remember to take these items with you: proof of identification, your exam registration paper, two sharp soft pencils (type B or HB is recommended), two pens and a rubber. You must use pencil for the optically scanned answer sheets (Reading, Use of English and Listening) and pen for the question paper booklet (Writing). You may use correction fluid or tape in the question paper booklet (Writing), but not on the answer sheets (Reading, Use of English and Listening). You are NOT allowed to take these items with you: books, notes, bags.

You may be asked to write your name, centre number and candidate number on answer sheets; you can find these on your exam registration paper. If this information is already on the answer sheets, check that it is correct; inform the person in charge if it is not. Do not turn over or open test papers until told. While you are writing, the person in charge informs you of the time at regular intervals. You can ask for scrap paper to make notes during some of the exams. You are not allowed to speak to another student during the exam; copies of the seating plan are kept. When you finish, leave all test papers, answer sheets and scrap papers on your desk.

Marking

A grade of A, B or C is a pass. Most students pass with a C. A grade of D, E or U is a fail. There is no 'set' pass grade for each paper. In general, the expected level for the typical C candidate is 60% for all papers, except for the Writing Paper, for which it is 40%.

You do not have to pass all the papers in order to pass the First Certificate. Your overall performance is evaluated and an average is taken from all of your papers. If there is any doubt about your marks, the papers are checked by other examiners.

The information given in this book is correct at the time of printing. However, it is sometimes necessary for the University of Cambridge Local Exams Syndicate to make changes. Please read all literature released by the Exams Syndicate to stay up-to-date.

Letter to the student

Dear Student,

You are learning English because you want to communicate with other English-speaking people. However, how do you know if you have learnt English well? One quick and fairly reliable way is to take a test.

In the final year of preparation for the Cambridge First Certificate in English examination, our experience has shown that students have to concentrate on three main areas:

1 revising grammar
2 building vocabulary
3 learning the test format

This book deals with the test format; the more familiar a student is with the format, the better he or she does. We have tried to include all of the suggestions we make to our students in the course of a school year. Read the suggestions in each unit, and then try to follow them while working on the material provided.

At first it may seem strange to structure your work – for example, to make a plan for your composition – but if you do it every time, you will see that you will get much faster at it. Soon you will be doing it automatically.

This book TEACHES you how to approach the exam tasks, and then TESTS how well you perform. We wish you success in the final test, the Cambridge First Certificate in English.

Best regards,

Kathryn Lukey-Coutsocostas   Despena Dalmaris

TEST 1

Paper 1 Reading (1 hour 15 minutes)

PART 1

*You are going to read a newspaper article about jeans. Choose from the list **A–I** the heading which best summarises each part (**1–7**) of the article. There is one extra heading which you do not need to use. There is an example at the beginning (**0**).*

A	The changes are many
B	Jeans make money
C	A film star start
D	A reflection of character
E	Teenagers love them
F	Three brands lead
G	Two things required
H	Styles come and go
I	Owned by many

HOW THE WEST HAS WON

0	B	**I**

One in two men and four in 10 women under 45 buy at least one pair of jeans each year.

1	C

That's a whole lot of denim, with Levi's flattening all in its wake with 22 per cent of the entire market, followed by Pepe and Wrangler with an annual battle for second place and the serried ranks of countless lesser-known brands bringing up the rear. We have become so used to the presence of this western uniform that we have forgotten what an amazing achievement it is for any single piece of clothing to be so popular for so many years.

2	

Few people know or care about the social origins of neck-ties or short skirts, but the purely functional roots of jeans as good old boy American workwear remain

PAPER 1
Reading

The Paper
This paper has four parts, each with a long text (or two or more shorter related texts) and questions. Parts 1 and 4 are multiple matching questions. Part 2 is a multiple choice question, and Part 3 is a gap filling question. There are 35 questions in the paper.

This paper tests you on how well you can understand general meanings as well as specific information. You may also be tested on information that you can deduce from the text ('reading between the lines'). It takes 1 hour 15 minutes.

PART 1

General hints
Question types

This part is multiple matching. You are given a list of prompts (paragraph headings, summary sentences or visuals) and must match them to the correct paragraphs (six or seven). The first question is always the example and is numbered (0). There is always one extra prompt.

Answering strategy

1 Look at the instructions, title and layout for information about the text. Cross off the example that has been used.
2 Read the whole list of prompts, circling key words/ideas which might match key words/ideas in the text.
3 Read the text under the first missing heading to get the gist (the general meaning). Read down the list of prompts until you find

one which fits. Underline the key words/ideas in the text which match the key words/ideas in the prompt. The key words/ideas in the text usually come after the missing heading.
4 Read the other prompts. Then mark the right answer on the answer sheet. Cross off prompts as you use them.
5 When finished, read the whole text through again, checking your answers. Do not use prompts twice.

vital to their popularity over a century later. Ever since Brando and Dean wore jeans (Levi's and Lee) in their cinematic refusal to accept society's rules of behaviour, they have been the most popular informal dress ever.

3 G

Designer jeans greatly increased in popularity after they were first introduced by Gloria Vanderbilt, and it has developed into an important branch of designer fashion. Paul Smith, whose own jeans check out at nearly 60 pounds, explains, 'Jeans have never really been out. They have more important periods than others but they are always around. Designers do their own because it's a good way of profiting from their brand name.' In other words, there's money in it and though it would take a colossal amount of the stuff to get rid of Levi's, the public is always ready to buy up new styles or change a particular brand's cool rating.

4 D

So effectively do jeans satisfy those two great and differing human needs, to be like everybody else and to be different from everybody else, that they will always find a way of reinventing themselves to fit every social and economic group.

5 A

I remember going to the first showing of black Levi's in the early eighties, before black had established itself as the colour of the '80s. They actually seemed far too strange at the time. Since then, jean styling has gone through several changes, from snow-washed through marbled, stretch, striped, torn, ankle-zipped, baggy and back to flared out at the ankle.

6 C

As Ashley Heath, associate editor of *The Face*, says, 'If anything is going to make masses of people look really stupid, it's jeans.' He calculates that it takes two months for these different designs to go from an idea in the designer's head to the shops; then they slowly fade out of the shops.

7 I

The single most important item of clothing to emerge in the last 50 years, the most widely-worn uniform ever to be adopted by successive generations, jeans still appear to say less about fashion than they do about you. No one wants to wear their heart on their sleeve but few people can resist wearing a little piece of their soul on their rear end.

PART 2

You are going to read an extract from a book. For questions 8–15, choose the answer (A, B, C or D) which you think fits best according to the text.

The car braked. One of its headlights had gone out, the one that had hit Lars, he supposed. It moved slowly, as if the driver were hesitating. Then it gathered speed and, one-eyed, it disappeared into the night.

Tyrin bent over Lars. The other sailors gathered around, speaking Swedish. Tyrin touched Lars' leg. He yelled out in pain.

'I think his leg is broken,' Tyrin said. *Thank God that's all.*

Lights were going on in some of the buildings around the square. One of the officers said something, and one ran off toward a house presumably to call for an ambulance. There was more rapid dialogue and somebody else went off in the direction of the dock.

Lars was bleeding, but not too heavily. The officer bent over him. He would not allow anyone to touch his leg.

The ambulance arrived within minutes, but it seemed forever to Tyrin: he had never killed a man, and he did not want to.

They put Lars on a stretcher. The officer got into the ambulance, and turned to speak to Tyrin. 'You had better come.'

'Yes.'

'You saved his life, I think.'

'Oh.'

He got into the ambulance with the officer.

They sped through the wet streets, the flashing blue light on the roof casting an unpleasant glow over the buildings. Tyrin sat in the back, unable to look at Lars or the officer, unwilling to look out of the windows like a tourist, not knowing where to direct his eyes. He had done many unkind things in the service of his country and Colonel Rostov – he had taped conversations of lovers for blackmail, he had shown terrorists how to make bombs, he had helped capture people who would later be tortured – but he had never been forced to ride in the ambulance with his victim. He did not like it.

They arrived at the hospital. The ambulance men carried the stretcher inside. Tyrin and the officer were shown where to wait. And, suddenly, the rush was over. They had nothing to do but worry. Tyrin was astonished to look at the plain electric clock on the hospital wall and see that it was not yet midnight. It seemed hours since they had left the pub.

Part 2

Specific hints
Question types

You are given multiple choice questions and must answer the questions or complete the sentences. The questions and correct answers often paraphrase what is in the text (express the meaning of the text in different words). The incorrect answers try to distract you by using incorrect facts or ideas. Incorrect answers can: say the opposite of what is true, use exactly the same words as the text, misuse some words from the text, or present believable (but wrong) answers.

Exercise on paraphrasing

As a small boy, I can remember being very bad. I would always get out of the small jobs my parents gave me to do around the house. I would also always get into fights with my brothers and sisters. I was not the perfect son, and must have made my parents very angry. They should have punished me more severely.
Question:
When the author was young,
A he was helpful.
B he was part of a large family.
C he did not know his father.
D he lived in a flat.
Answer:
A no: *I would always get out of the small jobs* means that he was not helpful, so this is incorrect.
B yes: *my brothers and sisters* is another way of saying the writer had a large family.
C no: *my parents . . . They should have punished me* means that he did know his father, so this is incorrect.
D no: *around the house* probably means that they lived in a house, and there is no other evidence proving that they lived in a flat, so this is incorrect.

PART 2

General hints
Question types

This part is multiple choice. You are asked to read a text and then answer seven or eight multiple choice questions. The questions either ask a direct question (e.g. *What does the actress believe?*), or ask you to complete a statement (e.g. *The actress believes that . . .*) You are given four options, A, B, C or D. Only *one* answer is correct.

Answering strategy

1 Look at the instructions, title and layout.
2 Read the whole text through carefully. Ask yourself: *What's this text about? What's the main point?*
3 Read the first question, but not the given A, B, C or D answers. They may confuse you.
4 Read the text through again, and find the lines or words that relate to the question. Underline them.

5 Read the four options given. When you find one which says the same as the text, mark it on the answer sheet.
6 Go on to read the next question, keeping in mind that the answers are usually found in the same order in the text.

8 Lars had been hit by
  A an elderly driver.
  B a vehicle.
  C someone who stayed to inquire about his health.
  D a flying object.

9 How did Tyrin feel about Lars' injury?
  A happy
  B unsympathetic
  C relieved
  D embarrassed

10 Where had the accident happened?
  A in the countryside
  B in a city or town
  C right next to a hospital
  D on the dock

11 Before the accident, Tyrin
  A had wanted to kill people.
  B had occasionally killed people.
  C hadn't killed anybody.
  D had killed many times.

12 Why did the officer ask Tyrin to come with him?
  A He was suspicious.
  B He thought Tyrin could give him some information.
  C He was worried about Lars' condition.
  D He wanted to arrest Tyrin.

13 What was Tyrin's opinion of the work he had done before this?
  A He did not like it.
  B He did not mind it.
  C He was proud of it.
  D He was shocked by it.

14 Who had planned Lars' accident?
  A the driver of the car
  B a Swedish sailor
  C Lars himself
  D Tyrin himself

15 In the hospital, how did Tyrin feel about Lars' condition?
  A unkind
  B astonished
  C anxious
  D satisfied

PART 3

You are going to read an extract from a book. Seven sentences have been removed from the extract. Choose from the sentences A–H the one which fits each gap (16–21). There is one extra sentence which you do not need to use. There is an example at the beginning (0).

Other guests were in the house. Several times while I was washing and changing I heard doors opening and closing. I put on my new blue slacks and sweater and picked up my bag, hoping that no one would notice how heavy it was. **0 H**

I intended to fight him in his own territory.

Finding a library in a large country house is not difficult when you've travelled widely and have quite a few wealthy friends. Libraries usually have double doors opening inwards and do not lead to anywhere else. **16** In a room nearby someone was playing the piano. **17**

'Surely people with your kind of job shouldn't sit with their backs to the door,' I said when I could see whom I was talking to. I already knew what he looked like. **18**

Sir George rose. He was of medium height, slightly fat, silver-haired and with a face surprisingly youthful for his sixty years. **19**

With not a second to spare, a word from him prevented huge dogs from attacking me. Grabbing collars, he said, 'Do help yourself to sherry while I get rid of this lot,' and crossed to another door as if floating in a sea of black and gold jumping gun dogs. Two elderly dogs followed with a couple of tail wags especially for me. **20**

I helped myself to sherry, a pale, dry luncheon sherry that would do nothing to dispel my tummy rumbles of hunger, and heard him despatch his dogs into the grounds with the weird cries people reserve for their pets when they don't think anyone else can hear.

Sir George returned, rubbing his hands, and warmed them before the blaze. 'God, it's cold out there.' **21** 'Am I wrong in assuming you prefer to be called Miss Langley?'

A His youngest daughter had recently married a television script writer and the wedding had been shown in all the newspapers.

B The whole lot, I could see now, had been asleep on the floor in front of the log fire.

C He reseated himself, waving me to a chair near the fire.

D There was just one set of double doors leading off the large square hall; I crossed the fancy wooden flooring, noticing Persian rugs and an arrangement of bronze flowers and copper branches in a brass jug.

E Instead of an old-fashioned smoking jacket and grey trousers he wore a sweater and woollen slacks from neither of which anyone had succeeded in removing the morning's harvest of dog hairs.

F I entered, prepared to apologise and leave immediately if necessary; for a moment I thought the room empty but then saw that one of the leather chairs was occupied, cigar smoke floating above it.

G I turned and ran towards the warmth of the kitchen.

H It seemed best to put it under my arm in a relaxed sort of way, relaxed and attractive according to the expensive mirror at the top of the stairs.

PART 3

General hints
Question types

This part is gap filling. You are given a text with six or seven gaps. Each gap must be filled in with given prompts (sentences or paragraphs). The first question is always the example and is numbered (0). There is always one extra prompt.

Answering strategy

1 Look at the instructions, title and layout. Cross off the example that has been used.
2 Read the whole text through. Ask yourself: *What's this text about? What's the main point?*
3 Start reading the text again until you get to the first missing gap. Read down the list of prompts until you find one which might fit and underline key words or ideas.

Underline the key words or ideas in the text which match. The key words in the text usually come before the missing gap.
4 Read the other prompts. Then mark the right answer on the answer sheet. Cross off prompts as you use them.
5 When finished, read the whole text through again, checking your answers. Do not use prompts twice.

PART 4

You are going to read some information about some endangered species. For questions 22–33, choose from the species (A–F). Some of the species may be chosen more than once. When more than one answer is required, these may be given in any order. There is an example at the beginning (0). For questions 34 and 35, choose the answer (A, B, C or D) which you think fits best according to the text.

Which endangered species:

has had its products replaced by other products?	**0** B	
is sometimes killed for entertainment?	**22**	
is being threatened by nature itself?	**23**	
is killed in order to cure humans?	**24**	
seems in less danger of disappearing than the others?	**25**	
are often caught by accident?	**26**	**27**
do not live on land?	**28**	**29**
are eaten?	**30**	**31**
live in only one area of the world?	**32**	**33**

34 What is the main aim of this text?
  A to inform
  B to frighten
  C to entertain
  D to sell

35 The World Wide Fund for Nature International must be
  A an association for educating hunters.
  B an institution for protesting.
  C an organisation for protecting animals.
  D a group for world peace.

PART 4

General hints
Question types

This part is multiple matching. You are given a list of questions and must find the answers in the following text(s). You may be asked to choose your answers from a list of given options. You may also be asked some multiple choice questions. Altogether there are 13–15 questions. The first question is always the example and is numbered (0).

Answering strategy

1 Look at the instructions, title and layout. Mark the section of text used in the example. You may need to use it again.
2 Read the whole list of questions, circling key words or ideas.
3 Scan the text, quickly looking for the specific information you need. Underline key words or ideas and mark the answers on the answer sheet. Tick the sections of text that you use. You may use each more than once.

4 Read the questions again, checking answers.
5 If there are multiple choice questions, ask yourself: *Where is this text from? Who was it written for? What is its main purpose?* (See Part 2.)

FACT SHEET
World Wide Fund for Nature International (WWF)

Tigers – A

The Tiger (Panthera tigris) is one of the cat Felidae family and lives only in Asia. Despite its wide range and adaptability, the tiger is severely threatened today. It is so dependent on cover that it cannot survive where people have cleared the land for agriculture.

The tiger is still widely hunted down, despite being legally protected in almost every country where it is found. In Chinese popular medicine, every part of a tiger's body is valued and this has made hunting even more popular.

Three of the eight tiger subspecies have already been wiped out and a fourth is very near extinction. WWF is promoting projects to save these subspecies.

Whales – B

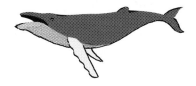

We know little about the earliest whales, but fossil remains and comparative anatomical studies indicate that they were probably descended from small, primitive, bear-like animals. Today's whales have evolved into mammals which live in the water.

Commercial whalers have exploited almost every whale species, causing many populations to come close to extinction. As a result, international trade in whale products, once of enormous volume, has now ended. Both natural and synthetic substitutes are available for all whale products and are competitively priced.

At the annual meeting in 1982, after many years of debate, the IWC (International Whaling Commission) voted to ban all commercial whaling for an indefinite period from 1986.

Elephants – C

The elephants we see today have been on the scene for some five million years. They are the only survivors of a once wide-spread group of animals with trunks, the Proboscidae, which produced more than 300 different species over a span of 50 million years.

At present, all international trade in elephant products, including ivory, is not permitted because all elephant populations are listed on Appendix I of the Convention on International Trade in Endangered Species of Wild Fauna and Flora (CITES) which prohibits all trade in elephant products such as meat and hides. The Asian elephant has been on this list since 1975. The African elephant was placed on Appendix I in 1990.

Giant Panda – D

In prehistoric times, the giant panda (Ailuropoda melanoleuca) was wide-spread in China. Today it is estimated that only 1,000 of these black-and-white bear-like animals remain, all living in the bamboo forests of southwestern China.

The main threats to the panda are destruction of its habitat and deliberate poaching for export of skins. Suitable habitat for the animals has shrunk by about 50 per cent in the last 15 years. Accidental snaring in traps set for other animals is also a major threat.

Another problem is bamboo flowering. It takes the bamboo plant about one year to regenerate from seed but it can take up to 20 years before it can support a panda population.

In total, WWF has spent SFr8 million on conservation in China.

Foxes and Wolves – E

Foxes and wolves belong to the Canidae, or wild dog, family.

Of the 14 fox subspecies, the red fox (Vulpes vulpes) is the most wide-spread. Though the red fox is heavily hunted and trapped for its fur, populations have remained the same.

The coyote or prairie wolf (Canis latrans) is found throughout the United States, southern Canada, and northern Central America. The population is large and increasing even though people hunt it for fur, sport, and to reduce loss of livestock and poultry.

WWF and IUCN (the World Conservation Union's Canid Specialist Group) both believe that most species require legally enforced protection measures. It is also necessary to protect their natural habitat and to increase the public's awareness of the problems confronting these animals.

Dolphins and Porpoises – F

Dolphins and porpoises are marine mammals belonging to the cetacean family which also includes whales. They are found in oceans, estuaries and rivers.

One of the threats facing dolphins and porpoises is hunting. As human populations have grown, more indigenous people fish in order to feed their families. More aggressive fishing methods have also been developed, such as the use of rifles.

Other serious threats include water pollution, destruction and fragmentation of habitat through such activities as dam building, and general disturbance by humans which reduce food supplies.

The largest catches of cetaceans, however, occur by chance while people are trying to catch other fish. Concern about this type of incidental catch led to the 1989 UN General Assembly adopting a resolution that called for the end of large-scale driftnet fishing by 30 June 1992.

Paper 2 Writing (1½ hours)

PART 1

*You **must** answer this question.*

1 While sightseeing in England you stop for lunch in a square in London with many different types of restaurants. You decide to eat at 'The Queen's Head Restaurant', which you have seen advertised. However, there are no children's meals available and your young children are forced to order a 3-course meal, which they cannot eat.

Below are three advertisements for restaurants in the square. Read them carefully and then look at the notes you made after your meal. Then write your letter to the Manager of the restaurant complaining. Cover the points in your notes and add any relevant information about your family.

Write a **letter** of **120–180** words in an appropriate style. Do not include addresses.

The Queen's Head Restaurant

Real English homecooking in a good old English pub. The best in local food and drink! Big servings and reasonable prices. (Children welcome.)

Live music.

Big Pizza House

Enjoy one of our many varieties of pizza. Try our mega-bite pizza! (Children-sized pizza also available.) For takeaway pizza,

ring us on 0171 675 849

ChoosyMeal ═══ **Express**

Wide selection of European dishes. We cater for all tastes, including (children's meals) and vegetarians. No reservations.

others do it

?

- Don't like home cooking
- meat and potatoes, no vegetables – healthy?
- children eat less than adults
- misleading advertising
- wanted quicker service, but waitress friendly

PAPER 2
Writing

The Paper
The paper has two parts. The question in Part 1 must be answered. It is always a transactional letter. In Part 2 you must answer one question out of four. You may be asked to write an article, a report, a non-transactional letter, a composition, or a question on the set books. Your answers must be 120–180 words.

This paper tests you on how well you can perform specific tasks. Think about the style and appropriateness of your writing, as well as answering the question. It takes one hour and 30 minutes.

Part 1

Specific hints
Identifying questions – letter

- *Semi-formal*
It deals with impersonal matters and can be written to people or organisations that you may not know. Use a polite style which is clear and straight to the point. Traditionally if you begin the letter *Dear Sir/Madam*, end it with *Yours faithfully*. If you know the person's name and you begin *Dear Mr/Mrs/Ms (Name)*, etc., end it *Yours sincerely* or *Best regards*. Then sign your name. Don't write addresses or the date.

Indent the paragraphs or leave a line between them. Use the same style throughout the letter. Do not use conversational language (*What's up?*) or contractions (*I'm*).

Letter of complaint
The problem should be clearly stated and supported by facts. To make your complaint more polite you may also include some points that were satisfactory. You may be asked to write about unsatisfactory service, damaged goods, etc.

Suggested plan:
Introduction: Para. 1: State your complaint.
Body: Para. 2: Explain the problem in detail.
Para. 3: State any additional problems (if necessary).
Conclusion: Para. 4: State what you feel should be done. Perhaps include some satisfactory points.

PART 1

General hints
Question types

Part 1 is always a transactional letter, and you must do it. It is usually semi-formal and it might include letters that complain, ask for information, give advice, invite or accept invitations. You are always given a specific task to do in a given situation. You may be given 1–3 short texts, some pictures, and some notes.

Answering strategy

1 Look over all the information carefully.
2 Underline the parts of the question that have to be answered.
3 Find the parts of the pictures and/or the text needed to answer the question. They might be marked by arrows.
4 Look at the notes and match the information with the pictures and/or text.

5 Decide on the level of formality. Write a letter in your own words based on the information in the question, the pictures/text, and the notes. Tick the points on the exam paper as you use them in your letter.
6 Check that you have used all of the necessary information and answered the question within the word limit.

PART 2

*Write an answer to **one** of the questions 2–5 in this part. Write your answer in **120–180** words in an appropriate style.*

2 The company that you work for has transferred you to its branch in a small country town.

Write a **letter** to a friend saying why you were sent there and describe the differences between working in the city and working in the country. Do not include addresses.

3 You are studying English and your teacher has asked you to write a composition giving opinions and suggestions in answer to the following question: 'Are there too many advertisements on TV?'

Write your **composition**.

4 Your school is involved in a foreign exchange programme and some students from abroad will soon be coming to your school for a few weeks. Your headmaster wants you to write a description of a festival that takes place in your village or town.

Write a **description** giving the main details of the festival and explaining its importance.

5 **Background reading texts**

Answer **one** of the following two questions based on your reading of **one** of the set books:

(a) What do you learn about the character of the hero/heroine in the story? Give a brief **account** of his/her character and explain to someone who has not yet read the book how this affects the outcome of the story.

(b) When choosing a book does the front cover of the book influence your choice? Write an **article** for your school newspaper about this, using the front cover of the book which you have read as an example.

Part 2

Specific hints
Identifying questions

● *Letter – informal (see question 2)*
You are asked for a letter dealing with personal matters, and it is usually written to a person that you know, e.g. a penfriend. It is clear when the writing task is a letter, as the question states 'write a letter' or something similar. Your style should be friendly but the English should be clear and correct. You may use phrasal verbs (*hang about*), expressions (*a breath of fresh air*) and contractions (*I'm*). You are instructed not to write your address or the date.

Start with *Dear (Name)*, and end with something like *Love, Best wishes, With love*. Then sign your name. You should indent each paragraph so that they can be clearly seen and the layout of the letter looks tidy.

Some examples of informal letters are: invitations, refusals, advice and thanks to friends or family.

● *Discursive (see question 3)*
You are asked for your opinion and suggestions on something. It might be a balanced discussion or a discussion where you are asked to support one side of an argument. You may also be asked to give suggestions. Identify what kind of question it is. In this type of question you must have sufficient vocabulary to discuss the topic, and sufficient ideas and opinions to support your answer. Give examples where appropriate. Plan your answer and organise your ideas logically using linking words to connect and expand them. Remember why you are writing your opinion.

PART 2

General hints
Question types

In Part 2 you must choose one question out of four. These may include a non-transactional letter, an article, a report, a composition (descriptive, narrative, discursive) and a question on the set books. You are always given a specific task to do. You are told why you are writing and to whom.

Answering strategy

1 Choose the topics that you know the most about.
2 Copy the question that you have chosen on to your answer sheet. Refer back to the question often so that everything you write is relevant.
3 Underline the parts of the question that have to be dealt with and include all of them in your writing.

4 Decide on the most appropriate style and language. You are writing for a specific purpose and for a specific reader.
5 Decide on a main verb tense and use it throughout.
6 Make a quick plan of your answer, e.g. an introductory paragraph, the body and a concluding paragraph. You may change parts of it as you write.
7 Write according to the time limit and the word limit.

Paper 3 Use of English   (1 hour 15 minutes)

PART 1

For questions 1–15, read the text below and decide which answer A, B, C or D best fits each space. There is an example at the beginning (0).

Example:

0 (A) hardly   **B** nearly   **C** almost   **D** completely

A GREAT SUPPORTER

Jim Stopford is a man who can (0) __*hardly*__ read or write, but talks with a great deal (1) ___of___ feeling for something that he has (2) ___given___ his life to. He gives talks to a (3) ___large___ number of children every year on lizards, snakes, tortoises, turtles and (4) _____ crocodiles so that they can understand what a(n) (5) _____ part of the animal world this species is. He has set (6) _____ a free rescue service where trained people are ready to (7) _____ anyone who has been bitten by a snake. A good number of people have also been trained to catch poisonous snakes.

Jim, who (8) _____ in Sydney, goes to many schools giving talks and showing the children his snakes. He (9) _____ the snakes' habitat, what they eat and how they move. He is now preparing a book (10) _____ this subject. He believes that snakes should be (11) _____ because they are dying out. He (12) _____ believes that if snakes are (13) _____ alone they will not harm anyone. (14) _____ Australia has the greatest number of poisonous snakes on the planet, he has always (15) _____ people to be careful when they see one.

1 A about	**B** off	**C** of	**D** with
2 A taken	**B** given	**C** seen	**D** spent
3 A many	**B** lot	**C** much	**D** large
4 A surely	**B** probably	**C** undoubtedly	**D** even
5 A usual	**B** proper	**C** important	**D** specific
6 A about	**B** up	**C** out	**D** off
7 A help	**B** give	**C** organise	**D** provide
8 A lives	**B** stays	**C** settles	**D** remains
9 A draws	**B** shows	**C** describes	**D** tells

PAPER 3
Use of English

The Paper
This paper has five parts. Part 1 is a multiple choice cloze, Part 2 an open cloze, Part 3 a key word transformation, Part 4 an error correction task and Part 5 a word formation task There are 65 questions in the paper.

This paper tests you on how well you can use vocabulary and grammar. It takes one hour and 15 minutes.

Part 1

Specific hints
Question types

The words around the gaps often give grammatical and contextual clues about which word is missing. The forms of words you may be asked for include verbs, nouns, auxiliary verbs, modal verbs, determiners, adjectives, quantifiers, comparatives, articles, prepositions, demonstratives, adverbs, particles in phrasal verbs, link words or pronouns.

Identifying questions

● *Verbs*
These show state, action and time. They can be either regular or irregular. Make sure that you know the irregular forms of the verbs. They can be used on their own or with either an auxiliary verb or a modal verb.
Question:
When several people are _____ together, they can easily argue and any one of these arguments might cause serious problems.
A *lives*   B *lived*   C *living*   D *live*
Answer:
A no: present simple – third person
B no: past simple
C yes: *are living* (verb – present progressive)
D no: present simple

PART 1

General hints
Question types

This part is multiple choice cloze. You are given a text with 15 gaps, and it is followed by 15 four-option multiple choice answers. Questions focus on vocabulary. The first gap is always the example, and is numbered (0).

Answering strategy

1 Look at the title of the text to help you understand the central idea.
2 Read through the whole text to get the general meaning.
3 Underline the key words by looking closely at the words before and after the gap and within the passage.

4 Read the first set of options. If you cannot identify the correct answer easily, cross out the options that are obviously wrong. Write the answers on to the text in pencil.
5 Read the whole text again, checking your answers. Now mark the answers on to the answer sheet.

10	A for	B of	C by	D on
11	A protected	B cared	C guaranteed	D favoured
12	A apart from	B also	C too	D besides
13	A departed	B undisturbed	C left	D moved
14	A While	B Despite	C Although	D Since
15	A advised	B suggested	C claimed	D explained

PART 2

*For questions 16–30, read the text below and think of the word which best fits each space. Use only **one** word in each space. There is an example at the beginning (**0**).*

A GREAT WRITER

Every child has at some time (**0**) ____*or*____ other been thrilled by the stories that have been written by Jules Verne, (**16**) _____ was a very imaginative Frenchman.

Although he was (**17**) _____ in Nandi, France (**18**) _____ 1828, Jules Verne lived in Paris (**19**) _____ he studied law. However, (**20**) _____ knowledge of science soon made him realise that he (**21**) _____ use this in the writing of adventure stories centred around the use of inventions.

He found it difficult to have his books published (**22**) _____ first, but after his first book, *Five Weeks in a Balloon*, was published, it was (**23**) _____ a success that his publisher, Etzel, offered him a twenty-year contract. After that he wrote two novels a year. In (**24**) _____ over forty years he had written eighty novels.

All of Verne's stories, besides being adventure stories, are also to do with travel. (**25**) _____ of his books, *Around the World in Eighty Days*, is a very clever (**26**) _____ that takes us around the world and through all sorts of adventures. *Twenty Thousand Leagues Under the Sea* stirs the imagination as we travel in Captain Nemo's submarine to many parts of (**27**) _____ world.

Many of his stories (**28**) _____ been made into films (**29**) _____ besides reading the stories we can now see them on the screen. Much of what was fantasy then has now (**30**) _____ reality.

Part 2

Specific hints
Question types

The words around the gaps often give you grammatical and contextual clues about which type of word is missing. The types of words you may be asked for include verbs, auxiliary verbs, modal verbs, nouns, determiners, quantifiers, comparatives, articles, demonstratives, prepositions, adverbs, link words, pronouns or adjectives.

Identifying questions

• *Auxiliary verbs*
They are the verbs *to be, to have, to do*. They are used with other main verbs to express particular meanings or grammatical functions.
Question:
When several people ____ living together, they can easily argue and any one of these arguments might cause serious problems.
Answer:
are – the plural subject *people* needs the auxiliary verb *are* to complete the present progressive tense *are living*.

• *Modal verbs*
Modals are not complete verbs and therefore can only be used as auxiliaries. They add extra meaning to the sentence. They have to be used with the base form of a main verb. The modal verbs are *can, could, may, might, will, would, shall, should, must, ought to* and *used to*.
Question:
When several people are living together, they ____ easily argue and one of these arguments might cause serious problems.
Answer:
can – the plural subject *people* needs the modal *can*.

PART 2

General hints
Question types

This part is an open cloze. You are given a text containing 15 gaps. Questions focus on grammar and vocabulary. Each gap must be filled with one word. The first gap is always the example and is numbered (0).

Answering strategy

1 Look at the title of the text to help you understand the central idea.
2 Read through the whole text to get the general meaning.
3 Underline key words before or after the gap or within the sentence.
4 Try to work out the type of word that is missing: noun, verb, preposition, etc.
5 Write the answers on the text in pencil.
6 Read the whole text again with your answers. Now carefully write the answers on to the answer sheet.

PART 3

For questions 31–40, complete the second sentence so that it has a similar meaning to the first sentence, using the word given. **Do not change the word given.** *You must use between two and five words, including the word given. There is an example at the beginning (0).*

Example:

0   Mr Jones needn't go if he doesn't want to.
   obliged
   Mr Jones *is not obliged to go* if he doesn't want to.

31   The football match was postponed due to the rain.
   put
   The football match was _____ due to the rain.

32   There was no one here except John.
   apart
   There was no one here _____ John.

33   You will have to pay at least £500 to get that watch.
   impossible
   You'll find it _____ that watch for less than £500.

34   I don't want to eat this now.
   rather
   I _____ eat this now.

35   'Shall I turn on the light?' Sue asked Jill.
   wanted
   Sue asked Jill _____ the light turned on.

36   Mother walked in quietly so as to avoid waking the baby.
   order
   Mother walked in quietly _____ the baby.

37   It's possible that she didn't understand what I had said.
   might
   She _____ what I had said.

38   I couldn't concentrate fully because of the loud music.
   difficult
   The loud music _____ fully.

39   The tea is too hot to drink.
   enough
   The tea _____ to drink.

40   She is certain to have heard about it on the news.
   must
   She _____ about it on the news.

Part 3

Specific hints
Question types

There are three categories of matching sentences covered in this part. They are: phrasal verbs, verb structures and word sets (simple substitution and whole structural change). Within these categories you may find examples of: phrasal verbs, comparisons, *so/such*, direct/indirect speech, present perfect tense, conditionals, gerunds, infinitives, passive/active voice, causative forms, impersonal *it* and modals.

Identifying questions

● *Phrasal verbs*
You may be asked to complete a sentence with a suitable phrasal verb. Phrasal verbs consist of a verb and a particle or particles. In order to fill in the correct form of the phrasal verb, you need to understand the meaning of the sentence. There are four kinds of tasks you may be asked to perform.
1 Change a verb into a phrasal verb with one particle.
   Example: *meet* to *run into*
2 Change a verb into a phrasal verb with two particles.
   Example: *escape* to *get away with*
3 Change a verb into a phrasal verb with an object.
   Example: *go with somebody when he leaves* to *see somebody off*
4 Change a group of words into a phrasal verb.
   Example: *not go to bed* to *stay up*
You may also be asked to change a phrasal verb into an ordinary verb.
Example: *keep on* to *continue*
Question:
While running I accidentally met Tricia.
came
While running I _____ Tricia.
Answer:
came upon – phrasal verb with one particle to mean *accidentally met*

PART 3

General hints
Question types

This part is key word transformations. You are given 10 sentences and the beginning and end of 10 matching sentences. Using the key words given, you must fill in the gaps with phrases (2–5 words). The matching sentences must have the same meaning as the original sentences.

Questions focus on grammar and vocabulary. The example is numbered (0).

Answering strategy

1 Read the original sentence carefully for meaning.
2 Look at the word given and decide what part of speech it is (noun, adverb, verb, etc.).
3 Read the matching sentence.

4 Decide which part of the original sentence has to be transformed.
5 Fill in the blank using the given word in the right way. Use 2–5 words. Do not change the word in any way.
6 Re-read the sentence checking that all the ideas in the original sentence have been included in the matching sentence. Now carefully write the answers on to the answer sheet.

PART 4

For questions **41–55**, read the text below and look carefully at each line. Some of the lines are correct, and some have a word which should not be there.

If a line is correct put a tick (√) by the number. If a line has a word which should **not** be there, write the word next to the number. There are two examples at the beginning (**0** and **00**).

A DREAM

As I am a university student I study hard and each night when	**0**	√
I will finish my studies I put away my books and put on	**00**	*will*
my training shoes. My sister, who lives in another town, she	**41**	_____
brought them back my training shoes from Europe as a birthday	**42**	_____
present. They are just right for jogging around the track.	**43**	_____
After jogging for the first lap I push myself so harder	**44**	_____
and harder for the second lap. My running style soon becomes	**45**	_____
comfortable and effective for the rest of the whole way. I	**46**	_____
hope that to improve my style so that I do not feel any	**47**	_____
tightness in the leg muscles. I am really looking forward much	**48**	_____
to taking part in my first University Games where I will be	**49**	_____
representing my year. If all goes well then I can expect to	**50**	_____
achieve at a good time which will help me to be chosen for the	**51**	_____
Olympic Games. It will be a moment full of excitement feelings	**52**	_____
for me. I plan on to continue my studies as well as my training	**53**	_____
until my dream is being achieved. My free time will be limited	**54**	_____
but it will be worth it in the end.	**55**	_____

Part 4

Specific hints
Question types

The errors that you may be asked to identify are grammatical. You must look carefully at the context to understand what the errors are. They may include verbs (e.g. incorrect tenses and particles), adjectives followed by prepositions, subjects/objects, adverbs, prepositional phrases or noun phrases.

Identifying questions

● *Verbs*
(a) Tenses
In order to identify an incorrect verb form you have to look at the tense of the verb (present, past or future tense), whether it is perfect or progressive, active or passive voice.
Question:
Not everyone can be have a gold medal.
Error:
be – there is no tense *can be have*. Context shows that the correct tense in this case is *can have*, not *can be*.
(b) Tenses after time words
Time clauses are introduced by *when, while, until, as, after, since,* etc. A future tense is never used with a time clause.
Question:
When several people will run together competitively, it is called a 'race'.
Error:
will – after the time word *when*, the simple present tense *run* is used so *will run* is incorrect.

PART 4

General hints
Question types

This part deals with error correction. There is a text containing errors based on grammar. Some lines of the text are correct, other lines contain an extra, unnecessary word which must be identified. There are 15 lines of text that have to be identified as either correct or incorrect. The first two lines numbered 0 and 00 are always the examples.

Answering strategy

1 Look at the title of the text to help you understand the central idea.
2 Read through the whole text to get the general meaning.
3 Read through each sentence checking the grammatical structure of the sentence.
4 Tick the parts that are correct on the text in pencil.
5 Underline the parts that are incorrect on the text in pencil.
6 Read the whole text again leaving out the unnecessary words that you identified in order to check the meaning of the text. Carefully put the ticks and the incorrect word on the answer sheet.

PART 5

For questions 56–65, read the text below. Use the word given in capitals at the end of each line to form a word that fits in the space in the same line. There is an example at the beginning (0).

TIME-SHARING HOLIDAYS

Today the **(0)** *variety* of time-share resorts found   **VARY**

throughout the world is evident. The great **(56)** . . .   **IMPORTANT**

that is given to these resorts can be seen by the especially

(57) . . . manner of the personnel who are ready to help   **ATTENTION**

in any way.

   Many **(58)** . . . have now understood that time-   **CONSUME**

sharing can be **(59)** . . . . However, this was not so at   **BENEFIT**

the beginning as people thought it would be just another

(60) . . . business project.   **SUCCESSFUL**

   In America time-sharing began as an **(61)** . . . way of   **ENJOY**

organising family holidays. This **(62)** . . . to share houses   **WILLING**

and apartments developed **(63)** . . . world-wide into a   **QUICK**

profitable business. The **(64)** . . . side of things was   **PRACTICE**

examined thoroughly so that an **(65)** . . . number of people   **INCREASE**

who were buying shares in this new industry were

satisfied.

Part 5

Specific hints
Question types

Look at the position of the word in the sentence to see which form it has to be changed into, for example: a verb into a noun or adjective; a noun into an adjective; an adjective into a noun or adverb. The words next to the gaps often give you grammatical clues.
   A prefix or suffix may need to be used in order to change the word into a different form, often the negative or opposite. There are also some irregular word formations and compound words.

Identifying questions

● *Nouns*
Nouns are naming words. They are often formed from verbs, adjectives and other nouns by adding a suffix.

● *Suffixes*
A suffix is a syllable which is added to the end of a word. Learn the suffixes and their meanings. Some suffixes which make nouns are:
Verb to noun: *accept ance, agree ment, injur(e) y, protect ion*
Adjective to noun: *sad ness, genero(u)s ity, perfect ion*

● *Irregular forms*
Some verbs and adjectives form nouns when -*th* or -*t* is added. There is often a vowel change.
Verb to noun: *grow th, fl(y) ight*
Adjective to noun: *warm th, de(e)p th*
Question:
One of the _____ lost the keys to her car.
run
Answer:
runners – make verb *run* into plural noun *runners* using suffix -*er*.

PART 5

General hints
Question types

This part deals with word formation. You are given a text with 10 gaps. Each gap must be filled in with one word. The stems of the missing words are given beside the text and must be changed appropriately. The first gap is always the example and is numbered (0).

Answering strategy

1 Look at the title of the text to help you understand the central idea.
2 Treat the text as though you are reading a story. Read it through quickly to understand what it is about. It will help you to connect the words to the topic.
3 Decide which part of speech you have to change the word into according to the position of the word in the sentence.

4 Decide from the context whether the word is positive or negative and whether to use a prefix, a suffix or both.
5 Write the answers on to the text in pencil.
6 Read the whole text again after having filled it in. Now carefully write the answers on to the answer sheet.

Paper 4 Listening (approximately 35 minutes)

PART 1

You'll hear people talking in eight different situations. For questions 1–8, choose the best answer, A, B or C.

1 Listen to this conversation between a mother and son. How does he feel about doing school homework?
   A He likes it.
   B He doesn't like it.
   C He always wants to do it later.

   | 1 |

2 A businesswoman phones to arrange a meeting with you. Where will it be held?
   A at her office
   B at a hotel
   C at a restaurant

   | 2 |

3 You are waiting to see the dentist when the receptionist comes to speak to you. What does she suggest you do?
   A relax in the office
   B come back later
   C make another appointment

   | 3 |

4 You are at a supermarket, when you hear this announcement. The aim of this announcement is to
   A advertise a special offer.
   B welcome customers.
   C entertain customers.

   | 4 |

5 Listen to this man talking to a colleague. Who is the colleague?
   A his boss
   B a secretary
   C someone from a different company

   | 5 |

6 Listen to this young man talking to a friend on the phone about a problem. What is the problem?
   A He is busy on Friday night.
   B He wants to have two girlfriends.
   C He wants to end a relationship.

   | 6 |

PAPER 4
Listening

The Paper
This paper has four parts, each with recordings of spoken English in everyday situations and questions. Part 1 is a multiple choice question, Part 2 is a note taking or gap filling question, Part 3 is a multiple matching question, and Part 4 is a two or three choice question. You will hear each taped text twice. There are 30 questions in the paper.

This paper tests you on how well you can understand general meanings as well as specific information. You may also be tested on information that you can conclude from the taped text ('reading between the lines'). It takes approximately 40 minutes.

Part 1

Specific hints
Question types

You are given multiple choice questions and must answer the questions or complete the sentences. The questions and correct answers often paraphrase what is in the taped text. The incorrect answers try to distract you by using incorrect facts or ideas. Incorrect answers can: say the opposite of what is true, use exactly the same words as the listening text, misuse some of the words from the listening text or present believable (but wrong) answers. In the Listening Paper, identifying the correct answer can often depend on: intonation, stress, register and similar sounds.

Identifying questions

● *Intonation/tone of voice*
You can often understand how someone feels or thinks by listening to how the voice falls or rises. When the voice falls, it often shows a feeling of completion, e.g. a statement or order. When it rises, it often shows a feeling of incompletion or doubt, e.g. a question or doubtful remark. The tone of voice (expression) also provides clues.

(cont.)

PART 1

General hints
Question types

This part is multiple choice. There are eight questions on eight unrelated taped texts (about 30 seconds each). You are asked to choose from three answers, A, B or C.

Answering strategy

1 First pause. Check where this part ends. Read the questions and underline key words. These will catch your eye while you are listening to the tape, e.g. *Listen to this man talking to a colleague. Why didn't he go to the meeting?* Ask yourself *What's this listening text about? Who is talking? To whom? Where? Why?*

2 First playing. Fill in the easiest of the answers in the answer boxes.

3 Second pause. Answer some of the other questions, or at least cross off some of the answers that are obviously wrong. Put an 'x' over the words that make answers incorrect. **Do not sit and do nothing.**

4 Second playing. Complete the rest of the answers.

5 Third pause. Make sure that every question is answered.

7 You are waiting to have a haircut when you hear this conversation. The receptionist does not have any change because
   A the girls have taken it.
   B the customers have taken it.
   C there are no customers.

	7

8 Listen to this girl talking about a film. Who is Phillip Carrington?
   A an actor
   B a director
   C a writer

	8

(continued)

Exercise on intonation/tone of voice

Listen to this woman talking to someone about going out. How does she feel?
A surprised
B disappointed
C angry
Now listen to the explanation.

PART 2

You will hear a recorded telephone announcement giving a recipe for bacon soufflé. For questions 9–18, complete the notes which summarise what the speaker says about making soufflés. You will need to write a word or a short phrase in each box.

The oven must be	9
Make soufflé in	10
or in	11
Grease bottom and sides, then sprinkle with	12
This stops the soufflé	13
White sauce should be stirred	14
Beat egg whites until	15
Leave in the oven for	16
or until it	17
It's best to	18

PART 2

General hints
Question types

This part is note taking or blank filling. There are ten questions on one taped text (about 3 minutes long). You must fill in the answers, according to the information given on the tape.

Answering strategy

1 First pause. Read the instructions for information about the situation/speakers. Underline the key words in the questions.
2 First playing. Fill in the easiest of the answers in the answer boxes. If there is more than one way to write the correct answer, write it the shorter way. If there are two

answer boxes for the same sentence, the order in which you write the answers is not important.
3 Second pause. Answer some of the other questions.
4 Second playing. Complete the rest of the answers.
5 Third pause. Make sure that every question is answered.

PART 3

*You will hear five people talking about a place where they like to eat. For questions **19–23**, choose from the list of places **A–F** what each speaker is describing. Use the letter only once. There is one extra letter which you do not need to use.*

A a fast food restaurant	Speaker 1	19
B a steak-house	Speaker 2	20
C a Chinese restaurant	Speaker 3	21
D a pizza parlour	Speaker 4	22
E a fish and chip shop	Speaker 5	23
F a theatre restaurant		

PART 3

General hints
Question types

This part is multiple matching. You are asked to match six headings or summary sentences with five speakers (about 30 seconds each). There is always one extra heading or sentence which you do not need to use.

Answering strategy

1 First pause. Read the instructions for information about the situation/speakers. If there are summary sentences, underline the key words.
2 First playing. Fill in the easiest of the answers in the answer boxes. Make notes beside some obviously wrong answers, e.g. beside A, write *not (Speaker) 2*.

3 Second pause. Answer some of the other questions. Cross off the answers you have used.
4 Second playing. Complete the rest of the answers.
5 Third pause. Make sure that every question is answered.

PART 4

You will hear a father and a daughter talking about going on a picnic. For questions 24–30, decide which of the choices A, B or C is the correct answer.

24 The father thinks his wife
    A does not usually keep her promises.
    B always does what she says she will do.
    C referred to the picnic the previous night.

| 24 |

25 What is the wife's job?
    A lawyer
    B basketball player
    C judge

| 25 |

26 When is this conversation taking place?
    A spring
    B summer
    C winter

| 26 |

27 What did the doctor suggest to the father?
    A Eat as many eggs as possible.
    B Do not worry about the number of eggs eaten.
    C Do not eat a lot of eggs.

| 27 |

28 How does the father feel about crackers?
    A He loves them.
    B He doesn't like them.
    C He is angry that she has put some in.

| 28 |

29 What is the daughter taking on the picnic?
    A uncooked vegetables
    B salami
    C fried chicken

| 29 |

30 The daughter suggests that
    A food should never be wrapped in foil.
    B food should always be wrapped in foil.
    C food can occasionally be wrapped in foil.

| 30 |

Part 4

Specific hints
Question types

You are given a selection from two or three possible answers. It may be true/false, yes/no, multiple choice or 'identify the speaker' questions.

Identifying questions

● *Multiple choice*
You are asked to choose the best of three answers. You can be asked to answer a question or finish a statement. Read each question carefully and underline the key words. Choose which answer best matches what you have understood from the taped text. If you are not sure of an answer, try to identify the incorrect answers, and then choose from the ones you have left.

Question types

The questions and matching correct answers often paraphrase what is in the taped text. The incorrect answers present incorrect facts or ideas based on the taped text.

Exercise on paraphrasing

Speaker 1: I had boarded the train and was looking for my seat when I came across Scotty. My old friend was in a very bad temper.
Question:
What did the writer do?
A He got on the wrong train.
B He made his friend angry.
C He met someone he knew.
Answer:
A no: he boarded the train but it does not say it was the wrong train
B no: his friend was in a very bad temper, but it does not say the writer caused this
C yes: *came across Scotty* is another way of saying *met someone he knew.*

PART 4

General hints
Question types

This part gives a selection of two or three answers. There are seven questions on one taped text (about 3 minutes long). The questions might be: multiple choice; yes/no; true/false; or which speaker said what.

Answering strategy

1 First pause. Read the instructions for information about the situation/speakers. Underline the key words in the questions.
2 First playing. Fill in the easiest of the answers in the answer boxes. Make notes about the obviously wrong answers.

3 Second pause. Answer some of the other questions.
4 Second playing. Complete the rest of the answers.
5 Third pause. Make sure that every question is answered.

Paper 5 Speaking (approximately 15 minutes)

PART 1 (approximately 4 minutes)

Talk about yourself:

1 Where do you live? Did it take you long to get here?
  Talk about your neighbourhood.
  Where are you from and what is it like living there?

2 Do you live in a flat?
  Would you like to live in a flat or a house?
  Talk about your home.

PART 2 (approximately 4 minutes)

Look at the photographs on p. 123. They show different types of pollution. Work with your partner.

1 Student A: compare and contrast pictures 1 and 2, saying if you think those responsible for these examples of pollution should be punished and how.

2 Student B: talk about any examples of pollution you have ever seen, caused either by industry or by individuals.

3 Student B: compare and contrast pictures 3 and 4, saying if you think those responsible for these examples of pollution should be punished and how.

4 Student A: talk about any similar instances of pollution you have seen, either in person or in the media.

PAPER 5
Speaking

The Paper
This paper has four parts. Part 1 is an exchange of personal information, Part 2 is a response to pictures, Part 3 is a performance of a set task (based on a visual stimulus), and Part 4 is an opinion exchange (based on themes related to Part 3). There are two candidates and two examiners. The interviewer asks questions and the other examiner watches; both give you a mark, then decide on your final mark. This paper includes both long and short speaking turns.

This paper tests you on how well you can give and exchange information and opinions: if you can carry on a good conversation in English. You are not tested on how many facts you know, but on how well you can express yourself. It takes approximately 15 minutes.

Part 1

Specific hints
Identifying questions

● *Discussing your neighbourhood (see question 1)*
You could be asked to describe your neighbourhood and discuss some good points or bad points about living there. Use examples to support what you say.

● *Discussing your home (see question 2)*
You could be asked to talk about your home, e.g. its appearance inside or outside. Try to think of something that makes it unique. If you compare it to other places, do not be insulting.

Part 2

Specific hints
Identifying questions

● *Discussing your opinion (see questions 1 and 3)*
Decide quickly whether you are for or against something, then make a fairly strong statement along with your reasons. Use examples to support your view.

● *Discussing a personal experience (see questions 2 and 4)*
Choose to talk about familiar things. Use examples to add interest. If you use an example from the media, e.g. television, mention that.

PARTS 1 and 2

General hints – Part 1
Question types

This part is the 'warm-up': you are each asked questions about personal background. Topics could include: neighbourhood, home, family, customs, pastimes, travel, plans/career, and thoughts on learning English. The interviewer asks both short-answer and long-answer questions, and encourages you to talk to each other. It takes approximately four minutes.

General hints – Part 2
Question types

In this part, you are each asked questions about two different sets of theme-related pictures. You can be asked to compare and contrast the pictures or discuss personal experiences, opinions, wishes, feelings, or thoughts regarding the pictures. You have approximately one minute to respond to your pictures, plus approximately twenty seconds to respond to the other candidate's pictures. It takes approximately four minutes.

PART 3 (approximately 3 minutes)

Imagine that you live in a fishing village. A developer wants to turn it into a tourist resort, including hotels, an entertainment complex and a watersports centre. Look at the pictures below.

Work with your partner. Talk together and decide if you think this development would be a good or a bad thing for your village.

PART 4 (approximately 4 minutes)

Discuss the following questions with your partner:
1 What kind of activities do you enjoy doing in the holidays?
2 What are your favourite hobbies?
3 How have your hobbies changed since you were young?
4 Do you prefer to play individual or team sports? Why?
5 How much time should one spend on leisure activities?

Part 3

Specific hints
Identifying questions

● *Speculating*
You are asked to form an opinion, based on some pieces of information given. 'Think aloud' with the other candidate, discussing the facts which are presented. Then, based on those facts, make a guess about a logical outcome.

Useful vocabulary

● *Uncertainty*
I think/it looks as if/perhaps/maybe it's a good development.
It might/could/may be a good development.

● *Probability*
It's probably (not) a good development.

● *Certainty*
It must/has to/can't be a good development.
It's clear/obvious that it's a good development.

● *Opinion*
In my opinion/it seems to me that this is a good development.

Part 4

Specific hints
Identifying questions

● *Stating personal choices (see questions 1, 2, 4)*
You are asked to choose between two or more alternatives. For example, *Do you prefer chocolate or vanilla ice cream? What flavour of ice cream do you like best?* Quickly make a decision and then give your answer. Do not waste time trying to find the 'right' answer; the answer depends on you.

PARTS 3 and 4

General hints – Part 3
Question types

In this part, you are each given a visual stimulus to look at, like a photograph or line drawing. Then the interviewer asks you to carry out a specific task together. This task could be: speculating (guessing), prioritising (putting things in order of importance), solving a problem, planning, etc. It takes approximately three minutes.

Answering strategy

1 Quickly study the visual stimulus.

2 Answer the interviewer's questions. If there is anything you are not sure of, ask.
3 Discuss the problem with the other candidate.
4 Draw a logical conclusion together. If you can't agree, politely 'agree to disagree'.

General hints – Part 4
Question types

In this part, you are encouraged to have a conversation together, stating opinions about subjects related to Part 3. You could be asked to state

personal choices, make generalisations, state reasons, suggest solutions, or discuss advantages/disadvantages. It takes approximately four minutes.

Answering strategy

1 Listen carefully to the questions.
2 Quickly form your answers. Take turns speaking. You may disagree, but do so politely.

TEST 2

Paper 1 Reading   (1 hour 15 minutes)

PART 1

*You are going to read a newspaper article about losing your job. Choose from the list **A–I** the sentence which best summarises each part (**1–7**) of the article. There is one extra sentence which you do not need to use. There is an example at the beginning (**0**).*

A Others are often blamed for a situation seen as hopeless.
B Ignore the whole situation so that you do not do anything foolish.
C Finding a sympathetic ear is a positive step.
D See the situation as a step forward, not a step backward.
E Initial reactions are often a sense of shock and panic.
F Along with acceptance comes the decision to take control of your own life.
G Recognise that it is all right to feel sad.
H Organise your day in order to organise your life.
I Losing a job means more than just losing your income.

What do you do when you lose your job?

0	I

If you've recently become unemployed, you may be asking yourself, 'Why didn't I see it coming? What could I have done to keep my job? What's wrong with me?' When you lose a job, you lose far more than just a wage. You lose your faith that hard work pays off. You lose part of your identity, because, to some extent, you define yourself by your job. You are no longer sure who you are or what you can do. You lose some self-esteem.

1	

It is common to mourn the loss of a job and go through certain stages. At first you feel like you don't have the strength to do anything. During the first few weeks the thought of 'this can't be happening to me' sits in your mind. The longer you have spent with an employer, the longer the numbness may last. You can't imagine yourself working for anyone else. You tend to panic. You're afraid and you don't know what to do. You might start imagining selling your home or being forced to ask family or friends for a loan just to buy food. You worry about what to tell your relatives and friends. This nervousness could cause headaches and stomach problems.

2	

'After all the effort I put into my job,' you think, 'I don't deserve to lose it.' You find yourself venting your anger on innocent members of your family, the kids, shop assistants, even innocent bystanders. When you start searching for another job, it's not easy. 'Why apply for a job that's advertised in the paper,' you say to yourself. 'I'll never get it. Nobody wants me.'

3	

You slowly come to believe what has happened, and you begin looking for a job with a more realistic attitude, accepting you'll have good and bad experiences. You know you'll feel low when you've been turned down, but you're optimistic that one of these days, you'll find the right job. 'This is my life and I've got to get on with it,' becomes your attitude.

4	

There are some ways to help you handle the anxiety of going through these stages. Here are some suggestions. You must realise that feeling miserable when you've lost a job and are out of work is normal. It is not a sign of weakness.

5	

Friends, family members and acquaintances can sometimes help find you jobs, encourage you and cheer you on. Confide in your partner, but don't lean too hard on them. They may be feeling anxious too, and your fears will only add to theirs.

6	

If you're not ready to phone employers first thing in the morning, how about planning to do something else that's constructive. Take a brisk walk; exercise at home; you could even learn a foreign language. The more active you are, the less miserable you will feel.

7	

Don't blame yourself for losing your job. Keep your eyes on what you have to gain by this event, and not what you have to lose. You have a chance to rediscover other things in life and develop friendships; take this opportunity to do so. Be open, ready and waiting when the right career opportunity comes along.

PART 2

You are going to read a list of rules and a session programme from a roller skating rink. Then you are going to read a mother's note to her children. For questions 8–14, choose the answer (A, B, C or D) which you think fits best according to the text.

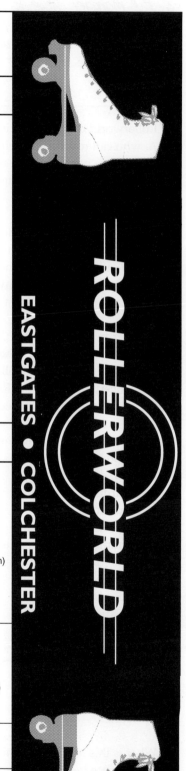

ROLLERWORLD

EASTGATES • COLCHESTER

Rollerworld is a public skating rink that welcomes everyone from individuals, couples and families to organised groups, from absolute beginners to experts.

CODE OF ENTRY

- – we keep all rights of admission
- – under 12's must be accompanied by an adult
- – over 14's on Friday and Saturday evenings
- – small fee for adults watching children
- – no chewing gum anywhere
- – no dirty, damaged, oiled or dangerous skates
- – no black wheels or toestops
- – all skates must have two good toestops
- – no street/hockey style skates during family time
- – dress must be neat
- – no jackets, hats, vests, open or torn clothing to be worn
- – all shoes, bags, etc. must be locked in lockers
- – lockers 20p per person per visit
- – no newspapers, books, magazines, games, etc. permitted in Roller Cafe or Roller Bar
- – no refreshments to be brought in
- – no smoking except in Roller Bar and part of Roller Cafe
- – over 18's only in Roller Bar (too much drinking is not allowed)
- – no swearing or rude behaviour
- – Rollerworld requests that you leave quietly and carefully

'Rollerskating fun for everyone'

SESSION PROGRAMME

TUESDAYS

Adult night	8.00–11.30	£3.00
		(before 9 pm)
		£3.50
		(after 9 pm)

A special night when we welcome adults from all over East Anglia to experience Rollerworld

WEDNESDAYS

| Allskate (term time) | 3.30–7.00 | £2.40 |
| Allskate | 7.30–11.00 | £2.80 |

THURSDAYS

| Allskate | 7.00–11.00 | £2.80 |

FRIDAYS

Roller Disco	7.00–12.00	£3.90
		(before 8 pm)
(Under 16's		£4.60
welcome until 11 pm)		(after 8 pm)

Rollerworld voucher for those leaving before 10.30 pm

Parents spectating	90p (not Roller Discos)
Roller Hire	60p per session
Lockers	20p (non-refundable)
all coats, bags, shoes, jumpers, etc., to be locked in	

SATURDAYS

Under 13's go wild	10.30–12.30	£2.20
(Under 13's only on the rink)		
Family Fun	2.30–5.00	£2.80
Roller Mania	7.30–12.30	£4.50
		(before 8.30 pm)
		£5.20
		(after 8.30 pm)

Rollerworld voucher for those leaving before 10.30 pm

SUNDAYS

Family Skating	10.30–1.00	£2.40
Family Skating	2.30–5.00	£3.00
Allskate	7.00–11.00	£3.20
		(before 8 pm)
		£3.70
		(after 8 pm)

MONDAYS

| Bank Holidays Allskate | 2.30–6.00 | £3.00 |

SCHOOL HOLIDAYS

Rollerskate covers Essex & Suffolk School Holidays

| Allskate | 2.30–5.00 | £2.80 |
| (every day Mon. to Fri.) | | |

Children:
I've left the money (£7·80) for you on the kitchen table. Make sure that you're both out of there by 11pm – don't make the manager have to throw you out again! I don't care if your older friends stay longer! And don't break any legs! Dad will be waiting in the car to take you home. This is your last chance.
Mum

8   Rollerworld can only be visited by people
   A who can rollerskate well.
   B who are not wearing jeans.
   C who are learning how to rollerskate.
   D who are tidily dressed.

9   If a parent wants to take her children to Rollerworld
   A she is allowed to watch them for free.
   B she can leave them alone, if they are teenagers.
   C she can take them Friday night, if they are young.
   D she can read and have a drink while she waits in the Roller Bar.

10   Where can people smoke?
   A in a certain section of the Roller Cafe
   B in all sections of the Roller Cafe
   C in a certain part of the Roller Bar
   D smoking is not permitted anywhere in Rollerworld

11   The best time for young children to go skating is
   A Tuesday night.
   B Thursday evening.
   C Saturday afternoon.
   D Saturday evening.

12   This mother's children must be going
   A on Wednesday evening.
   B on Thursday evening.
   C on Friday evening.
   D on Saturday evening.

13   What does 'there' in the mother's note refer to?
   A the kitchen
   B the car
   C the skating rink
   D home

14   What is this mother's opinion of her children?
   A They are her last chance.
   B They are always anxious to please her.
   C They are a little lazy.
   D They are rather naughty.

Part 2

Specific hints
Identifying texts

● *Practical text (see 'list of rules')*
This kind of text gives some kind of useful information, like facts, rules and instructions. In Part 2, the questions are often about the aim of the text, and for whom it was written. You may also be asked about the reasons and results of actions, as well as the actions themselves.

● *Personal text (see 'mother's note')*
This kind of text gives a personal message from someone to someone else. In Part 2, the questions are often about descriptions of persons, places, things or events. You may also be asked about the feelings of the writer and his or her reasons for doing something.

Identifying questions

● *Same word(s)*
Somtimes you are given incorrect answers which use some of the same words/phrases/sentences as the text. Try not to let these distract you.

Exercise on same word(s)

As a small boy, I can remember being very bad. I would always get out of the small jobs my parents gave me to do around the house. I would also always get into fights with my brothers and sisters. I was not the perfect son, and must have made my parents very angry. They should have punished me more severely.
Question:
When the author was young,
A he did some small jobs for money.
B he should have punished his brothers and sisters.
C he ran around the house.
D he avoided doing housework.
Answer:
A no: the writer mentions small jobs, but does not say that he got money for them
B no: the writer mentions that his parents should have punished him, and that he had brothers and sisters, but does not say that he should have punished his brothers and sisters
C no: the writer mentions small jobs around the house, but does not say that he ran around the house
D yes: *would always get out of the small jobs . . . around the house* is another way of saying he *avoided doing housework*

PART 3

*You are going to read an extract from a book. Seven paragraphs have been removed from the extract. Choose from the paragraphs **A–H** the one which fits each gap (**15–20**). There is one extra paragraph which you do not need to use. There is an example at the beginning (**0**).*

The luggage was to be sent up to the Royal Suite, which during the year had already been occupied by royalty, like Princess Grace of Monaco.

0	H

The Royal Suite is on the first floor at Claridge's and can be reached by an elegant staircase from the ground floor, or by a roomy lift with its own seat.

15	

The suite itself consists of four rooms: a small dressing-room, a bedroom, a bathroom, and an elegant drawing-room overlooking Brook Street. The furniture and pictures make it possible for you to believe that you are still in Victorian England. Only the telephone and television indicate otherwise.

16	

After a shower and change of clothes, Harvey glanced through his waiting mail and telexes from the bank, which were all routine. He took a short nap before going down to dine in the main restaurant.

17	

He had reached that time in life when he did not like change; the management of Claridge's, aware that the average age of their customers was over fifty, served accordingly.

18	

Harvey managed a little shrimp cocktail and a medium fillet steak with a bottle of Mouton Cadet. As he leaned forward to study the sweets trolley, he did not notice the four young men eating near the wall on the far side of the room.

19	

'Not exactly what I expected,' commented Stephen.

20	

A   Harvey always took the lift up and walked down. At least that way he convinced himself he was taking some exercise.

B   There in the large foyer was the usual small band, looking like hungry beggars. Harvey recognised the four musicians.

C   Francois, the head waiter, showed Harvey to his usual table.

D   Harvey was sure that they were extremely wealthy women. They could certainly afford to stay at Claridge's.

E   Stephen, Robin, Jean-Pierre and James all had an excellent view of Harvey Metcalfe. He would have had to bend double and move slightly backwards to have any sight of them.

F   'Put on a bit of weight since those photographs you supplied,' said Jean-Pierre.

G   The room is large enough to be used for cocktail parties or by visiting heads of state to entertain large parties. Henry Kissinger had received Harold Wilson there only the week before. Harvey enjoyed the thought of that. It was about as close as he was going to get to either man.

H   But Harvey still considered that his annual holiday at Claridge's was more certain than theirs.

PART 4

You are going to read some information about different kinds of holidays. For questions 21–33, choose from the holidays (A–H). Some of the holidays may be chosen more than once. When more than one answer is required, these may be given in any order. There is an example at the beginning (0). For questions 34 and 35, choose the answer (A, B, C or D) which you think fits best according to the text.

Which holiday or holidays would you recommend for someone who:

wants to travel in a small group?	**0** D	
loves books?	**21**	
likes travelling on water?	**22**	
wants to travel by coach?	**23**	
wants baby-sitting facilities?	**24**	
likes to avoid crowds?	**25**	
likes winter sports?	**26**	**27**
only has a week's holiday?	**28**	**29**
wants to know children are welcome?	**30**	**31**
wants to tour the world on foot?	**32**	**33**

34 Where might someone find this text?
  A in a tourist leaflet
  B in a tour programme
  C in a geography textbook
  D in a newspaper

35 What is the main purpose of this text?
  A to inform
  B to advertise
  C to instruct
  D to entertain

General hints
Answering strategy

Remember that only one answer is correct. Your opinion is unimportant; you must answer the questions according to what the text says. If you cannot recognise which answer is right, then look at the other possibilities and decide which answers are definitely wrong. If you are left with two answers you are not sure of, choose the one that seems the most logical. If you are still not sure, follow your instincts and choose the one that you first felt was correct.

TRAVEL AND LEISURE

Holiday A

SPAIN
10 days from only
£75
17 days from **£99**
Direct by V.I.P. Supercoach
● **Free child places still** available on many dates.

- **Castel Montgri** (*Spain's best leisure park*)
- **Estartit ● Calella De Palafrugell ● Salou**
- Camping, Mobile Homes, Apartments and Hotel
- **LOW DEPOSIT – £15** (*until Jan. 31st*)
- Travel by the world's finest double-decker Supercoaches from departure points throughout the country.

CALELLA SUPERDEAL
Up to £40 per person off our already low prices for all; dates incl. busy season if booked before January 31st.

No. A9701
51 Bank Street, Carlisle CA3 8HJ
INFORMATION HOTLINE (office hours)
01228 515383

Redcrest Holidays

Holiday B

SKI PEAK **offer catered chalet, hotel and self-catering holidays in Vaujany Alpe d'Huez.**

Genuine alpine village with top class skiing.

Please call for our New brochure on **(01428) 682272.**

Services include:
▲ guiding
▲ child-care
▲ 7 days skiing and
▲ short transfers.

MERIBEL is also featured.

Holiday C

WORLD-WIDE SMALL-GROUP EXPEDITIONS

EXODUS leads the field in adventurous travel.
We've over 200 trips, including high mountain treks,
lowland rambles, wildlife safaris,
exploratory expeditions and long-distance
transcontinental overlands.
8 days to 23 weeks, £450 to £3000+

DEPT. OD, 9 WEIR ROAD, LONDON SW12 0LT
0181-673 0859 (24 hrs)

Exodus
The Adventure Experts

CAA
ATTO

3 Worldwide brochures:
Walking, Adventure, Overland

Special brochures:
Morocco, China

Holiday D

Ramblers Holidays

Some of the most interesting holidays you'll ever find, walking, sightseeing, cross-country skiing. Easy through tough walking holidays throughout Europe. Treks in Nepal. Sightseeing and walking holidays all over the world. New Zealand, Chile, Canada and USA, Costa Rica, China, Nepal. Cross-country skiing in Europe.

RAMBLERS HOLIDAYS
Box 43, Welwyn Garden AL8 6PQ England Tel: (44) 1707 331133

Our winter brochure features **63** different holidays, including Christmas trips; our new brochure, due end September, around **130** – all designed to add a touch of interest, value, perhaps adventure ... all in small parties escorted by a Ramblers leader.
WEALTH WARNING: You may get hooked and keep coming back for more.

Just call or fax for a brochure.

Holiday E

ADRIFT

ADRIFT is the world's number one white water rafting company. Expeditions by raft along the arteries of the planet are offered for both

first-time adventurers and seasoned explorers. New Zealand, India, Ethiopia, Turkey, Nepal and Zimbabwe. Journeys as exotic as the rivers are wild, pushing back the boundaries of the imagination.

New brochure out now

APS-Select LTD
T-AS ADRIFT
ATOL 3556 ABTA E2851

0181 874 4969

Holiday F

Röhrsdorf Castle

A Renaissance Building at your disposal in Dresden

HOTEL ∗ RESTAURANT ∗ KULTURZENTRUM

- Rohrsdorf Castle is geographically located South-East of Dresden at a distance of roughly 6 km from the Saxonian capital. It is surrounded by fruit growing plantations which stretch over the hills from Dresden to the mountains of Swiss Saxony. The country is connected by road B172 which leads from Dresden to Heidenau – Pirna – Bad Schandau – Prague.

- A library contains approximately 3000 volumes in German, English and French covering Ancient History, Linguistics, Law and Economics.

- Horses are available at the castle. Long walks can be taken in the surrounding hills. The castle restaurant serves German and French specialities with first class wines.

Reservations: Mrs Kathi Lange
Tel. +49 351 285 770 Fax. +49 351 285 77 263
01809 Rohrsdorf (Dresden), Germany

Schlob Röhrsdorf

Holiday G

BRITISH VIRGIN ISLANDS CLUB

Escape the crowds

Luxurious villas with private pools and select hotels on secluded Caribbean islands. Inclusive year-round holidays for discerning escapists who feel they deserve a first-class break.

British Virgin Islands Club
66 High Street
Walton-on-Thames
Surrey KT12 1BU

Tel: (01932) 247617   ABTA AITO ATOL 848

Holiday H

TRADEWINDS

See the world without it costing the earth
THE FAR EAST
AFRICA
THE INDIAN OCEAN
AUSTRALIA
THE CARIBBEAN
FLORIDA
THE PACIFIC OCEAN

Pick up a brochure from your local travel agent or call

☎ **01235 832020**

TRW173

TRADEWINDS
Far & away better value

7 nights from £299

D E P A R T U R E S   F R O M   1 8   U . K .   A I R P O R T S

Paper 2 Writing   (1½ hours)

PART 1

*You **must** answer this question.*

1   Your family is interested in a holiday on a yacht but only has the advertisement shown below and so needs more information. You have the task of writing to the agency which handles yacht bookings.

Carefully read the advertisement and the notes which you have made below. Then write your letter to the agency, covering the points in your notes and adding any relevant information about your family.

Write a **letter** of **120–180** words in an appropriate style. Do not include addresses.

other activities ?

Any other choice ?

Islands Sailing Agency

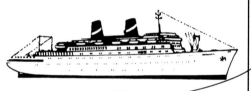

Visit the Caribbean islands in style on one of our luxury yachts. Swim in the clear waters off one of many isolated, sandy beaches. Traditional Caribbean food is served on board, cooked by a local. In the evenings relax in the best restaurants, taverns and bars in the Caribbean.

children?

- *must be late July or early August*
- *number of people on boat?*
- *weather at that time?*
- *length of cruise?*
- *price?*

PAPER 2
Writing
Part 1

Specific hints
Identifying questions

● *Letter asking for information*
Such letters can ask about time, dates, prices, travel arrangements, etc. Sometimes you already have some information but want more.

Suggested plan
Introduction: Para. 1: State the reason for writing.
Body: Para. 2: Ask for the information you want.
Para. 3: Ask for any further information needed.
Conclusion: Para. 4: Conclude politely (usually a formal expression of thanks).

Question types

In this question you often have to refer to the following: text, pictures, notes. Sometimes you are given all three, sometimes not. Check them carefully.

Identifying questions

● *Text*
Information can be given in the form of text. Use it to decide your next action. The information may be insufficient, misleading or try to make you form an opinion. There are often hand-written notes around the text which draw your attention to certain parts of the text where more explanation is needed.

PART 1

General hints
Answering strategy

Divide your paragraphs clearly so that each paragraph deals with a central idea. Use good structures to begin your sentences and your paragraphs and use a good range of vocabulary to suit each type of letter. Make sure that you cover all the points in the texts, pictures and instructions. If your letter is too short, you may not have included all of the points. If it is too long, you may have repeated things or written too many unnecessary details. Make sure your answer is complete. The reader should not have any difficulty understanding what your letter is about.

PART 2

*Write an answer to **one** of the questions 2–5 in this part. Write your answer in **120–180** words in an appropriate style.*

2

DELAWAY DEPARTMENT STORE

Requires Sales Managers for permanent employment.
Will pay top salaries for the right people.

Get on well with people? Have confidence in yourself? Able to work as part of a team?

To apply, write us a letter explaining why you think you would be right for such a position.

Write a **letter of application** to Delaway Department Store. Do not include addresses.

3 You have decided to enter a short story competition. The competition rules say that the story must begin or end with the following words: 'We never saw Angela again.'
Write your **story** for the competition.

4 A radio station is carrying out a survey and has asked its listeners to send in their opinions and suggestions on the following question: 'Should men and women do an equal amount of work in the house?'
Give your **opinion**, saying whether you agree or disagree with the statement.

5 **Background reading texts**
Answer **one** of the following two questions based on your reading of **one** of the set books:
(a) What is the central idea in the story? Describe the incident that you liked most and explain how this would sound interesting to someone who has not yet read the book.
(b) Describe the role of one of the heroes/heroines in the book. Would you have done things differently? Explain why or why not in a book **report** for your English lesson.

Part 2

Specific hints
Identifying questions

● *Letter of application (see question 2)*
You are asked for a semi-formal letter dealing with such things as applying for: a job, a course at a university, a scholarship, etc.
In this type of letter you should state what you are applying for, why you are applying, the details of your education/qualifications/skills/experience, a character description, the names of people that can be asked for a reference, and any other necessary information. You might put some of the details in point form. In the concluding paragraph you might ask them to send you some more information.
Start with *Dear Sir/Madam* and end with *Yours faithfully*, or *Dear Mr/Mrs/Ms (Name)* and end with *Yours sincerely* or *Best regards*. Then sign your name. You are instructed not to write addresses or the date.

● *Narrative composition (see question 3)*
You are asked to tell a story about a person or an event. Sometimes you are given the first or last sentence; do not change the wording. Your story should be developed in chronological order so that it is easy for the reader to follow. If possible use the simple past tense and build the other verb tenses around it. Set the scene in the first paragraph and develop the story in the following paragraphs. Each paragraph should concentrate on one idea. Try to give an interesting conclusion; it is just as important as the introduction.

PART 2

General hints
Answering strategy

Read the questions carefully and notice the type of writing task in each case. Choose a topic that you know enough to write about. It is a good idea to organise your ideas into a plan before you start writing. The points for each paragraph can be written down and then expanded with the use of link words and introductory words and phrases. Remember to include an introduction and a conclusion.
With a plan, writing becomes easier because you do not have to think of ideas as you write. You link, expand and add to the points in your plan. A plan organises your writing, and helps you answer all parts of the question.

Paper 3 Use of English   (1 hour 15 minutes)

PART 1

For questions 1–15, read the text below and decide which answer A, B, C or D best fits each space. There is an example at the beginning (0).

Example:

0   **A** born   **(B)** produced   **C** established   **D** encouraged

ENJOYING DRY-SKIING

Britain may not have **(0)** ___*produced*___ a downhill skiing champion, but there is **(1)** __*still*__ one area of the sport in which it is a leader: dry-skiing. As a **(2)** __*result*__ of this, more man-made ski slopes are found here than in the rest of the world. The first dry slope was **(3)** __*built/created*__ in London thirty-five years ago. Now there are a hundred and fifty slopes in Britain starting from the **(4)** __*smallest*__ size of 30 metres to one of 471 metres just outside Edinburgh. The bigger centres **(5)** __*operate*__ like golf **(6)** __*or*__ squash clubs because they offer their members a full **(7)** __*range*__ of well-organised facilities.

Many people want to **(8)** __*use*__ the dry-ski centres because they are close to the cities. For those who have never **(9)** __*skied*__ before, they can **(10)** __*without*__ doubt save a lot of time and money by going to one of the centres for beginners. Instructors will go **(11)** __*over*__ *explain* the equipment and teach the **(12)** __*basic*__ skills of skiing. For those that can ski, it is a(n) **(13)** __*really*__ good way of keeping fit and practising new techniques. For many **(14)** __*regular*__ skiers it has **(15)** __*become*__ a part of their entertainment.

1 A yet	**B** still	**C** then	**D** already
2 A development	**B** conclusion	**C** proof	**D** result
3 A built	**B** prepared	**C** formed	**D** created
4 A biggest	**B** longest	**C** smallest	**D** widest
5 A perform	**B** instruct	**C** operate	**D** conduct
6 A otherwise	**B** besides	**C** either	**D** or
7 A range	**B** row	**C** variety	**D** area
8 A do	**B** use	**C** go	**D** find
9 A skied	**B** skated	**C** climbed	**D** hiked
10 A with	**B** in	**C** without	**D** of
11 A to	**B** under	**C** round	**D** over
12 A thorough	**B** minimum	**C** true	**D** basic
13 A rarely	**B** really	**C** excellent	**D** seldom
14 A regular	**B** reliable	**C** continuous	**D** continual
15 A made	**B** become	**C** developed	**D** achieved

PART 1

General hints
Answering strategy

Some texts describe things or give information. They often use words that are related to that topic. Try to understand the meaning of such words from the context of the word in the passage. Although many words have a similar meaning, only one word will have the right meaning for that sentence. By understanding this, you will be able to choose the word that fits the sentence.

PAPER 3
Use of English
Part 1

Specific hints
Identifying questions

- *Nouns*
Nouns are naming words. They usually have a plural form that ends in *-(e)s*. Some have an irregular form, e.g. *man – men*. Nouns can be countable, uncountable, concrete, abstract, common or refer to a group. They might be used as part of an expression. It is important to match the type of noun with the verb and other words in the sentence, such as articles or determiners.
Question:
When several _____ are living together, they can easily argue and one of these arguments might cause serious problems.
A *neighbours* B *people*
C *crowds* D *audiences*
Answer:
A no: *neighbours* live near or next to each other
B yes: *people* (noun – general noun for a group): *people . . . living together*
C no: *crowds* collect in public places
D no: *audiences* watch plays

PART 2

For questions 16–30, read the text below and think of the word which best fits each space.
*Use only **one** word in each space. There is an example at the beginning (0).*

PARTY TIME

Joe called **(0)** ___*for*___ Sandra at half past seven. The barbecue
(16) ___was___ to begin at eight but they had decided to get there about half past eight.

Sandra had opened her wardrobe **(17)** ___and___ had looked through her clothes. She had spent a long **(18)** ___time___ trying to decide what to wear. As it was summer time, she had **(19)** ___finally___ chosen a flowered skirt **(20)** ___and___ a short-sleeved blouse. She had combed **(21)** ___her___ hair into the **(22)** ___latest___ modern style and tied it with a bright red ribbon. **(23)** ___However___, as she now sat in the car waiting for Joe to start the engine, she began to have doubts. Was she **(24)** ___too___ formally dressed for the occasion? What if everyone else came in casual clothes? Should she have worn a pair of jeans instead? Joe tried his best to assure her that she looked beautiful and that a lot of girls **(25)** ___would___ be wearing skirts and blouses like her. Sandra continued to be uncertain.

In the end, Sandra got out of the car and went back **(26)** _____ the house. She quickly **(27)** _____ into a pair of jeans and a blue T-shirt. She also put on a pair of shoes **(28)** _____ matched her clothes. Now she felt **(29)** _____ comfortable. She would be able to enjoy **(30)** _____ without feeling the odd one out.

Part 2

Specific hints
Identifying questions

● *Quantifiers*
Quantifiers show how many things or how much of something we are talking about. Some quantifiers are used with countable nouns, some with uncountable nouns and some with both kinds. Some examples are *several, few, little, plenty of, both, some, enough, every* and *most*.
Question:
When _____ people are living together, they can easily argue and one of these arguments might cause serious problems.
Answer:
several – the plural subject *people* needs a quantifier like *several* to show more than three or four.

● *Comparatives*
When we compare people or things that are separate from each other, we use the comparative form with *more* or *-er*, often followed by *than*.
Example:
He always runs *more* quickly *than* the others.
  When you compare one member of a group with a whole group you use the superlative form with *most* or *-est*.
Example:
It was the *most* horrible race he had ever run.
  The opposites of *more* and *most* are *less* and *least*.
Example:
He runs the *least* amount of time possible.

PART 2

General hints
Answering strategy

When you answer this question you should not waste time on one particular gap. If you cannot work it out immediately, leave it. Work out the rest of the gaps and then come back to the one that you have not completed. Before filling in the gap, read the whole sentence.
  Sometimes you may need to think about what comes right before or after the part that is missing. The more you read the text, the more familiar you become with the contents. This will help you understand what type of word is missing.

  Remember that the word you choose must not only be grammatically correct but also appropriate in meaning. You can use only one word in each gap.

PART 3

*For questions **31–40**, complete the second sentence so that it has a similar meaning to the first sentence, using the word given. **Do not change the word given.** You must use between two and five words, including the word given. There is an example at the beginning (0).*

Example:

 0 Mr Jones needn't go if he doesn't want to.
   obliged
 0 Mr Jones *is not obliged to go* if he doesn't want to.

31 We would rather stop than continue in this manner.
   prefer
   We _____ than to continue in this manner.

32 Mother told Tom that he had to go to bed early.
   must
   'You _____ to bed early,' Mother told Tom.

33 I last saw her at the end of May.
   since
   I _____ the end of May.

34 I'll never be able to persuade her to agree with the idea.
   bring
   I'll never _____ to the idea.

35 She could not understand how they were related.
   connection
   She could not understand _____ to her.

36 I don't think I can afford to buy this dress.
   have
   I don't think I _____ money to buy this dress.

37 He is helping his mother so that they can finish quickly.
   order
   He is helping his mother _____ quickly.

38 I found my old diary by chance.
   came
   I _____ my old diary by chance.

39 He was very rude when he spoke to the old man.
   politely
   He _____ the old man.

40 She caught the early bus so that she would not be late for work.
   avoid
   She caught the early bus _____ late for work.

Part 3

Specific hints
Identifying questions

● *Verb structures with similar meaning*
You may be asked to complete a sentence with a suitable verb form. You must change from one verb form to another.
Example:
is certain to have gone to *must have gone*
Question:
Perhaps they ran yesterday.
may
They _____ yesterday.
Answer:
may have run – *may* + perfect infinitive to mean *perhaps they ran*

PART 3   ***General hints***
Answering strategy

As this part contains some of the basic grammatical transformations that can take place in the English language, make sure that you are familiar with these changes. Learn all the sentence types and the structures which are used to form them.

PART 4

For questions 41–55, read the text below and look carefully at each line. Some of the lines are correct, and some have a word which should not be there.

*If a line is correct put a tick (√) by the number. If a line has a word which should **not** be there, write the word next to the number. There are two examples at the beginning (**0** and **00**).*

RACE AGAINST TIME

Soon a rather low sound was being heard and the float plane	**0**	*being*
appeared, flying towards us. It landed gently on the lake, turned	**00**	√
and then came slowly up along the landing stage. We loaded	**41**	
equipment while Jim was been talking with the pilot, wanting	**42**	
to know how about the weather was ahead of us. The pilot said	**43**	
that the conditions in the valley were all right at the moment for	**44**	
landing and taking it off, but that the weather was rapidly	**45**	
getting more worse and we would have to get away as quickly as	**46**	
possible. We all worked silently for quite a while, because of we	**47**	
did not want to waste time. Finally the plane was being ready.	**48**	
Jim he also boarded it so that there was one less person to take	**49**	
on the next trip. The plane moved over the surface of the water	**50**	
and rose into the air. The plane came back on the time and it was	**51**	
Chris' turn to go, with the rest of the film gear. Unless the plane	**52**	
was not back in time, we would be in trouble. The clouds	**53**	
were getting so thicker and blacker. We began to be anxious	**54**	
about our safety and whether the plane would be back to pick us up.	**55**	

Part 4

Specific hints
Identifying questions

● *Verbs followed by prepositions*
Some examples of verbs often used with prepositions are *agree with*, *believe in*, *arrive at*, *decide on*, *choose between*, *belong to*, *ask for*, *laugh at*. However, you must always look at the context to see if the verb should be followed by a preposition or not.
Example:
He *reached* the finish line.
He *reached for* the jug of water.
Question:
Athletes must train for hard.
Error:
for – athletes can *train for a competition*, but context shows that it is incorrect here.

● *Adjectives followed by prepositions*
Some adjectives usually take prepositions, like *afraid of*, *ashamed of*, *aware of*, *anxious about*, *sorry about*, *angry with*, *bored with*, *annoyed at*, *keen on*, *famous for*. However, you must always look at the context to see if the adjectives should be followed by a preposition or not.
Example:
He was *afraid of* the race.
He was *afraid that* he couldn't finish the race.

PART 4

General hints
Answering strategy

This part tests how good you are at grammar. You must identify any extra words, just as you would if you were re-reading your own written work. Be careful to look at the whole sentence because sometimes a word might fit, and sometimes it might not. For example: My sister and I are *becoming so* close. But: My sister and I are *becoming ~~so~~* closer and closer.

PART 5

For questions 56–65, read the text below. Use the word given in capitals at the end of each line to form a word that fits in the space in the same line. There is an example at the beginning (0).

MEMORIES

I will never forget the most **(0)** _wonderful_ moment in our career	**WONDER**
when we were given the highest score for our **(56)** ...	**PERFORM**
in the ice-skating championship **(57)** ... at Helsinki.	**COMPETE**
We received the **(58)** ... score of nine marks	**BELIEVABLE**
of 6.0, which was the maximum score that could be given.	
The **(59)** ... of time that we had spent practising	**LONG**
our dance routine finally paid off. The **(60)** ... that	**DIFFICULT**
we had found with some of the **(61)** ... pieces we	**MUSIC**
had chosen was soon overcome and becoming **(62)** ...	**FAME**
was only a matter of time.	
Those were the **(63)** ... days of being young and	**EXCITE**
(64) ... about everything and having the feeling that	**OPTIMISM**
our **(65)** ... would never lessen.	**POPULAR**

Part 5

Specific hints
Identifying questions

● *Adjectives*
Adjectives are describing words. Some of them are formed from nouns and verbs. They describe the qualities of people, things, places, etc. They usually come before the noun or after the verb *to be*. By knowing the position of the adjective in the sentence you will be able to understand how to change the given word with the appropriate suffix. Some suffixes which make adjectives are:
Noun to adjective: *histor(y) ic, dirt y, month ly, humour ours, continent al*
Verb to adjective: *enjoy able, act ive, excite d, surpris(e) ing, creat(e) ive*

● *Prefixes*
A prefix is a syllable which is added to the front of a word. It often makes the word negative or gives the opposite meaning.
Some prefixes which can be used with adjectives are:
Adjective to adjective: *un able, in complete, il legal, im perfect, dis honest, ir regular.*
   Note that sometimes in Part 5, you do not have to change the form of the word, but just add a prefix. Think carefully about the right meaning.
Question:
It was certainly an _____ win by the weakest participant.
expect
Answer:
unexpected – make verb *expect* into adjective *unexpected* using suffix *-ed* and prefix *un-*.

PART 5   ***General hints***
Answering strategy

To decide which part of speech to change the word into, look at the position of the word in the sentence. For example, if the blank is followed by a noun you may have to change the word into an adjective. If it names something/someone and follows an article, it may be a noun. If it is just before or just after a verb, it may be an adverb. If it follows the subject of the sentence, it may be a verb.

Paper 4 Listening (approximately 35 minutes)

PART 1

*You'll hear people talking in eight different situations. For questions **1–8**, choose the best answer, A, B or C.*

1 Listen to this girl talking to her friends. What doesn't she want?
 A to go to a film
 B to go to a film with a certain boy
 C to pay to see a film

| | 1 |

2 You receive this phone call. Why is the man calling?
 A to sell something
 B to buy something
 C to give something away free

| | 2 |

3 Listen to these two women discussing a friend. Who is she dating?
 A a university student
 B a professional musician
 C a businessman

| | 3 |

4 You are walking down the street when someone stops you. What does he want?
 A the name of a street
 B the location of 'Highlife' supermarket
 C some directions

| | 4 |

5 You come home to find this message from your daughter on your answering machine. Where is she?
 A at a football stadium
 B at a bowling alley
 C at a skating rink

| | 5 |

6 Listen to this teacher phoning a colleague about a problem. She blames
 A the students.
 B the parents.
 C the headmaster.

| | 6 |

7 Listen to a woman talking to a group about 'Assertiveness Training'. What does she ask you to do?
 A leave the room for a short time
 B make a big fuss
 C imagine a situation at work

| | 7 |

8 You are in a shopping mall when you overhear this conversation. What does the man ask for?
 A some food
 B some money
 C directions

| | 8 |

**PARTS
1 and 3**

General hints
Question types

In Parts 1 and 3 you can be tested on: gist (the overall meaning or situation), main points (key pieces of

information), function (the reason for speaking), location (the place of communication), roles/relationships (the connection between the speakers), mood (the state of the speaker's mind), attitude (the

speaker's thoughts or behaviour), intention (the speaker's plans), feeling (the speaker's feelings), opinion (the speaker's thoughts or beliefs).

PAPER 4
Listening
Part 1

Specific hints
Question types

This part is always a multiple choice question.

Identifying questions

● *Multiple choice*
You are asked to choose the best of three answers. You can be asked to answer a question or finish a statement. Read each question carefully and underline the key words. Choose which answer best matches what you have understood from the taped text. If you are not sure of an answer, try to identify the incorrect answers, and then choose from the ones you have left.

● *Stress*
You can often understand how someone feels or thinks by listening to the words that are stressed. When a speaker stresses a word, it means he thinks that word is important. This can give the sentence different shades of meaning.

Exercise on stress

Listen to this man talking to someone about going out. What is he thinking?
A I don't care about the other people.
B I'm too tired to go out again.
C Which place are we going to?
Now listen to the explanation.

PART 2

*You will hear a writer talking to a producer about a film script. For questions **9–18**, complete the notes which summarise what the producer says. You will need to write a word or a short phrase in each box.*

Kind of film:

Features modern spies who are [ ] **9**

and [ ] **10**

Actors:

Elizabeth Kingston – she'll attract crowds, but is [ ] **11**

Paul Downing – no, because the character isn't [ ] **12**

Luke Fairy – good, as he'll [ ] **13**

Climax:

Old climax – too much like [ ] **14**

Chase starts off in [ ] **15**

Big struggle takes place [ ] **16**

Hero gets away in [ ] **17**

Whole script must be [ ] **18**

Part 2

Specific hints
Question types

This part is always a note taking or blank filling question.

Identifying questions

● *Note taking*
You are asked to complete some summary sentences, for example about a course you are interested in or some rules you must follow. You are usually asked to write what you hear in a different, shorter form. There may be more than one way to write the correct answer. Choose the shorter way, but make sure you include all of the necessary information. If there are two answer boxes for one sentence, it does not matter in which order you write the answers.

As you read over the test, try to guess what kind of information you are being asked for. For example, it may be obvious that an adjective is missing. Answers may require one word or a phrase. It saves you time if you use acceptable abbreviations, for example, if you answer *8* instead of writing *eight* or *kms* instead of *kilometres*.

PARTS 2 and 4

General hints
Question types

In Parts 2 and 4 you can be tested on: gist (the overall meaning or situation), main points (key pieces of information), details (specific items), deduced meanings (logical conclusions drawn from the material given).

PART 3

You will hear five women talking about the jobs they do. For questions **19–23**, choose from the pictures of jobs **A–F** what each speaker is describing. Use the letter only once. There is one extra letter which you do not need to use.

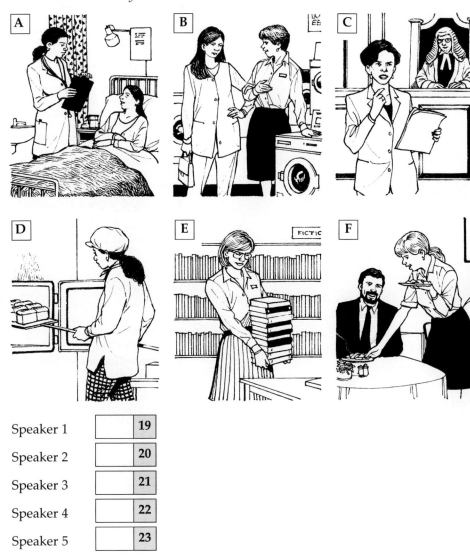

Speaker 1		**19**
Speaker 2		**20**
Speaker 3		**21**
Speaker 4		**22**
Speaker 5		**23**

PART 4

You will hear a car salesman describing a car. For questions **24–30**, answer the questions by ticking one of the boxes to show whether the answer to each question is **yes** or **no**.

Does the car have the following features?

24	an air bag	Y	N	**24**
25	front and rear mudflaps	Y	N	**25**
26	a CD player	Y	N	**26**
27	a leather steering wheel	Y	N	**27**
28	floor maps	Y	N	**28**
29	Does the salesman use 'safety' to sell the car?	Y	N	**29**
30	Is his sales talk cold and distant?	Y	N	**30**

Part 3

Specific hints
Question types

This part is always a matching question.

Identifying questions

● *Matching*
You are asked to match items in one list with speakers in another list. You might be asked to match words, sentences, or pictures to the speakers. If the information is in word or sentence form, listen for the words given or their synonyms. You are asked to choose from a group of similar items, so listen carefully for descriptive words or phrases that help to identify the differences. If it is in picture form, try to identify each picture: think of each item's name and use(s), and then listen for these words or their synonyms.

Part 4

Specific hints
Identifying questions

● *Yes/no*
You are asked to answer some questions with *yes* or *no*. Your own opinions are not important here, so listen carefully to the speaker(s). Do not forget that each time you answer there's a 50 per cent chance of getting it correct, so do not leave any questions unanswered, even if you are not sure.

Question types

The questions ask you to find information. You must listen carefully to the words that are said and how they are said. Pay special attention to: vocabulary, register (formal or informal), sounds, intonation/tone of voice and word stress. The questions often paraphrase the taped text.

Exercise on paraphrasing

Speaker 1: *I had boarded the train and was looking for my seat when I came across Scotty. My old friend was in a very bad temper.*
Question:
Answer the questions with *yes* or *no*.
1 Did the speaker meet his friend on the train?
2 Did the speaker meet two friends?
Answer:
1 yes: *I had boarded the train … when I came across Scotty* is another way of saying that the speaker met his friend while on the train
2 no: *Scotty* and *my old friend* are the same person, so this is incorrect

Paper 5 Speaking (approximately 15 minutes)

PART 1 (approximately 4 minutes)

Talk about yourself:

1 Do you have a large family?
Do you think a small family is better, or a large family?
Why?

2 What nationality are you?
Tell us about one or two interesting customs or traditions in your country.
As you have probably been studying English for some time now, can you compare one or two of your customs to English customs?

PART 2 (approximately 4 minutes)

Look at the photographs on p. 124 and p. 125. They show different groups of people. Work with your partner.

1 Student A: compare and contrast pictures 1 and 2, saying which situation you wish you could change and why.

2 Student B: talk about how you feel about these two situations.

3 Student B: compare and contrast pictures 3 and 4, saying which situation you might want to change and why.

4 Student A: talk about which situation you would feel more comfortable in and why.

PAPER 5
Speaking

Part 1

Specific hints
Identifying questions

● *Discussing your family (see question 1)*
If asked to describe your family and you're not married, start with your parents, then brothers/sisters, and then anyone else whom you might feel especially close to. If you're living with somebody, start with your partner, then your children. To make the discussion more interesting, perhaps describe a peculiar habit or mannerism. Some useful vocabulary might include: *grandfather, grandmother, aunt, uncle, cousin, mother-in-law, father-in-law, godfather, godmother, godchild.*

● *Discussing customs (see question 2)*
Customs are an important part of culture, and are often linked with historic or religious holidays. Speak about them respectfully. Include some personal examples of what your family does.

Part 2

Specific hints
Identifying questions

● *Discussing your wishes (see questions 1 and 3)*
Wishes generally show dissatisfaction or unhappiness with reality. Listen carefully to the question to decide what kind of wish you are being asked for. Use the right verb tenses.

● *Discussing your feelings (see questions 2 and 4)*
Decide how you feel about the subject. It might help to decide whether you feel positively (excited, curious) or negatively (angry, frustrated), and how strongly. Give the reason for your feelings, if you can. If asked about how other people might feel, put yourself in their shoes.

PART 2

General hints
Answering strategy

When talking about what is happening in the pictures, use the present continuous tense *They are eating breakfast.* If you do not know the verb you need, then try to say it in different words. For example, you can say *They're taking a slow walk through the park,* instead of *They're strolling through the park.*

When you first see the pictures, try to identify quickly what the general theme is. It is usually a broad subject, like technology,

sports or the performing arts. Look at the places, objects or people for clues. You may be asked to comment on them or compare/contrast them.

Places: In order to identify where the picture was taken, think about the people (their clothes, the colour of their skin, their features), buildings (architectural style), level of technology (advanced or not), plants and trees, etc.

Objects: If you need to describe an object in a picture, start by making a general statement and then describe it in detail by moving

from one side of it to the other, or from the top to the bottom. Useful vocabulary might include: *circular, square, oval, rectangular,* etc. If you are not sure of what something is, use expressions like *It looks like . . .* or *Perhaps it's a . . .*

People: When describing a person, think about his or her age, sex and general appearance. Focus on the most unusual feature, like uncommon clothes or expression. You might suggest a possible reason for this.

PART 3 (approximately 3 minutes)

Imagine that you work for a market research company. Look at the picture below; it gives some suggestions of things a thirty-year-old single man might like to have.

Work with your partner. Talk together and decide which thing he'd most like to have and which thing he'd least like to have. Then talk about what you think a seventy-year-old single man would most/least like to have.

PART 4 (approximately 4 minutes)

Discuss the following questions with your partner:

1 Why might a person's needs change because of age?
2 Do people sometimes think material things are more valuable than their family or friends?
3 How important is good health?
4 Is money the source of happiness?
5 What is the most important thing in your life?

Part 3

Specific hints
Identifying questions

● *Prioritising*
You are asked to put some things in the order of their importance. This might be as you see it, or as someone else sees it. If you are prioritising for someone else, think about that person's point of view. Consider the information given. Give good reasons for your choices. Keep in mind that a 'right' order may not exist.

Useful vocabulary

● *Agreement*
I agree (with you)/you're absolutely right/yes, I think so too.

● *Reluctant agreement*
I suppose so/I suppose not/you may be right/perhaps you're right.

● *Disagreement*
I'm afraid I can't agree with you/I don't really think so/I'm sorry, but I don't agree.
You may have a point there.

Part 4

Specific hints
Identifying questions

● *Making generalisations (see questions 2, 3, 4)*
You are asked to draw a general conclusion about a particular aspect of life. Use your own experience and knowledge to help you draw a logical conclusion. Make a statement, then give specific examples or evidence (something you have heard, read or experienced) to support your statement.

General hints
Answering strategy

The interviewer doesn't want to trick you. He or she wants to encourage you to speak. Be polite, diplomatic and as honest as possible. Try to open up new subjects with which you are familiar, just as you would in a real-life conversation.

Speak loud enough and with confidence. Look at the examiners and other candidate during the conversation. Speak in turn. Do not

talk all the time. Try not to say *er*. If you make a mistake and realise it immediately, correct your mistake and then go on talking.

When someone asks you a question, the answer is usually in the same verb tense. For example, the question *Would you like to visit Australia one day?* should be answered *Yes, I would.*

Answer the question appropriately. For example, if the examiner asks for advantages and

disadvantages, list some. If the examiner asks for your preference, state one. This is important. In many cases, there is no 'right' or 'wrong' answer. The examiner wants to see if you can try to do the task properly.

If you do not understand what the interviewer says, or if you need some more time to think, say something like *Pardon me? Would you mind repeating that?* or *I'm sorry, I didn't quite catch that.*

TEST 3

Paper 1 Reading   (1 hour 15 minutes)

PART 1

*You are going to read a magazine article about shoes. Choose from the list **A–I** the heading which best summarises each part (**1–7**) of the article. There is one extra heading which you do not need to use. There is an example at the beginning (**0**).*

> **A** Shoe designs are simple
> **B** Right and left
> **C** Some feet are bigger than others
> **D** Function turns to fashion
> **E** Expensive shoes are not always the best
> **F** Women like to look taller
> **G** Shoes sheltered the feet
> **H** Factories take over production
> **I** Know your history

DR MIX ON FOOT CARE: IF THE SHOE FITS

0	I

If you perform pedicures on your clients' feet, they will probably ask you about shoes. By understanding the history of shoes, the basics of shoe fitting, and the mechanics of shoe wear, you will be able knowledgeably to counsel your clients on how to choose the right footwear.

1	G

It is thought that the first shoes were worn more than 12,000 years ago by our ancestors who lived in a colder climate. These first shoes were probably an early version of moccasin made of leather and lined with fur or grass for insulation. They were to protect the foot more from the cold than from the harsh terrain.

2	D

Sandals appear to be the next development in foot coverings. Drawings dating back to 6000–9000 BC show craftsmen constructing this type of 'shoe'. The earliest existing example is an Egyptian sandal dating back to 2000 BC. From this simple design the Egyptians and Mesopotamians introduced fashion by adding colour ornamentation, and different shapes to their sandals.

3	A

All footwear fashions come from only seven basic designs. The newest of these designs, the laced oxford, dates back 300 years! And not one of these basic designs was created by or for women. Up until about 70 years ago, when shoes became more affordable and available to the masses because of mass production, only about 10 per cent of the population even wore shoes.

4 F

In the 16th century the 'high heel' shoe was introduced into women's fashion. It is recorded that Catherine de Medici, a 17-year-old Italian, was sent to marry King Henry II of France. Because of her short stature, she wore shoes with 2- to 3-inch heels. High heels became the rage of Europe, to the point that the church clergy branded them 'devices of Satan to stir the lusts of men'.

5 B

Early 19th-century America gave the world three great innovations in footwear construction and fit. Until then, all shoes were made from straight moulds, which meant the shoe could be worn on either foot. The idea of a left shoe and a right shoe was first introduced in 1824 but was rejected by the public because the shoes looked 'crooked'. It was not until around 1900 that left and right shoes gained a firm foothold in the commercial marketplace.

6 H

The second thing that revolutionised shoe manufacturing was Elias Howe's invention of the sewing machine in 1845. This allowed the upper pieces of the shoe to be sewn by machine instead of by hand. The McKay sewing machine was then developed to stitch the sole to the upper pieces. This allowed mass production of footwear, making shoes affordable to the general population.

7 C

The third innovation was the first common-sense system of shoe sizing, put forth by Edwin B. Simpson of New York in 1886. Until this time, shoes were generally available in only two sizes: large and small, fat and slim, or men's and women's. Simpson's system of progressive measurements applied separately to men's, women's, children's, and infants' shoes. By the turn of the century this system finally gave the world uniformity in shoe sizing.

PART 2

You are going to read an article about a policewoman. For questions 8–14, choose the answer (A, B, C or D) which you think fits best according to the text.

This is WPC Sue Porter's third year as a member of Avon and Somerset's task force, a specialised 'hit-squad' providing support for her colleagues. Her job is physically and mentally taxing. From disarming a knife attacker to bringing round the victim of a car crash she is expected to perform as well as the boys.

Her 119 male colleagues in the squad would doubtless recognise that the words 'task force' are usually associated with males. To try to remedy this the unit was renamed 'support team' on January 1. Porter, 26, is one of three women working in it. 'I'm not out to prove something because I'm a woman. I'm out to be me. They

Part 2

Specific hints
Identifying texts

● *Factual descriptive text*
This kind of text gives a detailed, impersonal description of something (a place, a process or a sociological trend). In Part 2, the questions are often about descriptions of behaviour or actions, thoughts and feelings.

General hints
Answering strategy

Note that the questions are usually in the same order as the information in the text. It is very important to learn how to identify key related words, in order to match *what is said* in the text *with the questions or prompts.*

● *Finding related words*
Same word
A word or phrase might be used in the text (*engineer*) and then used again in the question or prompt (*engineer*).
Different forms of the same word
One form of the word might be used in the text (*apply* which is a verb), and another in the question or prompt (*application* which is a noun). Or, a word might be used in the text

(*bed*), and another with the same stem in the question or prompt (*bedroom*).
Synonym
A word or phrase might be used in the text (*their ambitions*) and another word or phrase meaning the same thing in the question or prompt (*what they aim for*).
You must recognise all of these related words in order to answer the questions correctly.

can't expect any more from me and if they do they're going to be disappointed,' she says.

Porter is less than 5ft 5in tall and weighs about nine stone. In a fight she says her colleagues would probably feel better with a 6ft well-built man behind them. 'If I know we are going where things are going to be difficult I offer to drive. The driver always stays with the van. But no-one else would ever ask me to drive, and often we don't have time to prepare and it's the ones in the back who get out and deal with it.' Last year, 'dealing with it' included having building blocks and bricks thrown at them in several protests and riots.

Porter says the violence is there, no matter what sex you are. 'Being a woman makes little difference. Sometimes people tell you that you shouldn't be in this job, but that's usually their way of explaining why they've hit you. But sometimes a couple of men will react better to a woman telling them to calm down: they see a big man as a good opportunity to fight.'

At the station Porter books in her struggling prisoner. He has no home address and is unemployed. He does not like being arrested by a woman and keeps swearing at her. 'I'll see you in court,' he shouts as he is dragged to a cell.

Porter looks on without emotion. It is 3.30 am and there is still the paperwork to do. The team will reassemble at 7.30 pm to prepare for Arsenal fans coming in to a sleepy Yeovil for an FA cup match. It could be a busy night.

8   What does 'taxing', in the third line, mean?
  A easy
  B difficult
  C terrible
  D satisfactory

9   Why didn't the men on the squad ask her to drive?
  A They respected her.
  B She wasn't a good driver.
  C She had to stay with the van.
  D They were afraid someone would hurt her.

10 What do we learn about the people in protests and riots?
  A They always throw things at the police.
  B They rarely throw things at the police.
  C They sometimes throw things at the police.
  D They never throw things at the police.

11 Why did some people say she shouldn't be on the hit-squad?
  A They wanted to explain how they felt.
  B They thought that men usually reacted better.
  C They felt guilty.
  D They were innocent.

12 How did the prisoner react to her arresting him?
  A He dragged her to a cell.
  B He asked her to read him his rights.
  C He tried to insult her.
  D He calmed down.

13 How did she feel about her prisoner?
  A She was frightened of him.
  B She was confused about her feelings.
  C She was pleased that she had arrested him.
  D She didn't feel anything at all.

Identifying questions

● *Incorrect usage of a single word*
Incorrect answers sometimes use words like modals (*may, could, must*) or quantifiers (*always, never, sometimes*) to distract you from the correct answer.

● *Opposite meanings*
Incorrect answers sometimes use the opposite of what has been said in the text to distract you from the correct answer.

Exercise on single words/opposites

As a small boy, I can remember being very bad. I would always get out of the small jobs my parents gave me to do around the house. I would also always get into fights with my brothers and sisters. I was not the perfect son, and must have made my parents very angry. They should have punished me more severely.
Question:
When the author was young,
A he rarely argued with his brothers and sisters.
B he behaved well.
C he constantly quarrelled with his brothers and sisters.
D he might have upset his parents.
Answer:
A no: the writer says he always got into fights, so it is incorrect to say he rarely argued
B no: the writer says he remembers being very bad, the opposite of behaving well
C yes: the writer says he always got into fights, which is another way of saying he constantly quarrelled
D no: the writer says he must have made his parents very angry with his misbehaviour, so it is incorrect to say he might have upset them

14 What would be the most suitable title for this article?
- **A** Hard night for a policewoman
- **B** No equality in the police force
- **C** Police officers like violence
- **D** Police work tough for beginners

PART 3

You are going to read a newspaper article about someone who works. Eight sentences have been removed from the article. Choose from the sentences A–I the one which fits each gap (15–21). There is one extra sentence which you do not need to use. There is an example at the beginning (0).

THE PIES HAVE IT AFTER A SLICE OF PART-TIME WORK
Interview by Charlotte Beugge

Paul Hutchinson did not have a full-time job for nearly two years. **0 | I**

Mr Hutchinson, 48, from Prestwich, Manchester, was a manager of a chain of car dealers before he was made redundant 20 months ago.

He was jobless for a few months and then started temporary work at a factory. Then he took a temporary job at the bakery. **15**

Mr Hutchinson said, 'When I was out of work, I joined a job club. **16** It is easy to sit around and do nothing and get depressed but I am a strong sort of person and fortunately, I was financially OK. **17** I started doing temporary jobs and got this job through that.'

Mr Hutchinson's new job is a complete career change for him: his previous work mainly involved administrative work and accounting. But he is hopeful that his new job will be the first step on the ladder to a new career. He said, 'There are a lot of choices available at my new company. **18**

'I know I am over-qualified for my current job. **19** I am really enjoying my new job: the company and the people are fantastic.'

Mr Hutchinson got his new job through an employment agency, Brook Street. **20**

'There is a huge pool of people out there so no-one should take any refusals too much to heart. **21**

PART 3

General hints
Answering strategy

It is very important to learn how to identify key related ideas and connectors in order to match what is *said* in the text *with the questions or prompts.*

● *Finding related ideas*
An idea or theme might be used in the text (*her kitchen was a warm, safe place,* which is a description) and the same idea or theme continued in the question or prompt

(*there were many pots and pans hanging up on the walls,* which continues the description).

● *Finding connectors*
Pronoun
A noun might be used in the text and the matching pronoun in the question or prompt (*Mary* in the text with *she* in the prompt, *the skill of typing* with *this skill, doctor, lawyer, engineer* with *these professions*).
Comparative or superlative
An idea might be used in the text

and then compared in the question or prompt (*mountain climbing is a very interesting hobby* with *but cycling is safer and watching TV is the safest*).
Link word/adverb
An idea might be used in the text and then continued in the question or prompt (*we should really wash the dishes now* with *but let's watch some TV first*).
You must recognise all of these related words in order to answer the questions correctly.

A 'There may be opportunities to move upwards or sideways.'
B 'I used their facilities to write my curriculum vitae and apply for jobs.'
C 'People should explore any opportunities that present themselves for work.'
D His employers were so impressed with his work, that they offered him a full-time post on the pie-packing production line.
E 'But you've got to start somewhere even at my time of life.'
F 'I got a golden handshake from my last job, but I didn't go out and spend it all.'
G Mr Hutchinson was strongly supported by his wife.
H Hamish Thompson, marketing executive of Brook Street, said, 'It is a difficult job market but people need to have a strong way of dealing with things in a difficult situation.'
I But he has just started a new job at a Manchester bakery.

PART 4

*You are going to read some information about some cultural events happening in different European cities. For questions 22–26, choose from the cities (A–I). Some of the cities may be chosen more than once. When more than one answer is required, these may be given in any order. There is an example at the beginning (0). For questions 27–35, indicate the answer to each question by choosing from the list of events A–D. Some of the events will be required more than once. **Note:** Where a city offers more than one event, you may give the answers in any order.*

Which city or cities would you recommend for someone who:

likes photography?	**0**	**H**	
enjoys folk music?	**22**		
is interested in stone carving?	**23**		
is interested in musical instruments?	**24**		
is interested in South America?	**25**		**26**

What are the events offered in the following cities?

Aachen	**27**	**28**	**29**
Amsterdam	**30**		
Antwerp	**31**		
Barcelona	**32**		
Basel	**33**		
Copenhagen	**34**	**35**	

A music
B dance
C art
D theatre

Part 4

Specific hints
Question types

You are given questions and must find the answers. The questions often paraphrase what is in the text. Sometimes the questions use exactly the same words/phrases as in the text. You must quickly scan the text for the specific information you need. Do not worry about any unknown words.

Exercise on paraphrasing

Question:
Which boy would you recommend for someone who:
1 likes to teach well-behaved children?
2 likes to teach active children?

Tom – A
As a small boy, I can remember being very bad. I would always get out of the small jobs my parents gave me to do around the house. I would also always get into fights with my brothers and sisters. I was not the perfect son, and must have made my parents very angry. They should have punished me more severely.

Harold – B
I was a quiet child, always well-behaved and doing what my parents and teachers told me to do. This never seemed to bother me, as I could understand the reason for following orders. It is only now that I have come to question authority.

Answer:
1 B Harold was *well-behaved*, and the question asks about *well-behaved* children
2 A Tom was *very bad* and got into many *fights*, which is another way of saying that he was an *active* child

CULTURAL EVENTS IN EUROPE

AACHEN – A

LUDWIG FORUM FUR INTERNATIONALE KUNST Julicher Str 97–109. **Die 5. Biennale von Havanna.** This is the first time that this event has been held in Europe. Visitors can see street theatre and dance from Colombia, music from Argentina, Uruguay, Cuba and Trinidad, and enjoy literature and film from Brazil. There will also be a two-day Latin-American market.

Until 11 December.
Tel +49 241–18070

AMSTERDAM – B

HET MUZIEKTHEATER Waterlooplein 22. Performances of Mozart's **Le nozze di Figaro** on 9, 11, 14 October. Conducted by Graeme Jenkins and directed by Jurgen Flimm. It features Dean Peterson as Figaro, Roberto Scaltriti as the Count of Almaviva and Joan Rodgers as the Countess of Almaviva. The music is provided by the Netherlands Chamber Orchestra.

Tel +31 20-5518922

ANTWERP – C

HESSENHUIS FALCONRUI 53. **Music and Painting in the Golden Age: Music and Graphics.** An outstanding collection of works from Flemish and Dutch artists of the 17th century. In addition to 55 paintings there are musical instruments and pieces of music on display. There are still lifes of instruments, portraits in which the subjects play music and pastoral settings. There are 120 prints, mostly from the 16th century, which portray the social and symbolic importance of music, song and dance at this time.

Until 30 October.
Tel +32 2-2269300

BARCELONA – D

CENTRE CULTURAL DE LA FUNDACIO LA CAIXA Passeig de Sant Joan. **Kandinsky/Mondrian – Two roads towards abstraction.** This exhibition celebrates the anniversary of the deaths of two great pioneers of modern art. One of its aims is to highlight the parallels as well as the differences which mark the stylistic development of the two artists. Among the works on display are 35 canvases by the Russian-born Kandinsky and 56 oils, drawings, watercolours and gouaches by the Dutch-born Mondrian.
Until 13 November.
Tel +34 3-4046073

BASEL – **E**

KUNSTMUSEUM BASEL St Alban-Graben 16. **Fernand Leger 1911–1924 – le rhythme de la vie moderne.** A collection which concentrates on major works and work groups dating back to the critical early years of Leger's career when he developed his style. He is considered a painter of the modern world, seeing the basis of modern art in the principle of opposites.
Until 27 November.
Tel +41 61-2710828

BUDAPEST – **F**

HUNGARIAN NATIONAL GALLERY, Buda Castle. Several museums in the Hungarian capital have permanent exhibitions and this gallery has an important collection of Hungarian art from all periods, medieval stone carvings as well as Renaissance and Baroque art.

HUNGARIAN NATIONAL MUSEUM, Muzeum Krt. 14 which has Hungarian coronation regalia on display is also worth a visit.

Tel. +36 1-1179800

COPENHAGEN – **G**

THE ROYAL THEATRE Kongens Nytorv. An adaptation of Bournonville's **La Sylphide** ballet by Peter Schaufuss can be seen on 5, 11 and 13 October. Musical adaptation is by Ole Norlyng and Graham Bond is the conductor. Tchaikovsky's **Onegin**, based on Pushkin's famous novel about the cynical antihero in the Russia of the 1820s, can be seen on 8 and 17 October.

Conducted by Graham Bond and choreographed by John Cranko.

Tel. +45-33141002

EDINBURGH – **H**

THE FRUITMARKET GALLERY 29 Market Street. **BT new contemporaries.** This is an exhibition designed to showcase student and new graduate art in the UK. There is a variety of work on show from 36 artists including the six prizewinners. A strong feature of the exhibition is photography, with a wide variety of examples of how this medium can be employed. The artists have used materials as diverse as wood and soap.

8 October–12 November.

Tel. +44 31-2252383

FRANKFURT – **I**

DEUTSCHES ARCHITEKTURE-MUSEUM Schaumainkai 43.
Zeitgenössische Architektur in Brasilien (Contemporary architecture in Brazil). The exhibition is devoted to architecture of the past ten years and the aim is to show how dynamically contemporary architecture has developed. The climate alone in Brazil – tropical temperature as well as frost and snow – means that architects must be very creative with their methods.
8 October–6 November.
Tel +49 69-2121847

Paper 2 Writing (1½ hours)

PART 1

*You **must** answer this question.*

1 A group of teenagers are going on their first hiking trip. They have written to your hiking club asking for advice. You are the secretary of the club and have the task of replying to the teenagers.

 Look at the pictures and the notes which you have made below. Then write to them about the route they should take and the equipment they will need.

 Write a **letter** of **120–180** words in an appropriate style. Do not include addresses.

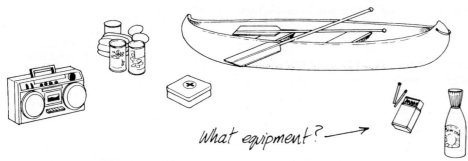

What equipment? ———➤

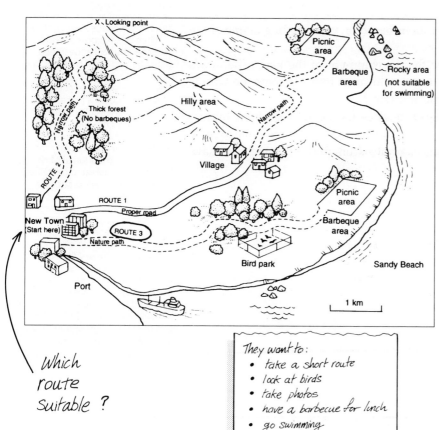

Which route suitable?

They want to:
- take a short route
- look at birds
- take photos
- have a barbecue for lunch
- go swimming

PAPER 2
Writing
Part 1

Specific hints
Identifying questions

● *Letter of advice*
This gives suggestions about how to deal with a problem. Advice can be given about choosing a job/accommodation/something to buy, solving a personal problem, etc. As the reader of the letter is usually a stranger, advice can only be given based on the information received.

Suggested plan:
Introduction: Para. 1: Refer to the problem (what it is, why you are writing).
Body: Para. 2: Give advice referring to the information received.
Para. 3: State your willingness to answer any further questions.
Conclusion: Para. 4: Conclude with a polite remark. Say that you look forward to hearing from the reader again if necessary.

Identifying questions

● *Pictures*
Information can be given in the form of a diagram, map, pictures, etc. In this type of question more information might be shown than is necessary. In your answer you should only use the information that you need to answer the question.

PART 1

General hints
Answering strategy

Use link words to connect the information. By doing this you will be able to 'save' on the number of words you use and make your answer more complete. Some link words are: *and, but, either ... or,* *since, if, although, however, so, so that.*

 As there is sometimes more than one correct answer you should always explain your choice by connecting it to the text. Do not invent ideas.

 You should also use suitable words and expressions so that your letter is either semi-formal or informal depending on the situation. Use grammar carefully and check for spelling mistakes. Your style should be clear and direct. Your letter should be neat and well presented.

PART 2

*Write an answer to one of the questions 2–5 in this part. Write your answer in **120–180** words in an appropriate style.*

2 A group of foreign exchange students have completed their stay in your area. You were one of the parents who put some students up in your home. Now you must write a report to the teacher in charge of the programme.

 Write your report. Describe the programme, what it offered the students, and comment on its good and bad points.

3 Your school is going to buy some toys for a local orphanage for children under six. You are on the school council and you must write a report on which toy(s) you recommend and why.

 Write a **description** of the toy or toys saying how it works and why it is ideal for children of this age.

4 You want to write an imaginative story to read to your young children at bed time. You pass a forest and this gives you the idea of making up an adventurous story about two children who make friends with the animals who live in the forest.

 Write the story for your children.

5 **Background reading texts**

 Answer **one** of the following two questions based on your reading of **one** of the set books:

 (a) How important is the setting to the development of the hero's/heroine's character? What part of the setting would most impress someone who is reading the book for the first time and why?

 (b) Do you think that reading a story teaches us something about human nature and life? Write a **letter** to a friend of yours who does not like to read, explaining your reasons and using examples from the book which you have read.

Part 2

Specific hints
Identifying questions

● *Report (see question 2)*
You are asked to write a formal description of something for someone. You have to write in a well-organised way using the information given. This information may be in the form of notes, a diagram, a chart, etc.

 Some examples of reports are: a report for your boss, a newspaper report, a biography of a well-known person, a book or film review or an experiment.

 You might start a report by stating the purpose:
To: (Name)
From: (Your Name)
Subject: (Brief description)

 Then you should make an introduction and list what you are asked to describe. You might use hyphens (-), numbers (1, 2, 3) or letters (a, b, c) for each new point. In the last paragraph you might comment on the points or reach a conclusion.

● *Descriptive (see question 3)*
You are asked to describe a person, a place, an object or a process. Use descriptive adjectives and watch the order in which they are written.

 When describing a person, describe physical appearance, character and behaviour. You might be asked to describe a family member or someone you admire. When describing a place, describe its general physical appearance and then go on to describe details, especially unusual features. Sometimes it is necessary to mention the importance of the place. You might be asked to describe a local area, a historical site or a monument.

 When describing an object, describe its size, weight, material, colour, use(s) and price. You might be asked to describe electrical appliances or toys. When describing a process, describe the materials needed, length of time needed and the order of the process. You might be asked to describe how to prepare a traditional meal or how to make a cup of coffee. Remember why you are writing the description.

PART 2

General hints
Answering strategy

Do not use words when you are not sure of the meaning. Use a wide range of vocabulary appropriate to the type of writing task you choose. Vary the length of your sentences. Use a simile, a pronoun or a phrase instead of repeating the same words. Use adjectives and adverbs

to make the story more interesting and alive. Use link words and phrases to expand an idea or connect ideas. Using direct speech in narrative writing can make the story more interesting.

 Set your paragraphs out clearly, each paragraph covering a separate point. Link your concluding paragraph to the introduction. This helps to sum up what you have written.

 For full marks, do not make your writing either too long or too short. A quick way to count your words is to count the number of words in a line and multiply it by the number of lines written.

Paper 3 Use of English (1 hour 15 minutes)

PART 1

For questions **1–15**, read the text below and decide which answer **A, B, C** or **D** best fits each space. There is an example at the beginning (**0**).

Example:

0	A thought	B tried	C dreamed	(D) wanted

AN UNDERWATER SWIM

I have always (**0**) _____*wanted*_____ to swim the English Channel underwater and as a former Olympic gold medallist I (**1**) _____*feel*_____ that I have the training to attempt (**2**) _____*such*_____ a swim. The Channel is, I suppose, the Mount Everest of the swimming world (**3**) _____*and*_____ to do it underwater will be an even greater (**4**) _*achievement*_ for me. Although many swimmers have (**5**) _____*C*_____ the Channel, it will be the first time that a former Olympic gold medallist has ever done it. I am (**6**) _____*D*_____ to do it in six to eight hours. I want to (**7**) _____*B*_____ money for a number of new charities and I am especially (**8**) _____*keen*_____ on the charities that protect the world's seas. I will be swimming (**9**) _____*B*_____ the Channel in the summer. In (**10**) _____*A*_____ to (**11**) _____*carry*_____ this out I have to follow a strict exercise programme. A usual training session for me would (**12**) _____*consist*_____ of thirty minutes in the weight room, thirty minutes doing different exercises and then three hours' straight swimming. I have to be (**13**) _*conscious*_ *(aware, think about)* of my diet so that it is a healthy and balanced one. I will (**14**) _____*be*_____ ready to set a record in something that has never been (**15**) _____*done*_____ before and which someone will have difficulty in breaking.

1	A feel	B regard	C sense	D propose
2	A quite	B so	C rather	D such
3	A but	B and	C as well as	D because
4	A prize	B work	C achievement	D duty
5	A moved	B passed	C crossed	D run
6	A forming	B willing	C agreeing	D hoping
7	A give	B raise	C save	D contribute
8	A keen	B interested	C thinking	D in favour
9	A through	B across	C over	D along
10	A order	B respect	C time	D regard

11	**A** cut	**B** check	**C** clear	**D** carry
12	**A** have	**B** spend	**C** amount	**D** consist
13	**A** capable	**B** conscious	**C** enthusiastic	**D** accustomed
14	**A** be	**B** have	**C** do	**D** try
15	**A** given	**B** made	**C** done	**D** kept

PART 2

*For questions **16–30**, read the text below and think of the word which best fits each space. Use only **one** word in each space. There is an example at the beginning (**0**).*

JUST IN TIME

The wind was stronger (**0**) ___*than*___ it had been earlier. I had (**16**) _____ *never* _____ been out in such a strong storm before. As we drove rapidly through the woods the branches swayed backwards and forwards above (**17**) _____ *us* _____. Lightning flashed.

'I wish we weren't out in (**18**) _____ *this* _____ storm,' I said to John. The words were hardly out of (**19**) _____ *my* _____ mouth when a branch from a tree came crashing down across the road in front of us. We leapt out of the car and ran quickly (**20**) _____ *towards* _____ the fallen branch. We had to move it, otherwise we (**21**) _____ *would* _____ not be able to continue our journey.

We pulled and pushed until we were finally able to move it (**22**) _____ *to* _____ the side of the road. We got back into the car and drove on down the road. We had to get to the house (**23**) _____ *on* _____ time. Lord Brenton, (**24**) _____ *who* _____ was dying, was the (**25**) _____ *only* _____ person who could give us the information we needed (**26**) _____ *so* _____ we could catch the murderers. He was a key witness.

At last we reached our destination. The house (**27**) _____ *was* _____ lit up inside like a Christmas (**28**) _____ *tree* _____. He must (**29**) _____ *still* _____ be alive, I thought, as we jumped out of the car and ran up the steps to (**30**) _____ *the* _____ entrance of the huge Victorian house. 'I think we've made it,' I called to John.

Part 2

Specific hints
Identifying questions

● *Demonstratives*
The words *this*, *that*, *these* and *those* are put before a noun. They identify something specific. We use *this* and *these* to talk about something that is near and *that* and *those* to talk about something that is farther away. *This/that* is used with singular nouns and *these/those* with plural nouns.
Question:
When several people are living together, they can easily argue and any one of _____ arguments can cause serious problems.
Answer:
these – arguments needs the plural determiner *these*

PART 2   ***General hints***
Answering strategy

Some texts tell stories. The story can be told in the first person or the third person. To understand the story, put yourself in the place of the story-teller. Try to form a picture of the action in your mind.

Always read the whole text before you attempt to fill in the gaps. Try to understand the central idea. This will help you choose the correct word. If you have lost the idea of the story, go back and read parts of it again until you can follow it clearly.

PART 3

For questions 31–40, complete the second sentence so that it has a similar meaning to the first sentence, using the word given. **Do not change the word given.** *You must use between two and five words, including the word given. There is an example at the beginning (0).*

Example:

0 Mr Jones needn't go if he doesn't want to.
obliged
Mr Jones *is not obliged to go* if he doesn't want to.

31 Sally has not come to school because she has been sick.
absent *adj*
Sally _____ is absent from _____ school because she has been sick.

32 It is often difficult to find an answer to a problem.
solution
Finding _____ the solution to _____ a problem is often difficult.

33 I was lucky you let me stay with you for the night.
put
I was lucky you _____ put me up _____ for the night.

34 I advised him to stop smoking.
suggested
I _____ suggested that he should _____ stop smoking.

35 They are going to do up my room.
have
I'm going _____ to have my room _____ decorated.

36 Jane doesn't often see Mike.
seldom
Jane _____ seldom sees _____ Mike.

37 I can understand this quite well.
easy
It's _____ easy t _____ understand this.

38 My mother doesn't like us to stay out late.
approve
My mother doesn't _____ approve of us staying _____ out late.

39 Mary is employed by IBM, isn't she?
works
Mary _____ works for IBM doesn't _____ she?

40 They could not understand what she said.
difficulty
They _____ found difficulty to understand _____ what she said.

Part 3

Specific hints
Identifying questions

● *Word sets – simple substitution*
You may be asked to complete a sentence with a suitable set of words. In this case, nothing in the matching sentence changes from the original except for the new set of words.
Example:
The tea is *too hot* to drink
The tea *isn't cool enough* to drink
Question:
He is running so that he can lose weight.
order
He is running _____ *lose weight.*
Answer:
in order to lose – this means *so that he can lose*

General hints
Question types

In Part 1, you are mainly tested on vocabulary (which words go with which other words). In Parts 2 and 3, you are tested on both grammar and vocabulary. In Part 4, you are mainly tested on grammatical items (finding mistakes). In Part 5, you are tested on word formation (understanding which form of the word is needed).

PART 4

For questions 41–55, read the text below and look carefully at each line. Some of the lines are correct, and some have a word which should not be there.

*If a line is correct put a (√) by the number. If a line has a word which should not be there, write the word next to the number. There are two examples at the beginning (**0** and **00**).*

FLOOD AND DROUGHT

If the experts could not agree on it the reason for the worst	**0**	*it*
floods of the century in northern Europe, they are no wiser	**00**	√
about the drought which hit is taking place in the south. The	**41**	
people are looking forward at the sky for the rain clouds which	**42**	
never come. A lot of people think it might be such a good idea if	**43**	
the planes do not fly over their areas so they do not frighten of	**44**	
the clouds away. In some areas the drought that has been going	**45**	
on for five long years. Swimming pools in resort areas lie empty	**46**	
because of residents have to put up with daily water cuts of up	**47**	
to 16 hours. On the other hand, in the northern part of Europe,	**48**	
thousands of residents have been left without some homes and	**49**	
have had to stay in other people's homes. Many farmers have lost a	**50**	
lot of money because their crops which were destroyed and could	**51**	
not be sold. Although some farmers tried to get back to their	**52**	
farms they were not allowed to by the police. Besides from the	**53**	
beautiful flowers, fruit and vegetables were also so badly hit that	**54**	
nothing could have be saved. Everyone in both the northern and	**55**	

southern part of the continent will be relieved when it is all over.

Part 4

Specific hints
Identifying questions

● *Subjects/objects*
In most sentences the subject is usually placed before the verb and is usually a noun or a pronoun. It cannot be both. A sentence can often have two objects, a direct object and an indirect object, but cannot have two of the same.
Example:
The man runs not *the man he runs.*
The man ran the race not *the man ran it the race.*
Question:
People they often run together because it's more enjoyable.
Error:
they – the subject of the verb *run* is *people*, so it is incorrect to use the pronoun *they* as well.

● *Adverbs*
Adverbs add information to a verb, an adjective or another adverb. There are three main positions of adverbs: before the subject, after the first auxiliary or after the verb *to be*, or at the end of the clause.
Example:
Clearly you've won the race.
You've *clearly* won the race.
You've won the race *clearly.*
Adverbs as modifiers always come before the word they modify, e.g. *very* wet, *too* late, *just* before, *so* far, *right* away.
Question:
It is obvious that those people are exercising much hard.
Error:
much – things are not done *much hard*. To be correct, it would have to be *exercising much too hard* or *much harder than someone else.*

PART 5

For questions 56–65, read the text below. Use the word given in capitals at the end of each line to form a word that fits in the space in the same line. There is an example at the beginning (0).

WHAT AN EXPERIENCE!

Every time I think of that **(0)** .terrifying. experience of the   **TERRIFY**

sinking cruise liner, the panic I felt then comes **(56)** ...   **LIVE**

again. The accident was tragic because of its **(57)** ...,   **SUDDEN**

causing the **(58)** ... of many passengers who would   **DEAD**

otherwise have been saved.

    All that some of the **(59)** ... could do, was to sit   **SURVIVE**

(60) ... in the lifeboats, waiting to be rescued.   **PATIENT**

    I became **(61)** ... many times during the long wait.   **CONSCIOUS**

I had to overcome any **(62)** ... I felt so I would not   **WEAK**

faint again. If I had not drawn another ship's **(63)** ...   **ATTEND**

our situation would have been **(64)** I   **HOPE**

try not to remember this **(65)** ... experience   **FRIGHT**

that only leaves me with unhappy thoughts.

Part 5

Specific hints
Identifying questions

● *Verbs*
Verbs are action words. They tell you what is being done in the sentence.
    Some suffixes which make verbs are:
Adjective to verb: *hard en,*
modern ise
    Some prefixes change the meaning of verbs:
Verb to verb: *un tie, out live,*
over eat, under estimate, en large
    Many verbs do not have prefixes or suffixes, and have the same form as nouns: *call, love, place, walk.*
    The position of the word in the sentence often tells you whether it is a noun or a verb.
Example:
Walks are good for a dog. (noun)
He *walks* the dog every day. (verb)
Question:
When you sprain your ankle, you can expect to _____.
sufferer
Answer:
suffer – make noun *sufferer* into verb *suffer* by dropping suffix *-er.*

PART 5   ***General hints***
Answering strategy

Look carefully at the context to decide if a word is positive or negative. If a word has to be changed into the negative, you need   to be aware of the prefixes and suffixes that are used in order to do this. Sometimes both a prefix and a suffix have to be used.

Paper 4 Listening (approximately 35 minutes)

PART 1

You'll hear people talking in eight different situations. For questions 1–8, choose the best answer, A, B or C.

1 Listen to this man phoning someone at his office. She is
A his boss.
B his assistant.
C in the same position as him.

1

2 You are at a family reunion when you hear this conversation between two cousins. What does the woman think the man has done?
A avoided her family
B insulted her mother
C cheated her family

2

3 Your air hostess makes this announcement on the plane. What does she ask you to do?
A do not block the runway
B do not open your travel bags
C do not move around

3

4 Listen to this man and this woman on a television talk show. Who is Julia?
A a librarian
B a writer
C a designer

4

5 Listen to this man on the radio talking about a woman. Why is he talking about her?
A He knows her personally.
B She is famous.
C He wants to introduce her.

5

6 Listen to this boy phoning his mother. Why has he called home?
A for a ride home
B to say he'll be late
C to say he needs money

6

7 You are having dinner at a friend's house. What does she tell you?
A a story about her pets
B a joke
C a lesson from school

7

PAPER 4
Listening
Part 1
Specific hints
Identifying questions

● *Register*
You can often understand how someone feels or thinks by listening to certain language factors, like formality and informality. We usually use polite language and more complex sentences when speaking to someone in authority or to someone we do not know well. When we speak to a friend or family member, we often use slang and incomplete sentences.

Exercise on register

Listen to this man talking to someone about going out. What is his relationship with this person?
A He doesn't feel very comfortable.
B He feels comfortable.
C He feels extremely comfortable.
Now listen to the explanation.

General hints
Answering strategy

Some of the difficulties you may face are:
1 *Unknown words*
Do not spend time worrying about a word you do not understand. Concentrate on understanding the general idea of the sentence. If you need to know the word to answer

the question, try to understand if the word has a positive or negative meaning.
2 *Finding specific details*
Listen for words that signal that the information you need is coming. These may be the exact words found in the test paper, or their synonyms.

3 *Accents*
In real-life situations there is a wide variety of English accents because it is spoken in so many regions and countries. The more you listen to different accents at home and in class, the easier it is for you in a test situation.

8 You are eating at a restaurant when a woman comes up to you. Who is she?

    A a former neighbour
    B a former teacher   **8**
    C a relative

PART 2

You will hear a woman registering at a hotel. For questions 9–18, fill in the registration form. You will need to write a word or a short phrase in each box.

Holly Hill Hotel
Jacob Lane
Southampton
Hants
SO2 3FL

Registration Card

First name:		**9**
Last name:		**10**
Date:	*on*	**11**
Type of room:		**12**
Number of occupants:		**13**
Room number:		**14**
Length of stay:	Friday,	**15**
Room rate (per night incl. VAT):		**16**
Breakfast: type		**17**
special arrangements required		**18**

PART 3

You will hear five people talking about a class which they are taking at a fitness-dance centre. For questions 19–23, choose from the list of alternatives A–F what each speaker is describing. Use the letter only once. There is one extra letter which you do not need to use.

A aerobics	Speaker 1 **19**
B ballet	Speaker 2 **20**
C jazz dance	Speaker 3 **21**
D self-defence	Speaker 4 **22**
E Latin and ballroom dance	Speaker 5 **23**
F birth and pregnancy classes	

PART 4

You will hear a radio bulletin for tourists giving local entertainment information for the City of Athens. For questions 24–30, tick one of the boxes to show whether each statement is true or false.

24 This bulletin is aimed at tourists under 25 years old. | T | | F | | 24 |

25 You can see Effy Gounela perform on Saturday night. | T | | F | | 25 |

26 Vincent Marsh is still painting pictures. | T | | F | | 26 |

27 You might see a painting of a forest at the Dada Gallery. | T | | F | | 27 |

28 All of the films mentioned have won prizes. | T | | F | | 28 |

29 The film *How the West Was Won* had three directors. | T | | F | | 29 |

30 The Greek Film Archives offer free entertainment. | T | | F | | 30 |

Part 4

Specific hints
Identifying questions

● *True/false*
You are asked to decide if some statements or pictures are true or not. Your own opinions are not important here, so listen carefully to the speaker(s). There is often only one detail which will make the statement or picture incorrect: identify it. Do not forget that each time you answer there is a 50 per cent chance of getting it correct, so do not leave any questions unanswered.

Question types

The correct answers often paraphrase what is in the taped text. Like the multiple choice questions, the incorrect answers try to distract your attention by using incorrect facts or ideas from the taped text.

Exercise on paraphrasing

Speaker 1: I had boarded the train and was looking for my seat when I came across Scotty. My old friend was in a very bad temper.
Question:
Decide if the following statements are true or false.
A He did not sit down immediately.
B He was expecting to see his friend, Scotty.
Answer:
A true: *was looking for my seat* is another way of saying that the speaker *did not sit down immediately*
B false: *I came across Scotty* means that the speaker was not expecting to see Scotty, so this is incorrect

General hints
Answering strategy

There are two ways of approaching a listening task. The first way is to answer the questions while you are listening. The second way is to listen to the text and answer the questions during the pauses. The first way is probably better because you might not have enough time to answer all of the questions during the pauses. However, if you are not doing well

with the first method, try the second.

Do not be anxious if you do not find all of the right answers the first time you hear the text. The second time you hear it, you know roughly when the right answer is coming. The questions are usually in the same order as the information in the text.

Sometimes background sounds can be heard before or after the speaking, but not during. Use them

to identify where the speaking is taking place.

Try to picture the whole situation in your mind: the characters, the setting, and what is happening. Practise doing this at home while listening to the radio or the television (with your eyes closed).

Paper 5 Speaking (approximately 15 minutes)

PART 1 (approximately 4 minutes)

Talk about yourself:

1 Do you know the other candidate? If you do, tell us what he/she does in his/her free time. If you don't, ask him/her about it.
Would you like more free time?
What would you do with more free time?

2 Many people travel in their free time. Have you ever travelled by plane/boat/bus/etc.?
Tell us about a memorable trip.
Have you ever travelled to an English-speaking country? If so, tell us your impressions. If not, which English-speaking country would you like to visit? Why?

PART 2 (approximately 4 minutes)

Look at the photographs on p. 126 and p. 127. They show different types of leisure activities. Work with your partner.

1 Student A: compare and contrast pictures 1 and 2, saying how the activity in the first picture is different from or similar to the activity in the second picture.

2 Student B: talk about which activity you would prefer to do.

3 Student B: compare and contrast pictures 3 and 4, saying how the activity in the first picture is different from or similar to the activity in the second picture.

4 Student A: talk about which activity you would prefer to do.

PAPER 5
Speaking

Part 1

Specific hints
Identifying questions

● *Discussing your pastimes (see question 1)*
Think of one or two hobbies/sports you enjoy. Explain why you like those pastimes. Try to be more creative than just saying 'watching TV'. If you do not have a hobby/favourite sport/any free time, explain why not.

● *Discussing travel (see question 2)*
Think of some trips you have made. Be honest; if you have not travelled by a certain means of transport, tell the interviewer. For example, *No, I have never travelled by plane, but I have travelled by boat.* This opens up a discussion on a familiar subject. Remember that we go on *a trip*, not *a travel*.

Part 2

Specific hints
Identifying questions

● *Making comparisons/contrasts (see questions 1 and 3)*
Find the most obvious similarity/difference. Then go on to look at other details. Think about: who, what, when, where and why.

Useful vocabulary

● *Comparison*
Chess is *more/less interesting than* draughts.
Chess is *the most/least interesting* board game.

● *Contrast*
On the one hand chess is extremely interesting *but on the other hand* it is very slow.

● *Discussing preferences (see questions 2 and 4)*
Quickly decide what you prefer and give your reason(s). Talk about why you do like something, and don't like something else.

General hints
Answering strategy

You are sharing this test with another candidate. Do not talk all the time or speak rudely to him or her. If the other candidate talks a lot, do not worry. The examiners will see that you are given an opportunity to talk too.

If you do not know the word for something, use other words to describe it. For example, use *a doctor who looks after people's eyes* instead of *an ophthalmologist*. If you find that you cannot do this, say something like *I'm afraid I've forgotten that word.* Then keep on talking.

If the interviewer uses a word that you do not know, decide whether you must know it in order to perform the task properly. If you feel you really need to know it, then say something like *I'm sorry, but I don't know the word 'hindrance'.* You might try to guess: *Does it mean 'something that makes you late'?* The interviewer might help you in some way, or he or she might move on to something else.

The interviewer may disagree with something you say, just to see how well you argue a point. Disagree politely. You can change your opinion, if you like, but remember to give reasons.

General hints – Part 2
Answering strategy

In Part 2, you are given some pictures and asked some questions. You are given two chances to speak, once for a long time (about one minute) and once for a short time (about twenty seconds).

You do not lose marks for not finishing on time, so do not worry if the examiner interrupts you. However, it does make a better impression if you can say what you want to say within the time limit.

Answer all points asked. If you do not have much to say about one point, admit that and perhaps explain why.

PART 3 (approximately 3 minutes)

Imagine that you are mountain climbing with friends and a fierce snow storm is just about to start. It will probably last for days. Look at the picture below which shows your position on the mountain.

Work with your partner. Talk together and decide what you should do. Then talk about some other problems you might face, and how you could solve them.

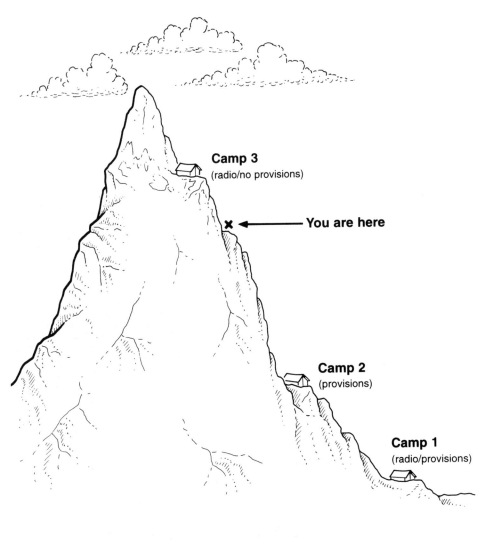

PART 4 (approximately 4 minutes)

Discuss the following questions with your partner:

1 Why is mountain climbing considered a dangerous hobby?

2 Why is it important for people to know how to work together as a team?

3 How do young people usually spend their free time in your town?

4 What are some solutions for people who want to travel in their free time, but do not have much money?

5 What are some healthy solutions for a young person who is feeling bored?

Part 3

Specific hints
Identifying questions

● *Problem solving*
You are asked to find a solution to a problem. Discuss the given facts with the other candidate. Then try to find a logical solution. There may be more than one, so be flexible. If one solution does not work, try another.

Useful vocabulary

● *Additional points*
Besides/as well as the shape, we *also* have to consider the number.

Part 4

Specific hints
Identifying questions

● *Stating reasons (see questions 1, 2)*
You are asked to give the reasons for something. Consider all of the facts involved. For example, if you are asked, *Why might someone choose to work in a circus?* consider the psychological reasons (he might find it exciting), the physical reasons (he might have the physical skills, like being acrobatic) and the practical reasons (he needs to earn a living somehow).

● *Suggesting solutions (see questions 4, 5)*
You are asked to solve a problem. Consider all of the facts involved. For broad subjects, like pollution, consider what can be done at these levels: personal (what can be done by you), small group (what can be done by a club, an association, etc.) and large group (what can be done by a town, a city, a country, etc.). It helps to give examples to support your point.

TEST 4

Paper 1 Reading   (1 hour 15 minutes)

PART 1

You are going to read a newspaper article about packaging. Choose from the list A–H the picture which best summarises each part (1–6) of the article. There is one extra picture which you do not need to use. There is an example at the beginning (0).

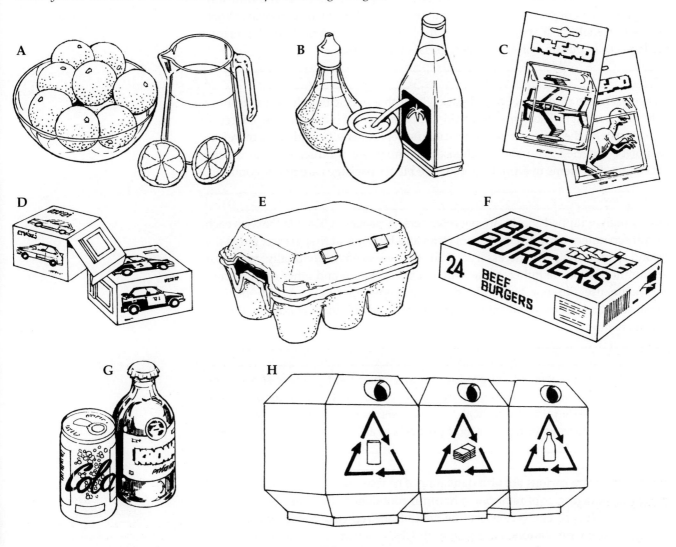

BAD PACKAGING – HOW TO FIGHT IT

0	H

At a time when we need to find ways to decrease the amount of rubbish we are producing, over-packaging of products should be against the law. Until it is, consumers can make an impact on both retailers and manufacturers by refusing to buy products that are over-packaged. Always remember to dispose of all rubbish properly and recycle as much as you can whenever possible.

1	

Tetra-packs are the square juice boxes you see in vast numbers on supermarket shelves. They can be neither reused nor recycled because they have an outer layer of plastic, a middle layer of cardboard and an inner layer of aluminium foil. Instead, make your own freshly squeezed juice; it's better for you anyway. When you're out, look for a shop that makes fresh juice on the spot. Look for ready-made juices in plastic – or even better, glass – containers.

2	

Blister packs are cardboard-backed packages with a plastic bubble on the front to hold the product. They are designed this way to let you see the contents. Unfortunately, the different materials can't be separated efficiently and therefore cannot be recycled. You should choose a comparable product without all the packaging. Buy items in a small shop where blister packages are not as common.

3	

Individually wrapped snacks are big offenders. A packet of biscuits that has each biscuit separately wrapped may seem clean and hygienic at first glance, but is the second wrapping truly necessary? And do we need individually wrapped restaurant portions of butter, sugar, salt, pepper, ketchup and other condiments? For home use, do not buy individually wrapped portions. Avoid them at restaurants as well, especially at fast food places, and complain about them to the management.

4	

Single-serving microwave food products or any other food product of this type are wasteful. The layers of packaging are simply excessive. Buy a larger pack, take out an appropriate portion and heat or cook it separately. Better still, don't buy ready-cooked microwave or other food products at all.

5	

Polystyrene foam cartons are also damaging. The issue here isn't so much one of reducing packaging as of replacing a harmful container with a harmless one. For example, cardboard egg cartons can be made from recycled paper, which saves resources. The foam cartons are made with CFCs, which harm the ozone layer. You should buy eggs only in cardboard egg cartons. If you buy them at a market, that's often what they use. You can even bring your old cartons for reuse.

6	

While it's a good idea to drink lots of water, especially on warm days, what happens to the hundreds of thousands of plastic bottles that are thrown away? They could be recycled but usually they are not. Choose glass bottles whenever possible. Glass is probably one of the most environmentally sound packaging forms around; it is recyclable and relatively harmless. Buy soft drinks in cans and recycle them, but try not to use straws, as they are difficult to recycle.

PART 2

*You are going to read an extract from an autobiography. For questions **7–14**, choose the answer (**A, B, C** or **D**) which you think fits best according to the text.*

The war was the most peaceful period of my life. The window of my bedroom faced southeast. My mother had curtained it, but that had small effect. I always woke with the first light and, with all the responsibilities of the previous day melted, feeling myself rather like the sun, ready to shine and feel joy. Life never seemed so simple and clear and full of possibilities as then. I put my feet out from under the clothes – I called them Mrs Left and Mrs Right – and invented dramatic situations for them in which they discussed the problems of the day. At least Mrs Right did; she easily showed her feelings, but I hadn't the same control of Mrs Left, so she mostly contented herself with nodding agreement.

They discussed what Mother and I should do during the day, what Santa Claus should give a fellow for Christmas, and what steps should be taken to brighten the home. There was that little matter of the baby, for instance. Mother and I could never agree about that. Ours was the only house in the neighbourhood without a new baby, and Mother said we couldn't afford one till Father came back from the war because they cost seventeen and six. That showed how foolish she was. The Geneys up the road had a baby, and everyone knew they couldn't afford seventeen and six. It was probably a cheap baby, and Mother wanted something really good, but I felt she was too hard to please. The Geneys' baby would have done us fine.

Having settled my plans for the day, I got up, put a chair under my window, and lifted the frame high enough to stick out my head. The window overlooked the front gardens of the homes behind ours, and beyond these it looked over a deep valley to the tall, red-brick houses up the opposite hillside, which were all still in shadow, while those at our side of the valley were all lit up, though with long strange shadows that made them seem unfamiliar; stiff and painted.

After that I went into Mother's room and climbed into the big bed. She woke and I began to tell her of my schemes. By this time, though I never seem to have noticed it, I was freezing in my nightshirt, and I warmed up as I talked until, the last frost melted, I fell asleep beside her and woke again only when I heard her below in the kitchen, making the breakfast.

7 The time the author spent as a child during the war was
A sad and frightening.
B happy and calm.
C peaceful and puzzling.
D violent and shocking.

8 When he woke up in the morning, he
A would call on Mrs Left and Mrs Right.
B would open up the curtains.
C would play with his feet.
D would agree with Mrs Left.

9 How did the writer and his mother feel about having a baby?
A They weren't able to agree.
B They sometimes agreed.
C They often agreed.
D They always agreed.

Part 2

Specific hints
Identifying texts

● *Fictional text*
This kind of text can give a real or imagined story of a personal experience in the first person (*I/we*). In Part 2, the questions are often about descriptions of persons, places or things.
This kind of text can also tell a story in the third person (*he/she/they*). In Part 2, the questions are often about the feelings and thoughts of the main character. You may also be asked about his or her reasons for doing something, or about some factual information.

Identifying questions

● *Acceptability*
Sometimes you are given incorrect answers which present points which seem believable or acceptable (according to what the text says or your general knowledge). Do not let this distract you from the right answer.

Exercise on acceptability

As a small boy, I can remember being very bad. I would always get out of the small jobs my parents gave me to do around the house. I would also always get into fights with my brothers and sisters. I was not the perfect son, and must have made my parents very angry. They should have punished me more severely.
Question:
When the author was young,
A he loved his brothers and sisters.
B he was the eldest child.
C he was the worst student in class.
D he misbehaved and quarrelled all the time.
Answer:
A no: it would be easy to assume that the writer loved his brothers and sisters since most people do, but there is no evidence to prove this
B no: it would be easy to assume that the writer was the eldest since he was always in fights, but there is no evidence to prove this
C no: it would be easy to assume that the writer was the worst student in class given his very bad behaviour, but there is no evidence to prove this
D yes: the writer says he was *bad* and *would always get into fights*, which is another way of saying he *misbehaved and quarrelled all the time.*

10 Why was the writer upset with his mother?
  A He could not understand her.
  B She was poor.
  C She was not very intelligent.
  D She did not love him enough.

11 The writer believed
  A that Santa Claus really existed.
  B that his father would never come home from the war.
  C that they were poorer than the Geneys.
  D that one could buy a baby.

12 The houses on his side of the valley were lit up because
  A they were facing the sun.
  B they were still all in shadow.
  C they had all turned their lights on.
  D they had odd shadows that made them look strange.

13 What was his mother's bed like?
  A freezing
  B uncomfortable
  C small
  D warm

14 What did the writer feel then that he does not feel now?
  A That everything is possible.
  B That war is ugly.
  C That his mother loves him deeply.
  D That life is complicated.

PART 3

You are going to read a letter from someone to her sister's family. Eight sentences have been removed from the letter. Choose from the sentences A–I the one which fits each gap (15–21). There is one extra sentence which you do not need to use. There is an example at the beginning (0).

April 22, 1994

Dear Kathy, John, Gigi,

Well, hello everybody!! **0** **I**

How's school, Gigi? I hear you've been studying hard. Have you made any earrings lately? Do you need any more jewellery backs, etc.? What are your plans for the summer? **15**

Brittany and Brendyn are doing well. They have so many friends here. There are kids all over the place at Whyte Ridge. Brittany knows some of her friends' phone numbers and sometimes calls them up and just invites them over. And Brendyn's latest is to ask any kid walking by if he/she wants to come to his house to spend the night. Either for that or for supper...

16

We had a nice time at Mom's in Saskatoon. **17** Unfortunately, she was sick, then we all were sick, so our energies weren't up to par.

Part 3

Specific hints
Question types

You are given a text and must choose the right sentences or paragraphs to complete it. The correct answers are connected to the text by related words/phrases/sentences/ideas. These key ideas might use synonyms or some of the same words as the text. Since you must choose from a whole list of items, more than one might look acceptable. Look carefully for matching or agreeing points.

(cont.)

This summer, we plan to go to Nick's second cousin's wedding in Yorkton first thing in July, then to the lake with MaryAnne (from Ohio), Theresa, Cathy, etc., for a week, then to Calgary for the 14th for Rosie's brother's anniversary. Then on our holiday to pick cherries. We'd also like to sneak in as many trips to the lake as possible with our caravan, and maybe to the Mall of America. We'll see.

Nick's back is slowly getting better; he sort of takes it easy, and uses the exercise bike all the time, as he says it helps his back. **18** [ ]

We love our house. Everything has turned out beautifully. **19** [ ] We just bought a lovely new purple sofa made in Italy (Natuzzi) for our lounge. We have not taken any pictures yet.

Well, Brittany and Brendyn can both ride two-wheelers now and can both whistle!

How are both your Mom and Dad feeling, John? Do they get out to Kanalia much? I know they love their village.

20 [ ]

Love,

JoAnn, Nick, Brittany, Brendyn

P.S. Bonnie and Phil had a girl – Tessa. **21** [ ]

A Then we brought her back here for awhile.

B And Patti is pregnant with her third!

C Black and white is the theme throughout.

D When can you convince your Mom and Dad to bring you here again?!

E I had it in mind while writing this letter, but my response may have been too late. Sorry about that!

F It was very painful and he thought he might need surgery.

G Got to go – so much to do as Nick and I are going out to supper tonight!

H Speaking of Whyte Ridge, there's a dalmatian dog who is the most popular dog in the neighbourhood; we have very nice neighbours, too!

I Sorry it's been so long but we've been getting settled in our new home.

(continued)

Exercise on agreement

Question:
Choose from the sentences A, B or C the one which fits each gap (1 and 2).

As a small boy, I can remember being very bad. I would always get out of the small jobs my parents gave me to do around the house. I would also always get into fights with my brothers and sisters. I was not the perfect son, and must have made my parents very angry. (1)

My parents would take us away on holiday. I suppose I should have been grateful. (2)

A *But every holiday I would get lost and my parents would have to contact the local police.*
B *I really wanted them to buy me a pet dog.*
C *They should have punished me more severely.*

Answer:
1 C *my parents* agrees with *They; angry* agrees with the result *They should have punished me*
2 A *My parents* agrees with *my parents*; their being *on holiday* agrees with an explanation of what happened *every holiday*
(Note that it would be easy to think that B was true, but it does not match the subject of either text.)

PART 4

You are going to read some information about your star sign. For questions 22–33, choose from the star signs (A–L). Some of the star signs may be chosen more than once. When more than one answer is required, these may be given in any order. There is an example at the beginning (0). For questions 34 and 35, choose the answer (A, B, C or D) which you think fits best according to the text.

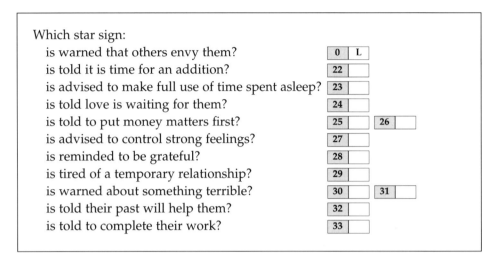

Which star sign:

is warned that others envy them?	**0** | L	
is told it is time for an addition?	**22**	
is advised to make full use of time spent asleep?	**23**	
is told love is waiting for them?	**24**	
is told to put money matters first?	**25**	**26**
is advised to control strong feelings?	**27**	
is reminded to be grateful?	**28**	
is tired of a temporary relationship?	**29**	
is warned about something terrible?	**30**	**31**
is told their past will help them?	**32**	
is told to complete their work?	**33**	

34 Where has this text come from?
   A a newspaper report
   B an advertisement
   C a magazine
   D a school textbook

35 What is the main aim of this text?
   A to offer advice to people with problems
   B to inform people about what may happen in the future
   C to recommend that people be careful
   D to encourage people to write to Richard Starr

YOUR HOROSCOPE THIS WEEK
by Richard Starr

Aries	A

Your family is going through the turmoil of many difficult changes. Not everyone is cooperating with these changes, which is resulting in feelings being hurt and relationships being threatened. A family crisis can be stopped if you unexpectedly change your mind. See if you can't be more understanding and lend a sympathetic ear to the members of your family who need it most.

Taurus	B

It may be time to start thinking about starting or adding to the family. But don't panic! Things will fall into place if you are calm and plan out your moves carefully. A bigger family will bring you the peace, joy and satisfaction that will fill that space within you which has been empty as of late.

Gemini | C

You are facing an overwhelmingly big job and you are feeling very distressed. Calm down! Why not invite in a group of friends or colleagues to assist you? Together you can tackle the job and enjoy yourselves along the way. Watch that you don't antagonise anyone, though – remember to say 'thank you' to all those who rally to support you.

Cancer | D

You are on an emotional roller coaster. You do not know if you are coming or going, and may consider turning to unsavoury companions for advice. Instead, look to your childhood for the answers. Happy memories will give you the moral strength to face what is to come, and even unhappy memories may comfort you in difficult moments.

Leo | E

Your passionate nature is going to get you into trouble. You like to let your emotions run free, but caution might be the better route to follow this week. Put the brake on and slow down. Do not get upset. Be especially watchful late in the week for incidents which will trigger misunderstandings in the future.

Virgo | F

You have always had a strong dream life, full of vivid colours and activities. Now it is time for you to put those dreams to good use. Write down your dreams and use them to come to an understanding of the inner workings of your mind. Your subconscious may help you solve problems in real-life situations.

Libra | G

You may be more interested in romance than in business, but an impressive business deal keeps dogging you. Do not ignore it. Cut down on romantic involvements and concentrate on business deals. You will have plenty of time for love, so now it is more productive to focus on finding the money with which to entertain your future romantic escapades!

Scorpio | H

A difficult health issue awaits you or someone who is very close to you. Pay close attention to the matter and have it looked into by an expert. Neglecting to do something now may prove disastrous in the years to come, so make sure that you look after everything that needs looking after.

Sagittarius | I

You have been working on a project for a very long time and the time has come for you to finish it. While it has been difficult for you to concentrate lately, you must put aside these distractions and get down to ending what you started. You may be surprised at how relieved you feel once it is done. And at how profitable it will be!

Capricorn	J

A lucky week for you! You have long wanted to become romantically involved with someone, and the time is right for you to be brave. Approach that person. Tell that person how long you have wanted to get better acquainted. Say how much you would like to become a part of that person's life. The outcome will pleasantly surprise you, and you will wish that you had spoken up sooner.

Aquarius	K

You will be expected to make a firm commitment, like marriage, and there will be tears if you do not. Although you are afraid of such a commitment, you also want something more permanent. Deal with this situation carefully, in order to avoid hurt feelings.

Pisces	L

Do not worry so much about what anyone else thinks. Follow what you think is the best course of action in the situation at hand. You are shining lately, and other people are jealous of your achievements. Do not listen to them, but rather follow your heart. In the end, this will pay off handsomely.

Paper 2 Writing (1½ hours)

PART 1

*You **must** answer this question.*

1 A well-known animal lover has been invited to speak to the local SA (Save the Animals) club about cruelty to animals. You have invited him to be interviewed for an article for your local newspaper about his talk. You have received the following reply:

> I shall be happy to be interviewed for your newspaper. It will have to be straight after my talk because I am booked to leave on the morning flight and it would therefore be difficult to see you at any other time. The talk is between 7 and 9 pm. Therefore, we could meet at 9.30 pm. Would that suit you? We could meet wherever you wanted. Just let me know where in advance so that I can organise my schedule.
>
> Would it be possible for you to send me a list of the questions you will be asking? It would save time and everything can be covered more thoroughly.
>
> If there is anything you would like me to bring to the interview please let me know.
>
> Yours sincerely,
> David Hammel

Read Mr Hammel's reply carefully and the following set of notes which you have made for yourself. Then write a letter to him setting up the appointment and answering his questions.

Write a **letter** of **120–180** words in an appropriate style. Do not include addresses.

Newspaper article

- general description of talk + points of interest
- why he came for the talk
- other clubs concerned about animals?
- his own photos of examples of cruelty?
- arrange photographs of interview

PART 2

Write an answer to **one** *of the questions 2–5 in this part. Write your answer in 120–180 words in an appropriate style.*

2 An international young people's magazine is investigating the question: 'Do non-smokers have as many rights as smokers?'

Write a short article for the magazine on this topic, based on your own experience.

3 You have witnessed a bank robbery. The police have asked you to give them the details of what happened.

Write a **description** of the incident giving all the necessary information.

4 This is part of a letter that you receive from an English penfriend.

We're doing a project at school on local conservation groups.

Could you please write me a short report on your local group to include in the project? Could you write about the type of people that take part and what kind of project they are involved in?

Write a **report** which your penfriend can include in the project.

5 **Background reading texts**

Answer **one** of the following two questions based on your reading of **one** of the set books:

(a) Give an example of conflict between the characters. Say how this helped to create the mood in the story and how it helped to arouse the interest of the reader. Give enough details for another student who may not have read the book.

(b) Many books are made into films. Which part of the book that you have read could be the climax of a film? What are the main plot points that build up to this climax?

Part 2

Specific hints
Identifying questions

● *Article (see question 2)*
You are asked to write something for a newspaper, magazine or newsletter. It can be about places, people, events, current news, etc. You can write an article based on what you know or on what someone else knows, e.g. from TV, books, magazines, etc. Description is often used along with a narrative style of writing. Give your article a title, e.g. *Do non-smokers have as many rights as smokers?* Remember who you are writing the article for, e.g. a magazine for women, young children, or a specialised group like doctors. Your language will change accordingly.

● *Descriptive narrative (see question 3)*
You are asked to give an account of how something happened, and it must include a lot of description to make the account interesting. Use colouful language so that the reader can picture what you are describing in his or her mind. Remember why you are writing the account.

● *Set books (see question 5)*
You are asked to write about one of the books prescribed by the University of Cambridge Local Examinations Syndicate. You must have a good knowledge of the story: the plot, the characters, the setting, the mood and how they all influence one another. Identify the task type (composition, letter, article or report) and write appropriately. Choose the parts of the story necessary to answer the question and/or support your answer. Be able to refer to different parts of the story to support your answer and to give the information in the right time order where necessary. Be careful not to use pieces of written material you have memorised in class; this is obvious to the examiner and marks are deducted for it. You may use quotations from the book to support your views.

General hints
Exam procedure

You are given a test paper, a piece of scrap paper and a question paper booklet. Check/write your name, centre number and candidate number. Use pen, not pencil, in the question paper booklet. Write the question numbers of the writing tasks you choose in the left-hand margin. Use the scrap paper to write down your ideas or to make a plan. It must be left with the other papers at the end of the test. Corrections are allowed. Write quickly but neatly so that the examiner can easily read your writing. Count the number of words you have written. Do not go over or under the word limit. Marks will be taken off if you do. Read through your work at the end and make any necessary corrections.

You have an hour and a half to write two writing tasks (45 minutes for each). Be careful not to spend too long on Part 1.

Marking

You do not lose marks for using American English or other 'standard Englishes', as long as you use the same kind of English throughout. Do not use memorised material: you will lose marks. Marks are given for good use of vocabulary, correct grammar, correct spelling and punctuation, good organisation, appropriate style and proper completion of the question. Each writing task is given a mark out of 20. The two marks are then added together to give a mark out of 40. The expected level for a typical 'C' mark is about 40 per cent of the total mark.

Paper 3 Use of English (1 hour 15 minutes)

PART 1

For questions 1–15, read the text below and decide which answer A, B, C or D best fits each space. There is an example at the beginning (0).

Example:

0 A opposite   **B** variable   Ⓒ different   **D** similar

A TYPICAL DAY

Nowadays, country kitchens are not very **(0)** __different__ from those in the city. **(1)** _____, in the past the differences could easily be **(2)** _____ By the 1940s most city homes had gas or electric cookers **(3)** _____ but in the country the farmer's wife still **(4)** _____ on a fuel cooker. This gave her more work because she had to **(5)** _____ at five o'clock in the morning and enter the kitchen with a candle which was always kept **(6)** _____ She then removed the ashes from the cooker and got some newspaper and pieces of wood from the box **(7)** _____ the side of the kitchen door.

Next, the kettle was filled and put over the fire in **(8)** _____ to make the first pot of tea of the day. Once this was **(9)** _____ she made sure she **(10)** _____ fed the animals **(11)** _____ the left-overs and then got **(12)** _____ with breakfast. After breakfast the plates would be **(13)** _____ and more wood put in the cooker. The only opportunity she had to rest next to the fire was after dinner. This **(14)** _____ of lighting the cooker was repeated every day. Wood was used in **(15)** _____ of petrol till the Second World War.

1 A However	**B** In spite of	**C** Because	**D** Despite
2 A glimpsed	**B** noticed	**C** understood	**D** made
3 A bought	**B** put	**C** connected	**D** installed
4 A baked	**B** stirred	**C** boiled	**D** cooked
5 A raise	**B** arise	**C** rise	**D** get
6 A handy	**B** far	**C** obvious	**D** reachable
7 A by	**B** next	**C** close	**D** outside
8 A so far as	**B** order	**C** view	**D** case
9 A ended	**B** done	**C** used up	**D** fulfilled

Specific hints
Identifying questions

● *Adverbs*
These words add information to another word, such as a verb, an adjective or another adverb. Adverbs have many different kinds of meaning. The most common are:
Manner: *well, hard, slowly, quickly*
Place: *above, below, up, down, here, there*
Time: *now, then, soon, recently, afterwards*
Degree: *very, much, really, quite, too, so*
Frequency: *always, never, often, sometimes*
Question:
When several people are living together, they can _____ argue and one of these arguments might cause serious problems.
A *nicely* B *easily* C *well*
D *slowly*
Answer:
A no: someone is dressed *nicely*
B yes: *easily argue* (adverb – without difficulty)
C no: someone works *well*
D no: someone walks *slowly*

● *Particles in phrasal verbs*
A phrasal verb is a verb with one or two particles added to give a specific meaning. These particles come straight after the verb or after the object. It is possible to understand which phrasal verb is needed from the context of the sentence. You can be asked for either the verb or the particle.
Question:
While running, they cut _____ the park.
A *across* B *back* C *off* D *down*
Answer:
A yes: *cut across* (phrasal verb – take a shorter way)
B no: someone cut *back* on expenses
C no: the city cut *off* the water supply
D no: someone cut *down* on smoking

PART 1

General hints
Exam procedure

You are given an answer sheet on which to write your answers. Check/write your name, centre number and candidate number. Use pencil on the answer sheet. Look at the sample answer sheet at the back of the book.
  You have 1 hour 15 minutes to do this paper, so you should spend

about 15 minutes on each part. If you have enough time at the end, check your work.

Marking

One mark is given for each correct answer. If you make a spelling mistake in Parts 2 and 5, you will receive zero for that question. If you make a spelling mistake in Part 3, some marks will be deducted. Marks

will not be deducted for mistakes made when copying words from the test paper. The total mark is then scaled to a mark out of 40. The expected level for a typical 'C' mark is about 60 per cent of the total mark.

10	**A** often	**B** sometimes	**C** always	**D** seldom
11	**A** at	**B** in	**C** without	**D** on
12	**A** down	**B** away	**C** along	**D** on
13	**A** cleaned	**B** removed	**C** washed	**D** polished
14	**A** time	**B** process	**C** procession	**D** progress
15	**A** place	**B** exchange	**C** favour	**D** position

PART 2

*For questions 16–30, read the text below and think of the word which best fits each space. Use only **one** word in each space. There is an example at the beginning (0).*

UNSOLVED MYSTERIES

I am going to visit one of the most famous prehistoric temples in Europe – Stonehenge. Ted, **(0)** ____*whose*____ father is an archaeologist, has invited me. Dr Millers, Ted's father, wants extra help **(16)** _____ the work that is going to be **(17)** _____ in the summer.

Stonehenge, **(18)** _____ means 'hanging stones', is said to be an open-air temple where the primitive people of the area worshipped the Sun-god. It faces the rising sun **(19)** _____ a midsummer day.

The temple is made of huge stones laid **(20)** _____ in a circle. There are two circles; the outer circle is made of sandstone and the inner circle is made of bluestone. On top of **(21)** _____ pillar is a horizontal block of stone. In the **(22)** _____ of this circle there was a place for the worshipping to take place.

I have **(23)** _____ wondered how **(24)** _____ giant stones were transported to that site as none of them are from there. They have come from **(25)** _____ area many miles away. Many theories have been put forward **(26)** _____ how the temple came to be there. **(27)** _____ theory is that living creatures from outer **(28)** _____ visited the area **(29)** _____ built the temple. They say that because the stones are so big they could not have been **(30)** _____ to the site of the temple in the ordinary way. Who knows? The work that will be done in the summer should give us more information.

Part 2

Specific hints
Identifying questions

● *Link words*
These are words that join two parts of a sentence. Some link words are *and, but, because, since, either, or, provided* and *although*.
Question:
When several people are living together, they can easily argue _____ one of these arguments might cause serious problems.
Answer:
and – the link word *and* links two simple sentences and expresses addition

● *Pronouns*
These are words used instead of a noun. The five groups of pronouns that you should know are subject pronouns, object pronouns, adjective pronouns, possessive pronouns and reflexive pronouns.
Question:
When several people are living together, _____ can easily argue and one of these arguments might cause serious problems.
Answer:
they – the personal pronoun *they* is used instead of a noun and refers to the noun *people* already mentioned

PART 3

*For questions **31–40**, complete the second sentence so that it has a similar meaning to the first sentence, using the word given. **Do not change the word given.** You must use between two and five words, including the word given. There is an example at the beginning (0).*

Example:

0 Mr Jones needn't go if he doesn't want to.
obliged
Mr Jones <u>is not obliged to go</u> if he doesn't want to.

31 He knows everything about flowers.
expert
He _____ flowers.

32 If you are not old enough you cannot watch certain films.
age
If you _____ you cannot watch certain films.

33 I regret that I gave him the money.
lent
If only _____ him the money.

34 It was such a boring movie that we left.
so
The movie _____ that we left.

35 People say that the pyramids are worth visiting.
supposed
The pyramids _____ worth visiting.

36 John cannot possibly borrow the car tonight.
question
It's _____ for John to borrow the car tonight.

37 Could I continue what I was doing?
get
Could I _____ what I was doing?

38 Mary is slower at doing things than Jill.
fast
Mary is _____ Jill at doing things.

39 I can't make up my mind about the colour.
decide
I _____ the colour.

40 There are times when you have to do things by yourself.
own
There are times when you have to do things _____

Part 3
Specific hints
Identifying questions

● *Word sets – whole structural change*
You may be asked to complete a sentence with a suitable set of words. In this case, the whole sentence is changed structurally in order to match the original sentence.
Question:
'Please let me run in this race!' she begged her mother.
let
She begged her mother _____
that race.
Answer:
to let her run in – this is needed to change the sentence from direct to indirect speech

PART 4

For questions 41–55, read the text below and look carefully at each line. Some of the lines are correct, and some have a word which should not be there.

If a line is correct put a tick (√) by the number. If a line has a word which should not be there, write the word next to the number. There are two examples at the beginning (0 and 00).

STUDYING ABROAD

There are two reasons why I had wanted to study in Paris. I wanted	0	√
to be in a place which it was at the centre of Europe, close to it	00	*it*
other countries such as England and Germany. The other reason	41	
was that I had been found it very difficult to find a place to	42	
study of medicine in my own country, where there were only	43	
three medical schools. I had spent my last two school years at a	44	
boarding school, where I was made a lot of friends and learned	45	
to look after myself. I was nineteen when I just left and I knew	46	
that I could deal with a student life. First of all, I had to learn	47	
the language of the country I would be living in there for quite	48	
a while. I learnt with the language quickly because I stayed	49	
with a family, which was a great deal help. I was expected to	50	
speak only their language and not mine. After that, I looked around	51	
for an apartment to rent. I found one very close to the university	52	
so I went on the foot every day. I was able to exercise a lot and	53	
therefore be fit all year round. My studies went very much well	54	
and I graduated at the top of the class with full honours.	55	

Part 4

Specific hints
Identifying questions

● *Prepositional phrases*
These are groups of words beginning with a preposition and usually followed by a noun or pronoun. They express many different concepts such as place or time. Some examples are: *at breakfast, at home, at sea, by hand, for love, for life, on holiday, on a journey, off duty, in a hurry, in pencil, in town, out of date.* However, you must always look at the context to see if a prepositional phrase should be used.
Examples:
My wife is *at home.*
I want to go *home.*

● *Noun phrases*
These usually begin with a determiner. They refer to a particular thing. Some noun phrases are: *the school, this problem, all the people in the country, that tree.* The difference between a prepositional phrase and a noun phrase is that with the first we are thinking of a general idea, e.g. *school* or *holiday,* and with the second we are referring to something specific, e.g. *the school we go to, the holiday we went on.*
Examples:
We like to go *to school.*
(prepositional phrase – in general)
We have to go *to the school* today to register for the race. (noun phrase – a specific school)
Question:
The people in my gym club jog together every day after the breakfast.
Error:
the – in this context, *after breakfast* has a general meaning, not *after one specific breakfast.*

PART 5

For questions 56–65, read the text below. Use the word given in capitals at the end of each line to form a word that fits in the space in the same line. There is an example at the beginning (0).

A GROWING CITY

Beaumont, Georgia's newest city, is a (0) .planned. city. **PLAN**

It is a (56) ... place all year round because of the great **LOVE**

(57) ... of flowers and trees which grow in the city centre. **VARY**

No one can be (58) ... with such natural surroundings. **SATISFY**

The (59) ... growing population includes not only the **QUICK**

many (60) ... who work there for an international computer **FOREIGN**

company, but also local officials. The (61) ... conditions are **LIVE**

excellent and all types of (62) ... and sport are available. **ENTERTAIN**

There are many (63) ... buildings to visit nearby and the **HISTORY**

wooded countryside which is (64) ... and particularly **PEACE**

beautiful in spring offers hours of cycling and walking.

A (65) ... will come back again and again to sample the **SIGHT**

pleasures Beaumont has to offer.

Part 5

Specific hints
Identifying questions

● *Adverbs*
Adverbs are used to add meaning to a verb. They tell you how, when, where or why something was done. They can also describe adjectives and other adverbs.
   Most adverbs are formed from adjectives by adding the suffix -*ly*. Sometimes spelling changes take place when the -*ly* is added.
1 No change: *bad ly, brave ly, hopeful ly, anxious ly*
2 If the adjective ends in *y* change the *y* to *i* and then add -*ly*: *hast ily, eas ily, wear ily*
3 If the adjective ends in -*le*, drop the -*le* and then add the -*ly*: *gent ly, sensib ly, probab ly*
Question:
In a short race, you must _____ pass the others.
quick
Answer:
quickly – make adjective *quick* into adverb *quickly* using suffix -*ly*

● *Compound nouns*
These are nouns which are made of two or more words. Some common ways to form them are: noun + noun – *doorstep*, noun + gerund – *hitchhiking*, gerund + noun – *steering wheel*, and verb + adverb – *runaway*.
Question:
The winner received a medal and a

_____
hand
Answer:
handshake – make noun *hand* into compound noun from noun *hand* + noun *shake*

Paper 4 Listening   (approximately 35 minutes)

PART 1

You'll hear people talking in eight different situations. For questions 1–8, choose the best answer, A, B or C.

1 Listen to this mother telling her children a story. She tells them she felt good when
   A she saw an animal.
   B she saw a boat
   C she fell asleep.

   | 1 |

2 Listen to this message on Catherine's answering machine. What does Andrew want her to do?
   A to give one presentation
   B to give three presentations
   C to phone him

   | 2 |

3 A friend phones to invite you to an anniversary party. Where will it be held?
   A at home
   B in a church hall
   C in a park

   | 3 |

4 Listen to this woman talking to someone in the street. What is she doing?
   A giving instructions
   B asking for directions
   C lending him a coin

   | 4 |

5 Listen to this man and wife. What does the wife want to do?
   A make her husband quit his job
   B join some clubs
   C enlarge the family

   | 5 |

6 Listen to a hairdresser talking to a customer. What is the problem?
   A Too much hair was cut off.
   B The haircut took too long.
   C The hairdresser was extremely rude.

   | 6 |

PAPER 4
Listening
Part 1

Specific hints
Identifying questions

● *Similar sounds*
To understand someone correctly, you must hear exactly what is being said. Several vowel sounds can be confused (e.g. *ship* and *sheep*) as well as consonant sounds (e.g. *pear* and *bear*). This can change the meaning of a sentence dramatically. Context (the surrounding words) can usually help you understand, but not always.

Exercise on similar sounds

Listen to this woman talking to someone about going out. When are they going?
A in less than half an hour
B in over half an hour
C in a few minutes
Now listen to the explanation.

General hints
Exam procedure

You are given a test paper and an answer sheet. Check/write your name, centre number and candidate number. While listening to the cassette, write your answers directly on to the test paper, in pen or pencil. At the end of the test, you are given five minutes to transfer your answers from the test paper to the answer sheet. Use pencil. It is not marked by computer, so if you have made a mistake in numbering and your answers are off by one, the marker will probably realise this and check your test paper. Look at the sample answer sheet given at the back of this book.

At the beginning of the exam, a short introduction is played on the tape. Then it is turned off to give you time to ask questions. This is when you should tell the person in charge if you cannot hear the tape well or if there is any other problem. Once the tape is turned on again, you are not allowed to talk and the tape is not turned off until the test is over. Everything is on the cassette, including the listening texts (twice), the pauses and the five-minute transfer time at the end. You may leave when the cassette finishes.

This paper takes about 35 minutes to complete, and then you are given 5 minutes to transfer your answers to the answer sheet.

Marking

Make sure that you answer all questions; marks are not subtracted for incorrect spelling or answers.

You are marked on your ability to make deductions and understand overall meanings (gist), main points, details or specific information. One mark is given for each correct answer. This gives a total of 30 marks which is then scaled to a mark out of 40. The expected level for a typical 'C' mark is about 60 per cent of the total mark.

7 Your favourite radio programme is interrupted for this news bulletin. Where is the reporter?

A outside a large building

B inside a factory

C at the fire station

[ ] 7

8 You are attending a class. What is the lesson about?

A reading

B history

C geography

[ ] 8

PART 2

You will hear a director of an English summer camp explaining the rules of the camp. For questions 9–18, complete the notes which summarise the rules. You will need to write a word or a short phrase in each box.

Rules

Students' washrooms/toilets:

Boys and girls must not [ ] 9

Keep them [ ] 10

Teachers' dormitory:

Only enter if [ ] 11

Teachers' washrooms/toilets:

Do not [ ] 12

Camp helpers:

Available for [ ] 13

Swimming pool:

Operating hours – [ ] 14

Don't make [ ] 15

Daily activities:

Lessons – students have [ ] 16

Leisure time – trips and [ ] 17

Main hall/dining hall:

Do not make [ ] 18

Part 2

Specific hints
Question types

You are given some gaps to fill in according to what you hear. The questions/prompts and some of the answers paraphrase what is on the taped text. Shorter or easier words are often required. For some of the answers, though, you may have to write down exactly what you hear. Be careful when you are asked for the opposite; for example, *he was not very polite* might become *he was rude.*

Exercise on paraphrasing

Speaker 1: I had boarded the train and was looking for my seat when I came across Scotty. My old friend was in a very bad temper.
Question:
Complete the notes which summarise what the speaker says.
Scotty felt _____.
Answer:
angry/upset
This is a shorter way of saying *in a very bad temper.*

PART 3

You will hear five people talking about a package holiday they have taken. For questions 19–23, choose from the list A–F of what happened to each on their holiday. Use the letter only once. There is one extra letter which you do not need to use.

A They couldn't find the coach.	Speaker 1 ☐ **19**
B They had one day free.	Speaker 2 ☐ **20**
C They found one of the sights closed.	Speaker 3 ☐ **21**
D They especially liked the food.	Speaker 4 ☐ **22**
E They all overslept.	Speaker 5 ☐ **23**
F They made new friends.	

PART 4

You will hear a conversation which takes place in an employment agency between two agents, Trevor and Carol, and Carol's husband. Answer questions 24–30, by writing T (for Trevor), C (for Carol) or H (for Husband) in the boxes provided.

24 Who is cheerful at first? ☐ **24**
25 Who knows everyone there? ☐ **25**
26 Who suggests they wait before making a decision? ☐ **26**
27 Who offers to stay alone? ☐ **27**
28 Who feels embarrassed? ☐ **28**
29 Who makes a threat? ☐ **29**
30 Who decides to leave? ☐ **30**

Part 4

Specific hints
Identifying questions

● *Which speaker said what*
You are asked to choose which speaker said what. In order to identify who is speaking, keep in mind the following points: gender (male/female), age (young/middle-aged/old), pitch (high/low), volume (loud/quiet), dialects (regional) and accents (national). Follow the conversation carefully so you do not miss what is happening and who is speaking.

Question types

The questions ask you to find out information about the speakers. You must listen carefully to the words that are said and how they are said. Pay attention to: vocabulary, register, sounds, intonation/tone of voice and word stress. The questions often paraphrase the taped text.

Exercise on paraphrasing

Speaker 1: I had boarded the train and was looking for my seat when I came across Scotty. My old friend was in a very bad temper.
Speaker 2: Well, I think he was probably in a very good mood until you came along!
Question:
Who blames the other?
Answer:
Speaker 2 – *I think he was probably in a very good mood until you came along* is another way of saying that Speaker 2 blames the other for making Scotty angry.

Paper 5 Speaking (approximately 15 minutes)

PART 1 (approximately 4 minutes)

Talk about yourself:

1 What are your plans for the future?
 Do you think you'll fulfil these plans? Why/why not?
 What might prevent you from fulfilling them?

2 How long have you been learning English?
 Why are you learning English?
 Tell us if your English has proved useful to you. If so, in what way? If not, how might you use it in the future?

PAPER 5
Speaking
Part 1

Specific hints
Identifying questions

● *Discussing your plans (see question 1)*
Try to have some kind of a future plan in mind so that if you are asked you do not have to say *er, I don't know.* Think about short-range plans (this year, next year) and long-range plans (five or ten years from now). Give your reasons. You might also think of some alternatives, for example *If I don't do this, I'll do that.*

● *Talking about learning English (see question 2)*
Obviously this subject interests the interviewer, so be prepared to answer it well. Talk about what has helped you and what has not helped you. You may offer constructive criticism, but be polite.

General hints
Exam procedure

The Standard Test Format is two candidates with two examiners. However, under approved circumstances (e.g. the last Speaking test of the day, or not enough interviewers available), some exam centres will use the Individual Test Format: one candidate with one examiner. Note that the Speaking paper and the Listening paper may be given on a different day to the other papers.
 Greet the examiners when you enter the room and ask them where to sit. Make regular eye contact with them and politely take turns during the conversation. Do not ask the examiners if you did well at the end of the exam; they are not allowed to tell you this.
 The Standard Test Format takes about 15 minutes to complete. The Individual Test Format takes about 10 minutes.

Marking

As in the Writing paper, you do not lose marks for using American English or other 'standard Englishes', as long as you always use the same kind of English. You do not lose marks for asking the interviewer to repeat something once, but you do lose marks for memorising 'speeches'. You will also lose marks if the interviewer has to keep reminding you what the question is. You are marked on how well you try, not on whether you reach a right or complete answer in the time available.
 You are marked on your ability to give and exchange information and opinions. Marks are given for correct use of grammar, appropriate use of vocabulary, good pronunciation (individual sounds, words and sentences), fluency, suitable communication skills (turn taking, holding someone's attention, negotiating meaning, starting conversation, responding to others)

and proper task achievement (appropriate responses). This gives you a mark out of 40. The expected level for a typical 'C' mark is about 60 per cent of the total mark.

Question types

In this paper you are tested on both interactional language (exchanging information) and transactional language (negotiating/reaching an agreement/coming to a conclusion). In Part 1 you are tested on giving information (about yourself) and socialising (relating to others). In Part 2 you are tested on giving and exchanging personal and factual information (about yourself in relation to the pictures). Part 3 tests you on information and opinion/attitude exchange (expressing what you know/think). Part 4 tests you on opinion exchange (expressing what you think/feel/believe) and how well you can justify your opinions (showing they are right).

PART 2 (approximately 4 minutes)

Look at the photographs on p. 128 and p. 129. They show different types of jobs. Work with your partner

1 Student A: compare and contrast pictures 1 and 2, saying what you might be thinking and feeling if you were these workers.

2 Student B: talk about the working conditions in your own country; are they similar?

3 Student B: compare and contrast pictures 3 and 4, saying what you might be thinking and feeling if you were these children.

4 Student A: talk about the situation for children in your own country; is it similar?

PART 3 (approximately 3 minutes)

Imagine that a citizens' committee has complained that the layout of the local airport isn't very efficient. Your council has decided to listen to them and make some changes. Look at the picture below. It is a ground plan showing two spaces (A and B), to be used as a cafeteria and a place for incoming luggage.

Work with your partner. Talk together and decide which space would be more suitable as a cafeteria and which as a place for the incoming luggage. Then talk about what you would need to put in each space.

Part 2

Specific hints
Identifying questions

● *Discussing thoughts (see questions 1 and 3)*
Consider the character and the situation. Thoughts might be in the past, the present, or the future. They might be in the first person, *I would rather be at the cinema*, or in the third person, *he's thinking he would rather be at the cinema*.

● *Making comparisons/contrasts with your own country (see questions 2 and 4)*
Identify the similarities and differences. Tell the interviewer if you are not very familiar with the subject, but then try to offer one or two ideas.

Part 3

Specific hints
Identifying questions

● *Planning*
You are asked to lay out or organise something, according to the information given. First, look over the whole picture. Then concentrate on the parts you need to answer the question. Think about uses and purposes. Draw a logical conclusion. Be flexible.

Useful vocabulary

● *Conclusions*
So/in the end/in other words this would be the best room for the kitchen.

PART 4 (approximately 4 minutes)

Discuss the following questions with your partner:

1 How important is a good public transport service?

2 What are the drawbacks of using non-renewable energy sources, like petrol, for transportation?

3 What are the advantages and disadvantages of travelling by aeroplane/boat/bus/train?

4 Would you be in favour of building more airports in your country?

5 What can a person learn by travelling?

Part 4

Specific hints
Identifying questions

● *Discussing advantages/disadvantages (see questions 2 and 3)*
You are asked for good points, bad points, or both. Quickly organise your thoughts into positive and negative. If asked for both, present one (e.g. all the positive points), and then the other. Try to make a balanced presentation.

TEST 5

Paper 1 Reading   (1 hour 15 minutes)

PART 1

You are going to read an advertisement for a theatre club. Choose from the list A–I the heading which best summarises each part (1–7) of the advertisement. There is one extra heading which you do not need to use. There is an example at the beginning (0). Mark your answers on the separate answer sheet at the back of the book.

> A   See excellent actors and actresses
> B   How to join the Theatre Club
> C   A choice of three
> D   Listen to an expert
> E   How to book a seat
> F   A show for the holiday season
> G   For those with a sweet tooth
> H   Performances held in different cities
> I   The Sunday Times: The Theatre Club

YOUR TICKET TO THE BEST SEATS

0	I

The Theatre Club now has 25,000 members, proving that it's one of the fastest growing clubs in the country.

1	

In the new year the club will introduce a series of weekend breaks, giving members the opportunity to visit and enjoy the rich variety of theatres around the country. From the oldest Georgian playhouse to the most modern auditorium, members will get the chance to go backstage and meet the people who make theatre happen, as well as to enjoy some sightseeing.

2	

This week's offers reflect the club's wide range of activities. There's a chance to meet one of the country's leading producers, go on a Chocoholic Theatre Weekend, or go to a special family ballet matinee.

3	

Call ahead to book seats for any of these shows at the Theatre Club's own booking service on 0171-413 1412, which is available 24 hours a day, or call the number given with each show during box-office hours.

4	

Send a cheque for £12.50, made payable to The Theatre Club, together with your name, address and telephone number to: The Theatre Club, PO Box 2, Owen Road, Diss, Norfolk, 1P22 3HH. If you need more information, please telephone 0171-387 9673.

| **5** | |

LONDON: English National Ballet performs *The Nutcracker* at the Royal Festival Hall
New Year's Day matinée 2.30 pm.

Tchaikovsky's magical ballet features flying cooks, a Christmas tree that grows and grows, a magic Santa's sleigh and dolls that come to life. Members are offered a special tea party after the matinée performance. The cost is just £30 a ticket for adults and half price for children.
Telephone 0171-928 8800.

| **6** | |

LONDON: *An Ideal Husband* by Oscar Wilde at the Globe Theatre
Tuesday, January 19

Meet the producer, Bill Kenwright, before a performance of Sir Peter Hall's production of *An Ideal Husband*. Bill Kenwright is one of the five most prolific producers in the country. He currently has five shows in the West End and produces at two regional theatres. Members have the chance to learn at first hand the producer's role in the theatre. Tickets are available to members at £26, which includes a pre-theatre buffet and top price seats for the show.
Telephone 0171-240 1690.

| **7** | |

BIRMINGHAM: A Chocoholic's Theatre Weekend with *The Wizard of Oz* at the Repertory Theatre
January 2, 9, 16, 23 and 30

Enjoy a weekend full of chocolate and fun. Members will stay at the Hyatt Regency Hotel and will receive a bundle of chocolate sweets before relaxing in the best seats in the theatre for *The Wizard of Oz*. Later, a cup of hot chocolate before bed finishes off the evening, which is followed the next day by a tempting trip to Cadbury World. Tickets for the weekend cost £62.75 for adults (based on two people sharing a room), £26.75 for children under 14, and £4.50 for children under five, staying in their parents' room (babysitters are available). The price includes bed and breakfast, theatre tickets and the trip to Cadbury World.
Telephone 0121-236 2302 for details and to book ahead.

PART 2

*You are going to read an extract from a book. For questions 8–15, choose the answer (A, B, C or D) which you think fits best according to the text. Mark your answers **on the separate answer sheet** at the back of the book.*

Just after midnight the last of the lights had gone out and Boyd started the car, drove down to the coast road and turned so that the car would be facing the right way for when he left. They didn't look as if they would be a problem but the quicker he could leave the easier it would be. He stopped the car just past the entrance to the driveway. The nylon ropes and the torch were on the passenger seat beside him. His gun was in his right-hand jacket pocket. When he got out he opened all the car doors very slightly after he had switched off the parking lights.

   He walked up the road until he guessed he was opposite the house and then climbed over the low dry-stone wall. The moon was full, making the house look almost as if it were all lit up. Treading slowly and determinedly he moved down the slope towards the house, across the drive and over to the front door. It was in deep shadow and he shone the torch on the lock as he gently pushed in the key. It turned easily and when he moved the handle he felt a soft rush of cold air as the door opened. He left the door slightly open and he shone the torch around the big square hall.

The stairs made a lot of noise despite his keeping well against the wall, but nobody stirred. The bedroom facing the top of the stairs was locked, and he tried several keys in the lock. The third one unlocked it and he opened the door slowly. There was a smell of stale smoke, and he guessed it was not used as a bedroom. He shaded the torch with his hand and saw that the room was unoccupied. He found the switch, turned on the light and closed the door.

There were two long tables in the centre of the room. The kind that decorators use. They were piled with papers and books, with a space cleared for a portable typewriter. Against the far wall was a projection screen on a metal stand. A slide projector and a 16mm sound projector were on a metal stand at the side of metal shelves. There were three worn armchairs and on an otherwise empty bookshelf was a small portable radio.

8 Why did Boyd wait to park his car?
   A to let the others go to bed
   B to make sure his car was facing the right way
   C to get the ropes and torch ready
   D to let the moon go behind a cloud

9 Why did Boyd turn the car around?
   A He wanted to be able to leave quickly and easily.
   B He was worried that he might have problems with the car.
   C He wanted to park just past the entrance to the driveway.
   D He couldn't see well because the lights had gone out.

10 How did he feel as he got near the house?
   A guilty and fearful
   B disappointed and determined
   C nervous and frightened
   D confident and calm

11 What does 'it' in line 10 refer to?
   A the low dry-stone wall
   B the moon
   C the house
   D the slope

12 What does 'treading' in line 10 mean?
   A running
   B walking
   C escaping
   D racing

13 While going up the stairs, he thought that
   A he should keep away from the wall.
   B he might be heard.
   C he must have lost his keys.
   D he was the only one in the house.

14 What do we learn about the bedroom facing the top of the stairs?
  A It had just been decorated.
  B It was unlocked.
  C It had been used by smokers.
  D It had been used as a cinema.

15 What would be the most suitable title for this extract?
  A Caught as a spy
  B An ordinary burglar
  C Looking for information
  D Telling secrets

PART 3

*You are going to read a newspaper article about bats. Seven sentences have been removed from the article. Choose from the sentences **A–H** the one which fits each gap (**16–21**). There is one extra sentence which you do not need to use. There is an example at the beginning (**0**). Mark your answers **on the separate answer sheet** at the back of the book.*

BATS ARE NOCTURNAL, BUT NOT AS BLACK AS PAINTED
By Anna Harrisson

Bats may play an essential part in horror films, but they suffer from an undeserved reputation. Just as strange is the preference of some, but not all, bat species to hang upside-down when resting. [0 | H]

Let's start at the beginning; first things first. Our friends the bats don't wish to get knotted up in our hair; they don't suck blood; they don't spread disease! Most bats are gentle and kindly, more keen on helping farmers than biting the necks of young women dressed in their nightdresses.
[16 |]

In pre-historic times, the cavemen noticed bats hanging like bunches of grapes, from the roofs of caves. Their first reactions were feelings of fear, which changed to respect when watching the tender care with which the mother looked after her baby bats, cleaning them and feeding them all day. [17 |]

The classical Greeks, who were great naturalists, were the ones to give bats their name, 'chiroptera'. [18 |]

While we humans are meat-eating, of the more than 1,000 kinds of bats on our planet, only one, the vampire bat from the Carpathian mountains, sucks blood. [19 |] Mosquitoes also suck blood and people are much less afraid of them, although they may be much more dangerous, spreading the disease malaria. The tiger mosquito in Central America spreads encephalitis.

Bats in Europe are 100 per cent insect eaters. In Greece, at the beginning of this century, there were great communities of bats living around the plains of Thessaly. [20 |] Then they would clean up the insects, many of which were harmful to the farmers' crops, acting like 'flying vacuum cleaners'. Now things are changing fast, and not all for the better!

Bats have been living on our planet for about 40 million years, and they move from place to place, living sometimes in caves, forests, old buildings, and every once in a while in a church bell tower. [21 |]

A This means 'hands with wings'.

B But unless we've been introduced and got to know someone, how can we love them – isn't this the case with bears, wolves and street dogs?

C In the evenings and nights, they would fly over the wet ditches and the wheat fields.

D How is it that just one out of more than one thousand species can give all bats such a bad name, considering that there are many, such as fruit bats and flying-foxes, which are completely vegetarian?

E Fools are described as 'batty' or have 'bats in the belfry'.

F All the ancient civilisations were sympathetic towards bats, respected them and considered them to have magic powers.

G Needless to say, we have a great responsibility towards them.

H Hopefully this is not too confusing!

PART 4

You are going to read some information about some companies. For questions 22–34, choose from the companies (A–H). Some of the companies may be chosen more than once. When more than one answer is required, these may be given in any order. There is an example at the beginning (0). For question 35, choose the answer (A, B, C or D) which you think fits best according to the text. Mark your answers on the separate answer sheet.

Which company or companies:

is proud of their research programme?	**0** F	
deals with a precious metal?	**22**	
deals with communication links?	**23**	
is partly owned by management?	**24**	
states it does not work in Europe?	**25**	
states it is concerned with the whole family?	**26**	
profit from natural resources?	**27**	**28**
directly exchange money?	**29**	**30**
mention how many people they employ?	**31**	**32**
make medicine?	**33**	**34**

35 Why would someone read this text?
   A to invest in a business
   B to look for a job
   C to order a report
   D to buy a product

FINANCIAL TIMES ANNUAL REPORT SERVICE

Choose which of the following reports you wish to have sent to you:

TVX Gold Inc. – A

TVX GOLD INC. is a Canadian-based growth-oriented international mining company with 1993 gold and gold equivalent production of a record 439,000 ounces at an average cash cost of $172 per ounce from its interests in six operating gold mines located in North and South America. The strengths of TVX Gold include quality reserves, long mine life, low average cash costs and increase in production, and a new, experienced and aggressive management team.

Statoil – B

Statoil is an integrated Norwegian oil and gas company and ranks as the leading operator on Norway's continental shelf. Operations are also pursued in 20 other countries. The group reported a profit before taxation of NOK 12 billion in 1993 as against NOK 9.9 billion the year before. This increase was due to a high level of production, a reduction in operating costs and improved financial results.

Statoil is organised in four business areas – Exploration and Production, Natural Gas, Oil Trading and Shipping, and Refining and Marketing. From 1994 Statoil's involvement in Petrochemicals has been transferred to Borealis, a new petrochemical company owned 50 per cent by Statoil and 50 per cent by Neste. After the hive-off of its petrochemical operations in 1994, the group has about 12,000 employees.

The Rabobank Group – C

With total assets of NLG 253.2 billion the Dutch Rabobank Group ranks among the top 20 banks in Europe and the top 50 worldwide. Over the past two decades, the bank has gradually expanded its international network to cover strategic geographic areas. It comprises now 47 offices in the world's major financial and commercial centres. The Group's 'central bank', Rabobank Nederland, operates as a wholesale house, specialising in serving major national and international corporations and in operations on the financial markets. Besides dealing room and treasury activities, the bank offers corporate financial services (including consultancy on mergers, acquisitions and participations) as well as a comprehensive package of international services through its international network.

Roberts Pharmaceuticals – D

Roberts Pharmaceuticals (NASDAZ: RPCX) is fast realising its goal of becoming a major pharmaceutical company whose diverse products contribute to the health and well-being of all age groups. Roberts has successfully combined an aggressive product development programme with strategic acquisitions, to create a profitable company with a well-balanced product portfolio concentrated in six major therapeutic categories.

Telia – E

The Telia Group offers public and private networks for telephony, data communications and mobile telephony. Together with PTT Netherlands and Swiss PTT, Telia is a co-owner of Unisource. In 1993, the Telia Group's revenues totalled USD $4.5 billion. Return on capital employed was 14.5 per cent. Telia invested a total of USD 910 million.

Roche – F

Roche is a Swiss-based international health-care group employing 56,000 people worldwide. It is a research-driven company with a leading position in biotechnology and activities covering the entire health spectrum of prevention, diagnosis and treatment of disease. Roche has gained a high reputation for the quality of its innovative research and the original contributions it has made to the development of new drugs. In addition to pharmaceuticals Roche is engaged in the fields of vitamins and fine chemicals, diagnostics, fragrances and flavours.

BSS – G

BSS is a Swiss bank with all that this applies in terms of tradition, experience, security and confidentiality. BSS is owned by the 'Fondation de Famille Sandoz' and by key executives of the bank. The bank focuses on asset management for private and institutional clients and offers a wide range of securities and banking services including global custody, forex and stock exchange operations.

Saga Petroleum a.s. – H

In 1993, Saga Petroleum had an operating profit of NOK 1694 million and a profit before taxes of NOK 1006 million. The Group's proved and probable oil and gas reserves total 1,474 million tonnes of oil equivalent, of which 44 per cent is oil. In terms of reserves, Saga is among the largest independent upstream companies in the world. It is Saga's intention further to strengthen its position on the Norwegian shelf, and to utilise the company's expertise and capacity gradually to develop its international activities.

Saga's objective is to give the company's shareholders the highest possible return on their investment through efficient operations and strict requirements to the profitability of new products.

Paper 2 Writing (1½ hours)

PART 1

*You **must** answer this question.*

1 You went to a cinema with your family to see one of the latest films. However, you could not follow the development of the story because of various problems during the showing. You also noticed various safety hazards. You were all extremely disappointed.

   Look at the diagram of the cinema and the notes that you have made. Then write your letter of complaint to the cinema manager. Cover the points in your notes and add any relevant information.

   Write a **letter** of **120–180** words in an appropriate style. Do not include an address.

PART 2

*Write an answer to **one** of the questions 2–5 in this part. Write your answer in **120–180** words in an appropriate style.*

2 A local young people's newspaper carried out a survey on the following question: 'Should school holidays be broken up or given together?'

   Write a short **article** for the newspaper on this topic, based on your own experience.

3 You have learned that a publisher of short stories is looking for a new author. You have decided to enter the short story competition. The competition rules say that the story must begin or end with the following words: 'I could not believe it.'

   Write your **story** for the publisher.

4 You work for a travel agent and this is part of a letter you receive.

> We are collecting information for our monthly travel magazine on the type of holidays that young people (15–25 years old) prefer. Could you please write us a short report on your country? Please include length, time of year and type of holiday.

   Write a **report** which could be included in the travel magazine.

5 **Background reading texts**
   Answer **one** of the following two questions based on your reading of **one** of the set books:
   (a) Describe an important turning point in the story and how this affects the characters. Does it make the book interesting for someone who has not yet read it?
   (b) Do any of the events of the book that you have read remind you of things that you have experienced or heard about from others? Describe these events by connecting them to your personal experiences.

Paper 3 Use of English (1 hour 15 minutes)

PART 1

For questions **1–15**, read the text below and decide which answer **A, B, C** or **D** best fits each space. There is an example at the beginning **(0)**. Mark your answers **on the separate answer sheet** at the back of the book.

Example:

| 0 | **A** ages | **B** lives | **C** years | **D** dates |

| 0 | <u>A</u> | B | C | D |

A PLACE WITH A DIFFERENCE

This is a place where people of all **(0)** _____ can come and be entertained and never want to **(1)** _____. It is Disneyland, **(2)** _____ outside Paris, especially **(3)** _____ to provide the best for Europe and the **(4)** _____ of its new guests. The park is **(5)** _____ into five areas, each one representing a special theme. **(6)** _____ in a film, the **(7)** _____ are taken along through a series of magical sets to relive the past, visit wonderful faraway places **(8)** _____ of excitement and fantasy, and even **(9)** _____ into the future. The trees that have been **(10)** _____ around the park protect the guest from the real world outside.

  The resort area, beyond the park, has six hotels to suit the needs of every guest. In **(11)** _____ to these six hotels there are campsites and fully equipped caravans for rental. There is no **(12)** _____ of sporting opportunities and, besides many health clubs in the actual hotels, there is a variety of fascinating nature trails you may **(13)** _____ to follow. The Disneyland Resort is easily **(14)** _____ by road or rail. Whichever way you choose to arrive, you will be **(15)** _____ enough to enjoy all the wonderful things that the park has to offer.

1	**A** leave	**B** go	**C** depart	**D** set off
2	**A** nearly	**B** almost	**C** just	**D** recently
3	**A** composed	**B** created	**C** consisted	**D** placed
4	**A** rights	**B** demands	**C** consideration	**D** dealings
5	**A** shared	**B** distributed	**C** calculated	**D** divided
6	**A** Whereas	**B** Unless	**C** As if	**D** Wherever
7	**A** staff	**B** guests	**C** members	**D** teams
8	**A** full	**B** crowded	**C** complete	**D** packed
9	**A** look	**B** go	**C** run	**D** turn
10	**A** dug	**B** planted	**C** grown	**D** stuck
11	**A** answer	**B** reply	**C** debt	**D** addition
12	**A** supply	**B** shortage	**C** amount	**D** quantity
13	**A** expect	**B** hope	**C** wish	**D** order
14	**A** contacted	**B** arrived	**C** reached	**D** entered
15	**A** relaxed	**B** unhurried	**C** easy	**D** lazy

PART 2

*For questions **16–30**, read the text below and think of the word which best fits each space. Use only **one** word in each space. There is an example at the beginning (**0**). Write your word **on the separate answer sheet** at the back of the book.*

Example:

0	*and*	▭ **0** ▬

CARNIVAL TIME

It was carnival time again. It was time for fun **(0)** ___*and*___ laughter. Although I had seen carnival processions on television, I had never taken part in **(16)** _____ before so I was looking forward to it.

The procession began and we went singing and dancing **(17)** _____ the street watched by crowds of people. Balloons flew up in the air and everyone was having **(18)** _____ wonderful time.

Just then I realised that my young brother, who had **(19)** _____ with me to the procession, was **(20)** _____ longer with me. I asked one of my friends to help me find him. It was a difficult thing to do because everyone was dressed up and many of them were also wearing masks over their **(21)** _____.

Suddenly, I saw him. I could **(22)** _____ believe my eyes. He was sitting on the very first float right next to the 'King of the Carnival'. He **(23)** _____ smiling and enjoying every minute of it.

I shouted to him **(24)** _____ because there was **(25)** _____ much noise, he did not hear me at first. I kept **(26)** _____ shouting until he finally **(27)** _____ me and waved. I yelled out to **(28)** _____ that he should wait for me at the end of the street when the **(29)** _____ was over. He nodded his head **(30)** _____ agreement and went back to waving and smiling at the crowd.

PART 3

For questions 31–40, complete the second sentence so that it has a similar meaning to the first sentence, using the word given. **Do not change the word given.** *You must use between two and five words, including the word given. There is an example at the beginning (0). Write only the missing words* **on the separate answer sheet** *at the back of the book.*

Example:

  0 Mr Jones needn't go if he doesn't want to.
     obliged
     Mr Jones _____ if he doesn't want to.

The gap can be filled by the words 'is not obliged to go' so you write:

0	*is not obliged to go*	0

31 He really likes correcting her English.
    pleasure
    He _____ correcting her English.

32 It's not necessary to take a lot of luggage when going on holiday.
    much
    You _____ luggage when going on holiday.

33 Perhaps he hasn't received the doctor's results yet.
    may
    He _____ the doctor's results yet.

34 All I want you to do is to look after my dog.
    care
    All I want you to do is to _____ my dog.

35 She was not certain about the trip.
    decide
    She _____ about the trip.

36 He locked the gate so that the dog wouldn't escape.
    prevent
    He locked the gate _____ escaping.

37 They did not like to pay extra taxes.
    objected
    They _____ extra taxes.

38 The day was so nice that we went on a picnic.
    such
    It was _____ that we went on a picnic.

39 The only person I didn't see was Jane.
    except
    I _____ Jane.

40 She decided to visit her friend and tell her the news.
    drop
    She decided to _____ her friend and tell her the news.

PART 4

*For questions **41–55**, read the text below and look carefully at each line. Some of the lines are correct, and some have a word which should not be there.*

*If a line is correct put a tick (√) by the number **on the separate answer sheet** at the back of the book. If a line has a word which should **not** be there, write the word **on the separate answer sheet**. There are two examples at the beginning (**0** and **00**).*

Examples:

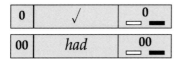

AN UNEXPECTED ACCIDENT

  0   We had just arrived in a village on the way to meet some friends

 00   who we were going hiking with when we had had a flat tyre. We got

 41   out of the car and walked towards a shop so that we could have

 42   ask if there was a someone who could change the flat tyre. The

 43   shop-owner agreed that to help us by sending a boy to fetch a

 44   man to look at the tyre. He explained that it would cost a lot of

 45   money because the materials for doing such jobs were expensive

 46   and difficult to get them. All we could do was to sit around and

 47   wait for the job to be done. While we were waiting we decided to

 48   spend some time playing a game of our football. However, as it was

 49   the middle of summer it soon became so hot that we had to stop.

 50   We sat on some chairs and ordered a cold drink and had looked

 51   at the view. When the man finally he came, we asked him to

 52   finish quickly because we were in a hurry to meet our friends. Even

 53   though he worked quickly it still took a few of hours for him

 54   to be finish. We could only hope that our friends had not set off

 55   without us. We would have to drive quickly to make it up for lost time.

PART 5

For questions 56–65, read the text below. Use the word given in capitals at the end of each line to form a word that fits in the space in the same line. There is an example at the beginning (0). Write your word on the separate answer sheet at the back of the book.

Example:

0	*impossible*	0

SURVIVAL

The weather made their progress **(0)** .... As it	**POSSIBLE**
had been raining **(56)** ... all night they had to	**HEAVY**
be very **(57)** ... as they walked through the	**CARE**
thick jungle. Their good **(58)** ... would help	**JUDGE**
them overcome the **(59)** ... and get back to	**SET**
civilisation with only minor injuries.	
Although things were **(60)** ... they had to be	**BEARABLE**
(61) ... because it was the only way they could	**OPTIMIST**
help each other through this difficult situation.	
Their **(62)** ..., chosen for his knowledge, would help	**LEAD**
them in every way. The **(63)** ... of this training	**IMPORTANT**
was to **(64)** ... them for the special task ahead	**HARD**
of them. However, they had never imagined how **(65)** ...	**DANGER**
it would turn out to be.	

Paper 4 Listening   (approximately 35 minutes)

PART 1

You'll hear people talking in eight different situations. For questions 1–8, choose the best answer, A, B or C.

1 A policeman has signalled for you to pull your car over to the pavement. What does he do?
   A check under the bonnet
   B check the boot
   C give you a ticket

   | 1 |

2 Listen to this woman on the radio. What is she trying to do?
   A encourage
   B inform
   C persuade

   | 2 |

3 Listen to this man phoning Quick Car Service. How does he feel about it?
   A suspicious
   B enthusiastic
   C satisfied

   | 3 |

4 Listen to this teacher talking to a student. He was certain the student
   A had done her homework.
   B hadn't done her homework.
   C could tell him the answer.

   | 4 |

5 Listen to the doctor talking to your wife. What does he tell her to do?
   A to bathe more often
   B to be careful with her diet
   C to take walks

   | 5 |

6 Listen to these two colleagues talking. Who are they?
   A players
   B coaches
   C referees

   | 6 |

7 You have phoned a cinema for information. Which film is playing on Friday evening?
   A Eye of the Hurricane
   B Last of the Cowboys
   C Gone with the Snow

   | 7 |

8 You are phoning someone from your office. He is
   A your boss.
   B your assistant.
   C someone in the same position as yourself.

   | 8 |

PART 2

You will hear part of a radio discussion about overweight children. For questions 9–18, complete the notes which summarise what the doctor says. You will need to write a word or a short phrase in each box.

Overweight children later have problems as		**9**
Best advice – don't let children		**10**
Mealtimes should be		**11**
Children don't feel hungry if they eat		**12**
Second helpings – make children		**13**
Babies know when to		**14**
If parents are overweight, children are probably		**15**
Snacks – give at certain		**16**
Sometimes, give children a		**17**
When with other people, don't		**18**

PART 3

You will hear five people leaving phone messages for a woman named Sylvia. For questions 19–23, choose from the list A–F what message each speaker is leaving. Use each letter only once. There is one extra letter which you do not need to use.

A She should not forget her date.	Speaker 1 **19**
B She should call home.	Speaker 2 **20**
C She should go for an interview.	Speaker 3 **21**
D She should expect a business phone call.	Speaker 4 **22**
E She should think about getting married.	Speaker 5 **23**
F She should make an appointment.	

PART 4

You will hear a radio discussion about writing picture books for children. For questions 24–30, tick one of the boxes to show whether each statement is true or false.

24 Mr Parker works for Night Publishers.   T ☐ F ☐ | 24 |

25 The interviewer probably doesn't know Mr Parker.   T ☐ F ☐ | 25 |

26 It is easy to write a picture book.   T ☐ F ☐ | 26 |

27 Jayne Fisher was a teenager when she wrote her first book. T ☐ F ☐ | 27 |

28 Listeners can post a book they've written to Mr Parker.   T ☐ F ☐ | 28 |

29 They must send a 'dummy'.   T ☐ F ☐ | 29 |

30 The publisher's logo looks like this: T ☐ F ☐ | 30 |

Now copy all your answers on to the separate answer sheet at the back of the book.

Paper 5 Speaking (approximately 15 minutes)

PART 1 (approximately 4 minutes)

Talk about yourself:

1 When you have free time, where do you like to go with your friends?

2 Which country would you like to visit? Why?

3 What are your job/career plans?

4 How long have you been learning English? Do you have a favourite teacher? What makes a teacher special?

PART 2 (approximately 4 minutes)

Look at the photographs on p. 130. They show different types of environment. Work with your partner.

1 Student A: compare and contrast pictures 1 and 2, saying what you might be thinking and feeling if you were these people.

2 Student B: tell us which type of environment you prefer.

3 Student B: compare and contrast pictures 3 and 4, saying what you might be thinking and feeling if you were these people.

4 Student A: talk about which place you would prefer to go to.

PART 3 (approximately 3 minutes)

Imagine that a new neighbour is designing her back garden. She wants to create a friendly environment for entertaining guests. Look at the picture below. It is a ground plan showing two areas (A and B) in a garden, to be used for a swimming pool and a cooking/eating area.

Work with your partner. Talk together and decide which area would be more suitable for a swimming pool and which as a place for cooking/eating. Then talk about what you would like to put in each area.

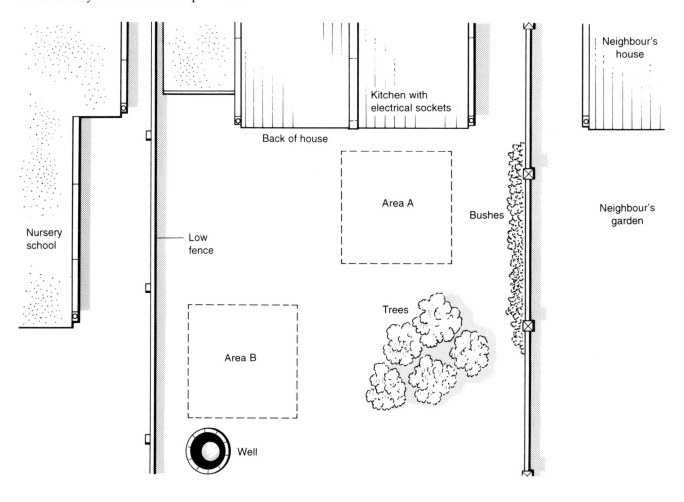

PART 4 (approximately 4 minutes)

Discuss the following questions with your partner.

1 What else would you like to see in an ideal back garden?

2 Do you prefer to be in a man-made environment or a natural environment? Why?

3 Why does a person's environment affect his or her mood?

4 What are some of the advantages and disadvantages of living in a large city/in a small town/on a farm?

5 What are some solutions for people who have to live in a big city?

TAPESCRIPTS

TEST 1

SPECIFIC HINTS SECTION

Exercise on intonation and tone of voice

Listen to this woman talking to someone about going out. How does she feel?

A surprised
B disappointed
C angry

Woman: Where are we going?

The speaker feels surprised. If the speaker had felt disappointed, she would have said:
(sigh) Where are we going?
If the speaker had felt angry, she would have said:
Where are we going?

PART 1

Question 1
Mum: I told you to leave that alone and to clean up your room! Don't you ever listen to me?
Son: Ah, Mum. *Now's* not the time for that. I've got to get this done. Mr Bridges wants it *done* by tomorrow.
Mum: That's what you always say when I tell you to tidy up your room. Day in and day out I have to cope with your dirty socks all over the house. You could at least clean up after yourself in your own room!
Son: Right, Mum. I mean, I really *like* doing homework. Yeah. That's why I'm not tidying up my room …

Question 2
Businesswoman: No, I can't possibly make it to the Hyatt Hotel by eleven – I've got a ten thirty appointment here at my office. Then I've got to get that report up to Simmons. By that time I'll be running pretty late … Let's make it down in the cafeteria at one, if that's all right with you. The food's not great, but as long as we steer clear of the chicken, we'll be all right. See you there.

Question 3
Dentist's receptionist: Excuse me, Mr Thompson? I'm very sorry, but I'm afraid that the dentist's in the middle of a very difficult case, and that he's going to be delayed. It might not be a bad idea to go to the café round the corner. At least there you can have a cup of coffee. He'll probably be at least another half an hour.

Question 4
Clerk: Attention, shoppers. Welcome to Thrifty's Supermarket, the supermarket where every deal is a steal. Today we'd like to draw your attention to aisle number nine, where several of our cheeses are available at special low prices. Thank you for shopping at Thrifty's.

Question 5
Clerk: That's absolutely correct, Mrs Townshend. Would you like to see the figures on the, uh, Underwood merger?
Boss: No, that's fine for the moment, Dave. I'm still waiting to see what turns up in the Prescott case.
Clerk: Can I get you some coffee? Uh, they've brought up some fine Danish pastries today, if you'd uh …
Boss: No. Hold all of my calls while I'm taking this meeting with Woodsworth.

Question 6
Young man: Yeah, I told her that it wouldn't work out, but she wouldn't take 'no' for an answer. Mmmm, that's right. Surprised me, too. So we're going out Friday night. No, I'm keeping Saturday free for Cindy. Yeah. So anyway, on Friday I'll tell Joan that I want to break it off … You're right, but I have to tell her sooner or later.

Question 7
Hair salon receptionist: Look, I'm afraid I can't possibly give you any change, luv, it's just out of the question. Everyone's been asking me for change to tip the girls. You'd think they'd bring change with them. Really! The things you have to put up with nowadays. Makes me want to work in a blooming flower shop!

Question 8
Girl: I almost *died* when Phillip Carrington came on screen. I mean, with those dark brown eyes and big, hunky muscles. And, I mean, the dialogue was so good, you know? I wish I could write like that. Miss Simpson would give me an 'A' in English. Instead of the 'D's I'm getting now. Oooof.

PART 2

Announcer: Hello! This is Dial-a-recipe. Today we have a recipe for you for a lovely, light bacon soufflé.
  To make this delicious soufflé, you'll need the following ingredients: 250 grams of bacon, 50 grams of grated cheese, 2 onions, a tomato, 4 eggs, 50 grams of flour, 70 grams of butter plus another 20 grams to grease the baking dish and a bit of salt and pepper for seasoning.
  Preheat the oven to 210 degrees centigrade. Be sure that your oven has been heated to the right temperature before you put the soufflé into it. Soufflés need quick heat so that they can rise swiftly and properly.
  Finely chop the onions. Skin the tomato and remove the core and the pips; chop finely. Cut the bacon into small pieces.
  Heat up 25 grams of butter in a frying-pan, and lightly fry the bacon for 5 minutes. Add the chopped onions and tomato to the bacon and let it all fry for another 7 minutes.
  Grease the soufflé baking dish. When making soufflés, you can use small, individual soufflé dishes to bake several soufflés in or you can use one, tall soufflé dish. Whatever you choose, grease the bottom and sides well with butter, and then coat the buttered bottom and sides with flour. This will help the soufflé climb up the sides of the dish, and it won't stick to the dish.

Make a white sauce by melting the remaining butter in a saucepan. Take care not to burn the butter. Carefully add the flour. Then stir constantly while slowly adding the milk. Cook over a low heat for 5 minutes until it thickens.

Take the eggs and separate the whites from the yolks. Remove the saucepan from the heat. Add the cheese, bacon, tomato, and onion mixture, and a little salt and pepper, and the 4 egg yolks.

Beat the egg whites until stiff. Carefully add them to the mixture in the saucepan.

Fill the soufflé dish with the mixture and bake for 15 minutes, or until it doubles in size. Soufflés are famous for their lightness; the heat and egg whites should make them double in size, but soufflés soon flatten after they leave the oven, so always serve them immediately.

Enjoy your soufflé.

PART 3

Speaker 1: I suppose I'm rather adventurous. I enjoy ethnic restaurants. I usually go to a quaint little spot in town. When you walk in it's like entering another world. There's oriental music and ornaments on the walls, and candles are lit in lanterns on the tables. The waitresses are all dressed up in costumes, and you don't understand half the things on the menu. I never use a knife and fork when I eat there.

Speaker 2: Me? I like to grab a quick burger on the way home from the pictures. Usually get a large chips to go with it. And a shake. I'm not big on salads, though they've got a big salad bar. I like it 'cause it's got lots of young people – lots of loud music, and all. Mind, my girlfriend prefers steak and kidney pudding . . .

Speaker 3: It's a fast, friendly solution to a meal out with friends. They've got a good wine list. Clean tables. Presentable waiters. And there's not just one choice of food, as you might think. When I read the menu I often need to ask the waiters what something is. Sometimes, if you're lucky and have a lively group sitting at the next table, they'll break out into an Italian song at the end of the meal. It's like a free performance! And if you've got food left over, they can always pack it up for you!

Speaker 4: When one goes out, one should enjoy oneself to the fullest. That's why I rather appreciate a good meal – a rare steak done to perfection, a baked potato, and a fine bottle of wine – followed by a superb performance. This week they're presenting 'China Town', by Vance Granger. I would highly recommend it.

Speaker 5: From the moment you arrive, the staff wait on you hand and foot. Light music accompanies your meal, while you enjoy your food. Not hamburgers slapped on the grill, but juicy beef fillets, done however you want. This is an excellent choice for anyone who likes first-class service.

PART 4

Father: Cindy, I'm home!
Daughter: Hi, Dad! How was your day?
Father: Exhausting. I'm really tired. Maybe I'm just getting old, but work gets harder every day.

Daughter: Sit down and relax for a couple of minutes. Come on. It'll do you good.
Father: Whew! I'm getting too old for television. Interviewing all of those boring people. I should have been a doctor! Or a pilot!
Daughter: Just forget about work. Anyway, the picnic will make you feel better.
Father: What picnic?
Daughter: You're joking! The picnic *we're* going on! You know, the family!
Father: *Our* family?
Daughter: Of course, *our* family!
Father: But Mum never mentioned anything last night about a picnic . . .
Daughter: I don't understand . . . she promised she'd call you at the studio.
Father: Oh, that explains it.
Daughter: Oh, come on. She probably didn't have time. She had another court case today. With her favourite judge. You know, the one who always interrupts her when she's speaking. Anyway, we're going to go out to Marble Hill Park . . . you *know* you love picnics.
Father: Yeah, I'm just feeling kind of tired. Recorded all morning. Lucky you – no school!
Daughter: Not for two more months! But let's not spoil the mood; I'm in the middle of packing some things for the picnic.
Father: Mmmm, what've you got there?
Daughter: Hey, don't mess it up!
Father: Well, I'm hungry. Where is the salami? We *always* have salami when we go on picnics! It's the best part!
Daughter: Well, today mum told *me* to cook. None of that unhealthy stuff! I boiled some chicken and wrapped it up, see?
Father: It looks so white.
Daughter: That's because I peeled the skin off. No cholesterol for you today!
Father: And where are my boiled eggs?
Daughter: Oh, Dad! Dr Wilson told you not to eat so many eggs. *He* would have a heart attack if he knew how many you ate! Instead, I've packed some salt-free crackers.
Father: Oh, I love crackers.
Daughter: And look at these!
Father: What are you going to do? Become a greengrocer?
Daughter: No, silly! We're going to eat carrots and peas.
Father: Oh, no.
Daughter: Oh, yes!
Father: But they're all raw.
Daughter: That's what makes them so healthy! Heat kills most of the vitamins, you know.
Father: And why have you got the cheese packed in these old yogurt containers? Have we run out of foil?
Daughter: No, but we shouldn't use foil very often. Only when we have to. We create *so* much rubbish – we should be reusing things.
Father: Is that why you don't have any plastic plates and cups in here?
Daughter: Yes! These are all reusable.
Father: Fine . . . but *you* can wash up afterwards!

TEST 2

SPECIFIC HINTS SECTION

Exercise on stress

Listen to this man talking to someone about going out. What is he thinking?

A I don't care about the other people.
B I'm too tired to go out again.
C Which place are we going to?

Man: Where are we going *now*?

The speaker is thinking that he is too tired to go out again. If the speaker had been thinking about himself and his companion, not the other people, he would have said:
  Where are *we* going now?
If the speaker had been thinking about the place, he would have said:
  Where are we going now?

PART 1

Question 1
Girl: There's a great new film on at the Odeon, but I don't want to go with *him*. He talks about his rugby coach all the time. Mind you, it's a good film. But I don't know ... Doesn't seem worth it. I know what will happen. We'll go and then he'll ask me out again.

Question 2
Salesman: Are you the woman of the house? I'm calling for Distributor's International to let you know that *you* have been chosen to enter our 'Win a Trip with Distributor's Contest'. That's an all-expenses-paid trip! Madam, your name will soon be on the grand entry list! Yes! Now, just tell me a convenient time when one of our representatives can come round and get all of the details from you. *And* he'll show you our wonderful line of electrical products. I know you'll just *love* our top-quality, low-priced products.

Question 3
Woman 1: Did you see who Elizabeth was out with last night?
Woman 2: Yeah. Wasn't he good-looking?
Woman 1: No. I don't mean that. Don't you know who he is?
Woman 2: Who?
Woman 1: You know. The guy that my sister used to go out with. Remember? Last year, when she was going out with that university student.
Woman 2: The one who was doing a degree in agriculture?
Woman 1: No. The one who dropped out. He used to play his guitar all the time. Now he owns his own business. Sells pianos.

Question 4
Man: Excuse me. I'm sorry to bother you, but I'm having trouble finding Pendleton Street. They told me to walk straight down Logan Crescent, and that I'd see a 'Chambers Supermarket' to my left, and that's Pendleton Street. But the only supermarket I've seen is a 'Highlife', and that's way back down *there*.

Question 5
Daughter: Hi, Mum? We've finished the game – our team won! Uh, Sandra got two strikes, and Peter even managed to, to knock down all the pins – with his new ball, you know? Uh, can you come and, come and pick me up when you get home? Uh, Sandra wants us to give her a lift, too. Bye.

Question 6
Teacher: So I send a student up to see the headmaster because he was disturbing my class – you know, the usual – throwing chalk. The next day, the boy's father comes storming into the headmaster's office and demands that I be sacked for harassing his son. Imagine! We have problems with the students *and the parents*. *They're* the real root of the problem.

Question 7
Lecturer: As you are all employees, you know that sometimes problems arise in the workplace. I want you all to close your eyes and picture yourself at work. You've just gone out for a moment, and when you come back, you find out that another worker has been rude to one of your regular customers. What do you do? Ignore the situation? Go over and make a big fuss? Talk to her about it later?

Question 8
Homeless person: Can I speak to you for a minute?
Shopper: What do you want?
Person: Well, it's like this. I've been travelling round the world. And I'm a bit short of cash.
Shopper: So you expect me to give you a handout?
Person: Oh, well I wouldn't look at it like that. Just enough so I can get something to eat. I wouldn't be asking if I didn't have to.

PART 2

Producer: So you must be ...
Writer: Kimberly MacDonald.
Producer: Yes, Sam King has spoken very highly of your writing. I'll give you exactly five minutes to convince me to buy your film script. Not that I mean to be rude, Ms MacDonald, but there's nothing new about a spy film.
Writer: You're absolutely right, Mr Golding. And why is that? Because people love an exciting spy story.
Producer: I agree, I've made millions of dollars out of them *myself*, but why should I invest in *yours*?
Writer: Because mine deals with a *new* kind of spy. Not the Cold War heroes of the past, but the technological and industrial spies of the future.
Producer: Yes, that *is* an interesting new approach ... However, a film is only as good as its leading actors. Who do you see as the leading names in *your* film?
Writer: For the female star I see someone who could portray an intelligent character. The heroine of the story is in her late twenties, with long black hair, neatly tied back. Very chic-looking and businesslike. Possibly glasses, and definitely wearing smart executive-style clothes, I think Elizabeth Kingston fits the bill perfectly.
Producer: She'd be expensive but she would draw the crowds, I suppose. What about your male lead?
Writer: Someone older – experienced, seen a bit of life. I see the character, the character in the story, in his late forties, short blond hair, thin moustache, smoking a pipe – how about Paul Downing to play that part?

Producer: No. Paul Downing is good but that character role is just too boring. We need someone that the young people can relate to. That's where the money is.

Writer: Er, no problem. The character could easily be younger – early twenties, long blond hair, wearing jeans and a T-shirt and with a cigarette hanging out of his mouth. I think Luke Fairy could play that part very well.

Producer: Yes, he would fit that role very well ... OK, your characters sound good, but what about the climax of the film – essential. What kind of chase scene have you developed?

Writer: Well, if you've read my script, you'll see that I've used a sports car and ...

Producer: Yes, yes, but it needs to be something rather different – more varied and exciting, I reckon. People are tired of the same old stuff. How about using a boat, like in Miami Vice? A real fast boat?

Writer: Yes, that would work well.

Producer: The chase will take place up and down the coast in boats, then Luke will plunge into the water as the boat breaks into a thousand pieces on the rocks. They all think he's dead, then they see him climbing out of the water onto the jetty and race after him. He jumps onto a passing bus and ... *no* ... a bicycle! Yes, a kid's bicycle. He charges along until he gets a flat tyre, and then he steals a lorry – a *big* lorry! No, on second thoughts, he sees a horse in a field and jumps onto the horse. He rides the horse toward the town with his pursuers right behind him on motorbikes. *Then* he steals the lorry but, with his enemies closing on him, he crashes the lorry into a railway bridge which is too low for the lorry. He climbs up the bank and throws himself onto a passing goods train! They do the same, and there is a fight on the train. He jumps off the train as it passes an airfield. He eventually escapes in a small private aeroplane. Yes. I like that! Make those changes, and I'll take a look at your script!

PART 3

Saleswoman: You have to be prepared to do a lot of talking. And you've got to like being with people – talking to them, trying to persuade them to do something they might not be ready to do, dealing with any difficult questions they might have. Most people don't like spending, so you've got to have a special ability to make people trust you. Believe in you. Believe in what you're saying.

Doctor: This kind of job demands someone who's strong – both emotionally and physically. You work long hours and often have to talk to people who are under a lot of stress. But you feel that you're really helping people every day. All the studying and books in the world don't prepare you for the challenges you face in this job.

Waitress: I don't recommend this job for someone with back problems. All the time it's lifting and carrying, lifting and carrying. And being polite to the customers. No matter how rude they are to you. They can be really difficult and then they don't even leave a tip.

Lawyer: Half of the game is talk, the other half is preparation. You have to constantly be in the library, checking out the latest case developments. It's not usually as exciting as it looks on TV, although you do have to look good in order to make a good impression. I try to wear a nice suit – not too expensive though. You don't want to annoy anyone and lose before you even begin to talk.

Librarian: I was surprised to find how much physical effort it involved; I carry quite heavy loads, especially at weekends when it's busier. Of course, a lot of my work is done behind a desk, but when people ask for help I have to show them where something is. I try to explain how the whole system works so that they can find it themselves the next time. It takes a little longer, but I find it pays off in the long run. I deal with all kinds of people. I really find it rewarding.

PART 4

Salesman: Ladies and gentlemen. Could I have your attention please. This afternoon I'd like to show you our latest baby – the SX50. It's an exquisite car with everything you could want.

Come in for a closer look. It's a deluxe model in a class of its own. How do you know that? By all the luxury features that this car automatically comes with.

You, sir, take a look at the aerodynamic shape of the body. Madam, just look at this boot ... it opens up high and out of the way, making the boot easy to load. And the rear seats fold down so that you can make your boot space even bigger if you need to.

Ladies and gentlemen, every little detail has been carefully thought about. Observe these mudflaps over the front and rear tyres. Yes, over all four wheels. Not those floppy, soft flaps that don't protect your car from the mud. No, they're made of durable hard plastic, guaranteed to look good and protect even better. Speaking of protection, may I draw your attention to the outer door handles; they have been fitted with protectors to ensure that your car continues to look good, year after year. Yes, this car is going to last so long that it's going to put us out of business!

Up on top the SX50 comes complete with a roof rack and come round to the front of the car ... look at the fog lamps, your choice of white or yellow. We've fitted them in neatly under the bumper so that you can drive safely in all weather conditions. And speaking of safety, let me open the driver's door so that you can take a look at the roomy interior.

All of the latest technology has been employed so that you will have a comfortable safe journey. An air bag has been installed to protect the driver in case of an accident. The back seats have been supplied with shoulder seat belts with a lap seat belt for the middle seat. Music? You'll be able to enjoy your trips, whether short or long, with this excellent cassette radio. Put in a cassette, and you're in heaven even in the middle of a Friday night traffic jam on the M1.

This car is a driver's dream come true. Look at the quality of the cover on the steering wheel. Come and touch it. Sir, don't be shy. Yes, that's pure leather, pure leather. You've also been provided with high-quality floor mats and a map lamp! Who would like to be the first to come and sit in the driver's seat? You, madam; how about you, sir?

TEST 3

SPECIFIC HINTS SECTION

Exercise on register

Listen to this man talking to someone about going out. What is his relationship with this person?

A He doesn't feel very comfortable.
B He feels comfortable.
C He feels extremely comfortable.

Man: Excuse me, but would you mind telling me where you would like to spend the evening?

The speaker doesn't feel very comfortable. If the speaker had felt comfortable, he would have said:
   Where do you want to go? *or* Where shall we go?
If the speaker had felt extremely comfortable, he would have said:
   Where are we going then? *or* Where to?

PART 1

Question 1
Man: Betty! Hi! Have you got a minute? Listen, I'll be in late for work today – no, I'm fine, but the neighbour who usually drives the kids to school is ill. Look, would you mind giving Mary my report on Chadwick Enterprises? Yeah, it should be right on top of my desk. And please ask her to type it up pronto. Sorry to ask you – you've got your own stuff to worry about. I owe you!

Question 2
Cousin 1: Bev! It's been a long time. What? Five years? How are you?
Cousin 2: I'm just fine, Kevin. How about you?
Cousin 1: Fine, just fine. Life's treating me well …
Cousin 2: I bet it is. Rolling in money, eh? After that little trick you played on my mother.
Cousin 1: I don't know what you mean.

Question 3
Air Hostess: Ladies and gentlemen, can you give me your attention, please. We have just been informed that the runway is blocked. This means that there will be some delay in taking off. Please stay in your seats. However, you may take down your hand luggage. Thank you.

Question 4
TV host: Why don't you tell us a little about yourself, Julia?
Julia: Well, there's not much to tell. I started out teaching English, but then I was approached by LUP to do a grammar book. I met with the team, including the editors and designers and …
TV host: And what about the financial side of it …

Question 5
Radio presenter: … and besides our main guest star, we have another little surprise in store for you today: MC Mad Dog's mother! Yes, even great rock stars have mothers! Mrs Ashworth, or should I say 'Mrs Mad Dog', will be on the air live and will let us in on some of Mad Dog's secrets. That is – if Mad Dog lets her! So pick up your phones and give us a ring if you've got any questions for Mad Dog – or his mum!

Question 6
Teenager: Hello, Mum? Is that you? It's me. Yeah, well the match finished, but instead of coming home right away, I was wondering if … The rest of the kids are all going for a hamburger … Yeah – Dad gave me some money. No, not too late. I'll get a ride home with one of the other kids. Pete. No, not with his brother. His dad is going to come and pick us up. No, you know we won't do *that*. OK, so around eleven then. Bye.

Question 7
Friend: I simply must tell you this one. Er, the birds were having a great time, picking up bits of food. But then a big cat spotted them. He was just going to pounce on one, when an owl called out from a tree: Woof Woof! Well, the cat ran away quick, as fast as it could. The owl looked down at the birds and wisely said, 'It never hurts to learn a foreign language.'

Question 8
Woman: I know you don't recognise me, but *I'd* know *you* anywhere! I surely would! You were no higher than my knee when you used to play outside my house. Day in and day out, you'd ride that skateboard back and forth on the sidewalk. How's your mum? I remember she used to get real mad when you didn't do your homework! I got kinda mad with you myself!! You always were a naughty little devil!

PART 2

Receptionist: Good evening, madam.
Guest: Good evening. I wonder if you have any rooms available for tonight?
Receptionist: Yes, we do. Let me just find a registration card … right, may I have your name, please?
Guest: Yes. Catherine Pool. That's Catherine spelt C-a-t-h-e-r-i-n-e.
Receptionist: All right, Catherine Pull.
Guest: No, sorry, *Pool*. P – double O – L.
Receptionist: Oh, right, Pool. Sorry. And will you be staying just the one night, Ms Pool?
Guest: No, actually I think it will be more than that.
Receptionist: How many nights do you think it will be?
Guest: Let's see … let me check my diary … today's Friday, then it'll be Saturday and Sunday so that's 3 nights altogether.
Receptionist: Right. And what kind of room would you like, a double or a single?
Guest: A double, please, if you've got one free. I always have trouble sleeping on those narrow single beds that some hotels have.
Receptionist: Well, you shouldn't have that trouble here, but we do have a double available. Are you by yourself?
Guest: Yes, I'm alone.
Receptionist: That will be £65 per night then, which includes breakfast and VAT, of course.
Guest: Right, that's fine.
Receptionist: Could I just make a note of what type of breakfast you would prefer. We offer a continental or a traditional English breakfast.
Guest: Well, I'm afraid I am rather used to bacon and eggs in the morning when I'm away.
Receptionist: Fine, traditional English breakfast then. Breakfast is served between 7.30 and 9.30. If that's inconvenient for you, just let us know the night before

and we will notify the cook to arrange for a better time for you.

Guest: It's all right. I'll be attending nine o'clock seminars, so I'll be eating at about 8.00.

Receptionist: Right. Now let me just fill in the date on here: 13th September 1993, and the room number – there. Your room is number 17. If you follow the corridor over there, you'll see it on your left. Just past the health club and the swimming pool. I'll ring a porter for your luggage.

PART 3

Speaker 1: Couples usually dance together. It's done to a variety of music. Some of the dances are of South American origin, or even of European origin, like the waltz or, for example, the polka. We also do the mambo and the cha-cha. It's a lot of fun. My wife and I never miss a class, if we can help it.

Speaker 2: We wear a certain kind of soft shoe and we usually start our class with different exercises at the bar to classical music. Then we go to the centre of the floor where we do different steps and techniques. And then we move on to combinations of choreographic pieces to classical music, like the waltz.

Speaker 3: In this class we usually wear running shoes. We normally start with a warm-up, and then we gradually build up the work rate. Once we're at full stretch, we take our pulses to see how much the heart has worked. Then we proceed to do a warm-down. Once that's done we go ahead and do different exercises on mats on the floor. Of course, it's all done to quick dance music.

Speaker 4: This class is often called a 'Lamaze class', after the system Lamaze which teaches breathing techniques, relaxation, and prepares women for the happy event. We've seen some slide presentations and different breathing exercises that the women have to do at home, away from class, to prepare themselves. We husbands also get involved in some of the classes to be prepared to help our wives when the time comes. I don't know if we can ever *really* be prepared, though!

Speaker 5: We move or dance to modern music, like Whitney Houston or Phil Collins or whatever. We usually do different exercises in technique, on the bar and in the centre. And then we do different steps and combinations or dances to modern-type music. I like this class, because I use a lot of these steps to impress my friends at parties!

PART 4

Announcer: Good morning, ladies and gentlemen. As a service of the Greek Organisation of Tourism here is an overview of what is available for your entertainment in Athens this weekend, Friday the 3rd, Saturday the 4th, and Sunday the 5th of March.

From tonight until Sunday evening, there will be a musical tribute to the famous Greek opera diva, Maria Callas, at the Athens Concert Hall. Effy Gounela will perform the role of Santuzza in this performance of Pietro Mascagni's *Cavaliere Rusticana*. Seats start at 2,000 drachmas, and you may book your tickets by using your Visa, Diners, or American Express card. Call the Athens Concert Hall on: 729 2333.

If you are interested in art there is a first-class exhibition of sketches by Vincent Marsh on display at the Aenaon Gallery in Katehaki. These sketches were the models for Marsh's world-famous paintings of dogs. This will be the first exhibition since his death in 1991. The gallery is open from 10.00 am until 2.00 pm, and from 6.00 pm until 9.30 pm. It is closed on Sundays. Admission fees are: 1,000 drachmas for adults, and 500 drachmas for children under 16, the over-sixties and the unemployed. Further information can be obtained by calling the gallery on 671 1264.

Another exhibition of paintings well worth seeing is being held by local artist, Voula Makopoulou, at the Dada Gallery. Makopoulou's use of natural themes and colour is considered by many to be magical. The gallery is open from 9.00 am until 1.00 pm, and again from 5.00 until 9.00 pm. It is not open on Saturday and Sunday afternoons. There is no charge for admission. For further information, call the gallery on 722 2929.

Several classic Oscar award-winning films are being shown at the Greek Film Archives this weekend. Friday features *A Pocketful of Miracles*, directed by Frank Capra, starring Bette Davis and Glenn Ford. On Saturday *How the West Was Won*, directed by Henry Hathaway, John Ford and George Marshall, and on Sunday, *Superman*, directed by Richard Donner. All screenings begin at 8.15 pm, and there's an admission charge of 600 drachmas. Ring 361 2046 for more information.

TEST 4

SPECIFIC HINTS SECTION

Exercise on similar sounds

Listen to this woman talking to someone about going out. When are they going?

A in less than half an hour
B in over half an hour
C in a few minutes

Woman: Are we going in fifty minutes?

The speaker is leaving in over half an hour. If the speaker had been leaving in less than half an hour, she would have said:
   Are we going in fifteen minutes?
If the speaker had been leaving in a few minutes, she would have said:
   Are we going in a few minutes?

PART 1

Question 1
Mother: When I was a young girl, I used to go out into the fields and play. You didn't know that, did you? My best friend and I would gather up huge bales of hay and make straw huts. Then we'd crawl into the huts – they were pretty dark – and have picnics. Some of the berries we'd picked. Or boiled eggs. Sometimes we could see a sheep or two in the distance! Then we'd be really happy!

Question 2
Andrew: Um, Catherine, it's Andrew again. I just wanted to say that, um, I was wondering if you'd be interested in

also giving a professional presentation at the book exhibition. Um, this is so that we make the most of, you know, what they offer. We can give a commercial *and* a professional. Um, if you call me, then we can discuss it. OK? Speak to you soon. Bye.

Question 3

Friend: Just a few close friends and some family members. So we'd like it if you could come too, if you've got nothing else planned. Good. It's this Saturday night at eight. Well, at first we thought we'd make it at our house, but then if we get fifty or sixty coming out, Martha won't be able to handle it. So then we booked St Michael's hall. Uh huh, that's the one. To the left of the park.

Question 4

Woman: Having trouble? Hmmm. I don't think that's where you put it. Look – there's an arrow over there. Try putting your coin in there . . . Right, mm, the picture shows a finger pushing the green button. Yes! There's your ticket!

Question 5

Wife: I've been feeling very depressed lately, and I just can't seem to snap out of it. I mean, the children have grown up and gone. And you're away all the time on business.
Husband: Well, you know I can't work any less . . . Perhaps if you joined some clubs you'd feel better. Have some companionship.
Wife: I miss the children. I wonder if we should have . . . It's still not too late to have another . . .

Question 6

Hairdresser: But that's the way you, you *told* me to do it.
Customer: I didn't want it *so* short. Just, just a little shorter. Here – at the sides.
Hairdresser: But if it's short at the sides, it has to be short all over to look balanced – see?
Customer: Well, I didn't th–, I didn't think it was going to look *this* short.
Hairdresser: Let's dry it and have another look at it. Then we'll see what can be done.

Question 7

Presenter: We interrupt this programme in order to bring you the following news bulletin.
News reporter: This is Carole Kimbel, reporting live, from the scene of the fire. The Hornby chemical factory is up in flames, and hundreds of workers are now trapped inside. Out here is the fire chief, who has consented . . .

Question 8

Teacher: The history of the world is a violent one, and some will argue that the world was once joined. Then it was torn apart. The earth now has several main land masses. In this lesson, we shall read about the features of each in detail. These continents are: Africa, Australia, Europe and Asia (the conventional divisions of the Eurasian land mass), North America, South America and, usually, Antarctica.

PART 2

Camp Director: Could I have your attention please . . . thank you . . . thank you! Welcome to the Plymouth Institute Summer Camp, 1995. Thank you. The camp has been set up so that you can attend your lessons and enjoy yourselves at the same time and I know you are going to have a wonderful time with us. I'd like to start by running through a few of the camp rules first. Could you stand so that you can see the big map of the grounds that's in front of you. OK. As you know, as well as being by the sea here we also have a large wooded area where you will do some of your activities. The woods are shown in the top left-hand corner of the map.

To the right of the woods is the girls' dormitory. The boys' dormitory is directly below the woods on the map and below the boys' dormitory are the boys' washrooms. The boys' toilets are obviously here too. The girls' washrooms and toilets are to the right of the boys'. At no time may boys enter the girls' washrooms, or the other way around!

Please keep the toilets and showers clean, and remember that somebody else has to use the facilities after you.

To the right of the girls' dormitory is the teachers' dormitory. Please stay out of here unless accompanied by a member of staff. Also, please don't use the teachers' washrooms or toilets which you can see marked on the map below their dormitory.

There will be several assistant helpers sleeping in your dormitories with you. So . . . so, if you have any questions or problems, or if there is an emergency, please speak to them.

In the middle of the camp is our superb swimming pool. Now, swimming is allowed between 8.00 am and 8.00 pm when there is a lifeguard on duty. Please don't swim at other times without asking permission of a member of staff first. Please try not to make too much noise when you are in or around the pool as the classrooms are quite near the pool and others may be in lessons.

You can see the classroom block on the bottom right of the map. The classrooms are large and well equipped with videos and tape recorders, etc., to make your learning more enjoyable. You will all have four hours of lessons every day. If you check your timetables it should be fairly clear where you should be at what time. Please ask the assistants if you are not sure. The rest of the day will be filled with sporting activities and excursions. We'll tell you about those at breakfast tomorrow.

Lastly . . . Lastly, if you look at the map again you'll see to the right of the pool, facing the sea, the main hall which we also use as our dining hall. It's marked as main hall/dining hall on the map. Please don't leave a mess on the floor in there as we use it for other activities as well.

Thank you for your attention. If you'd like to make your way towards the main hall now, our evening meal should be ready.

PART 3

Speaker 1: In general, we were quite pleased with the tour. The driver took us to all of the famous spots – the museums and whatnot – we had all read about. The only problem was that every day we started out so early and went to bed so late. And one morning there was a mix up at the hotel reception desk and they forgot our wake-up calls. So we all missed breakfast too!

Speaker 2: I've been on quite a few of these tours, you know, but this time we had a bit of an adventure. The driver dropped us off for two free hours of shopping and told us to meet him at a certain square at a certain hour. Some of us even found time for a quick snack – and then we started to gather on the church steps. But no sign of the coach! After an hour, one of the group discovered it on the *other* side of the square. You can imagine our relief!

Speaker 3: It was the first time I'd gone on a package tour, and I was worried I wouldn't like the rigid schedules that you have to stick to: getting up at seven every morning, eating a quick continental breakfast, finding the coach in the car park, and then going off to see the sights. But I quite liked it. Even got the addresses of the other people on the tour.

Speaker 4: I was quite disappointed, actually. We got up early and travelled by coach for three hours, then we were dropped off in a square, with a list of places we should try to see. Well, most of us headed straight for the museum, as it holds some of the most famous work in the country. But as soon as we got there, we saw a notice on the gate: it didn't open until late afternoon. Much too late for our tour group!

Speaker 5: After paying all that money, I was expecting to have all of my days filled. But every extra tour cost money. They should have warned us. One day we chose not to visit an island, and we were stuck on the ship for the whole day with nothing to do. We ended up spending the whole day eating!

PART 4

Trevor: Well, we've had a lot of people in the agency looking for jobs this week. Let's have a look through the vacancies and draw up a list of who looks suited for which job. Most of them will be ringing up tomorrow.

Carol: I was thinking of this one for Helen Shaver: her forms show she's interested in cookery and she has some experience. Her last employer said she was clean and fast.

Trevor: Excellent. Shall we recommend her for the job of cook at Priors School then? ... What about Ellen Blake?

Husband: Hi there. Still working?

Carol: Hi, darling. James, this is Trevor.

Trevor: Pleased to meet you at last.

Husband: Likewise.

Carol: We've got to finish this off. Do you mind waiting a couple of minutes?

Husband: No problem. Just remember that we have to go home and change before the concert starts.

Carol: This won't take long.

Trevor: Please have a seat.

Husband: Thanks.

Carol: Yes, well, Ellen's a very interesting person. It says here she's good at karate and Tae Kwon Do! We could suggest she applies for the job of prison guard at Stony Mountain Women's Prison.

Trevor: Yeah, although Bea Murray is also interested in karate, so maybe she'd be a good applicant for the prison guard job.

Carol: Yes, but she has accounting experience. I thought of suggesting the senior cashier position at the National Bank for Bea. I'll just run a security check on her first.

Trevor: Oh yes, good idea. That leaves Sandra Taylor. Mmmm, with these qualifications it's a pity she didn't apply to the university to do medicine. How about suggesting she applies to Blacks just down the road? They are looking for a trainee pharmacist.

Husband: Have you got much more to do? We told the babysitter we'd pick her up at 7.30 ...

Carol: Just a couple more. I seem to remember having to wait for you several times when *you've* had office work to finish up.

Trevor: Uh, you two go on. I can stay and do up the rest of this lot.

Carol: That's not fair. You've stayed late every evening this week. Now, how about this Tommy Dickens? He's got no –

Husband: Darling, he said he didn't mind finishing up by himself. Next week *you* can stay late.

Trevor: Look, there's no, there's no reason for you to stay longer. I can uh, easily ...

Carol: There are only two more. Now, Tommy Dickens has got no qualifications. He lists his hobbies as sport, water skiing and riding. And he grew up on a farm.

Trevor: Well, um, how about stable hand up at the Meadow Club?

Carol: Sounds perfect. That just leaves Tammy Prime.

Husband: Darling, if this takes much longer, I'll have to go alone ...

Carol: Well, she's smart and elegant judging from her photo and she has some waitressing experience so we could suggest she applies to British Airways. What do you think?

Trevor: Yes, and she comes within their height specifications. Right, I think that's everyone.

Carol: Yes, I think so ...

Carol: Oh, hold on, I spoke too soon. I'll get that ... Good afternoon, Frogmore Employment Agency, how can I help you ...?

Husband: Well, *I'm* not going to sit here waiting.

TEST 5

PART 1

Question 1
Policeman: Can I see your driving licence? Uh, huh. Now would you please turn on the headlamps. The indicators? Left? Right? Good. Brake lights? Right, now, would you mind getting out of the car and opening the boot for me?

Thank you sir, you can go now.

Question 2
Woman: Want to look your very best on a summer's evening? You've put on your best clothes, but what about your tan? *Suretan* is the industry's technology leader in tanning beds. *Suretan's* line of systems offers state-of-the-art design and technology, giving you the brownest, most even tan in the city. At leading beauty salons everywhere.

Question 3
Man: Yes. I'm calling to find out some more information about your car service. What does your service include? Hmmm, anywhere in the city? The country! What about international service? I see ... And how much does it cost to become a member? Yes, yes. So if I become a member, no matter what trouble I'm in, you'll help me out for free? Hmmm. Well, it *sounds* good.

Question 4
Teacher: Elizabeth, why don't *you* tell the class the answer? Elizabeth ...? You haven't done your homework, have

you? You haven't even tried to do it, have you? What are we going to do with you?

Question 5

Doctor: I called you both in here because I want the two of you to hear what I have to say.

Wife: Is my health that bad?

Doctor: No, but it could be if you don't watch out. Now I want you to listen. You've got to eat foods that are full of iron, if we want to get you healthy again.

Wife: But the baby is due in three months.

Doctor: That gives you lots of time. Just follow my advice and you'll be fine.

Question 6

First referee: I must be getting older. I can't run as long and as hard as I used to.

Second referee: You're telling me! I'm not getting any younger – but the players are. Soon we'll be retired. Put out to pasture.

First referee: We're out to pasture *now* – we're running around that field the whole game.

Second referee: *And* nobody likes us: the players, the press, to say nothing of the fans ... The hooligans ...

Question 7

Woman: Odeon Cinema, Gunworth Road, Newcastle. This week we start with *Eye of the Hurricane*, Monday to Wednesday, at seven pm and nine pm. *Last of the Cowboys* is playing Thursday to Saturday, at six pm, eight pm, and eleven pm. On Sunday we have a matinée featuring *Gone with the Snow* at four pm, continuing at six pm, eight pm, and eleven pm.

Question 8

Man: Mr Worthington? This is Carl. From the office. Sorry to bother you at home, but we've just received the fax from Leeds you've been waiting for. Yes, sir. Yes. Right away, sir. Uh, was there anything else? No? Thank you then.

PART 2

Presenter: And a good morning to you. I hope you had a good start to your day, and that you got the children all dressed, fed and off to school on time. But not too well-fed, I hope. My guest this morning is child psychologist Dr Elspeth White who will be giving us advice on how to keep our children slim and healthy. Good morning, Dr White.

Doctor: Good morning, Dickie.

Presenter: So we need to be careful how many chips and burgers we let our children eat?

Doctor: That's right, Dickie. We don't want them hungry but we don't want them to overeat either as it is likely that they will then have weight problems in adult life.

Presenter: What is your advice for mothers and fathers of overweight children?

Doctor: Well, Dickie, they really shouldn't have let them get overweight in the first place. There are certain things you can do to prevent children from having weight problems, for instance ...

Presenter: So you're saying it's too late for them to do anything about it now?

Doctor: No, no, I'm not saying that at all. They can still help their children develop good eating habits – habits that will last a lifetime.

Presenter: Like what, for example?

Doctor: Like teaching your child that a mealtime is a pleasant, relaxed time when you can chat and spend time together, perhaps discussing what happened during his or her day. If the child eats slowly, he'll have the time to start feeling full. And if the child does eat quickly, let him or her wait before giving a second helping. The chances are that the child will start feeling full during that time and won't actually want any more. Or at least he or she won't want such a big helping.

Presenter: So you do believe in giving second helpings to children.

Doctor: Oh, yes! And I don't believe children should be put on diets. They have to learn how to judge how much food is right for them. This is essential. Babies know when they're full and they just stop eating. We have to help all children – thin and overweight – to realise how much food is right for them.

Presenter: What about chocolate and sweets? Do we keep them out of the house?

Doctor: No. If something is forbidden, it just makes the children all the more determined to eat it. But you don't put sweets out in bowls on the coffee table. This is a temptation, for the adults and children alike. By the way, studies show that if one parent is extremely overweight the child has a 40 per cent greater chance of also being overweight. If both parents are overweight the risk goes up to 80 per cent.

Presenter: So everyone in the household can help each other to keep the weight off?

Doctor: Exactly. The trick is to make it seem like eating less isn't punishment, but instead something that's natural and healthy. You know, children can still eat snacks, even ...

Presenter: Oh, can they?

Doctor: Oh, yes. But not at any time of the day. One study has shown that thinner children eat snacks and meals according to a more regular timetable.

Presenter: Are you suggesting then that at four o'clock you blow a whistle and pull out a snack?

Doctor: It sounds rather strange, but it does work. If the child is hungry, he knows that his snack is coming at four o'clock so he waits for it, rather than going to the cupboard and filling up on chocolate. Of course, you have to give him the occasional chocolate as well. You don't want him or her to feel different from the other children. And something else which can be a problem for overweight children, do be careful never to embarrass them in front of other people. This could cause them to eat even more.

Presenter: Well, all of your advice certainly sounds sensible and not all that hard to follow. Do you have anything else to add, Dr White, before I move on to my next guest this morning?

PART 3

Agent: Sylvia, Jack here. Where have you been? Look, I'm trying to set up a contract with *Mode* magazine. They want to photograph you all over the world. Now listen carefully: their photographer will call you to arrange for an appointment. Just to take some trial photos. And don't be late! Ciao, Sylvia darling ... love you.

Photographer: Hello, it's Palmer. *Mode* told me to set up a photo shoot with you, and they want it done quick. The only times I'm free next week are: Monday, 7.00–8.00 pm, Tuesday, 9.00–10.30 in the morning, Wednesday, 4.00–5.00 pm, Thursday 3.00 – no, make that 7.00–8.30 pm and Friday at noon. Leave a message on my machine at 723 3667. Oh, and make sure you wear something loose and flowing. Goodbye.

Mother: Sylvia ... Sylvia? Is this thing on? I don't know why you got one of these things, anyway. Is this what's happened to our relationship? We have to use a machine to communicate? Anyway, I'd better ring off. The sight of our phone bills makes your father go grey. Long distance isn't cheap, you know. But then you wouldn't know, because you haven't bothered to phone us for two weeks and this is the last time ...

Aunt: Sylvia? Aunt Maude. Let me fill you in on all the latest news. Since you haven't phoned your mother in two weeks. Kate went in on Wednesday morning, and the whole thing had finished by Wednesday evening. It's a girl! Kate's so happy about having the baby. Well, now everyone's asking about *you*. Don't you think the time is right, dear? What happened to that Jack you used to go out with? Bye.

Boyfriend: Sylvia, don't forget – we're going out at eight tonight. I've made reservations at the Blue Field. Go on ahead if you get there first. Order me a martini. I'll need one after that meeting today. Uh, so that's eight o'clock. Tonight. At the Blue Field. Bye.

PART 4

Announcer: My guest today on Making Contact is the Children's Book Managing Editor from one of the largest publishing houses in Europe, Light Publishers, Mr Mitch Parker.

Publisher: Hello. Thank you for inviting me on the programme.

Announcer: Mr Parker, the logo of Light Publishers must be one of the most famous in the country.

Publisher: Yes, everyone has seen our symbol – our logo – a candle with a flame in front of an open window. If they haven't seen it on one of our books, then I'm sure they've seen it on one of our posters or television advertisements.

Announcer: Why not start off by telling us about writing children's books. You deal with picture books, don't you?

Publisher: That's right. My department publishes picture books for children between the ages of two and eight. As you know, picture books usually have very little text.

Announcer: So it must be very easy to write a book like that!

Publisher: Well, that's what everybody *thinks*. Even children's books must have a well-developed plot or story-line. The setting and theme are important, and the characters are extremely important. Young children are fascinated by entertaining characters. Let's say you're creating a lead character for your book. You wouldn't want someone too unimaginative. Think of the possibilities for example of a lead character who has tiny glasses, wild grey hair, and a big bushy black beard! And as Mary Louisa Molesworth, one of Britain's most famous writers for children, pointed out, you must get to know your characters very well before you sit down and write a word about them!

Announcer: So it's a lot more complicated than it appears.

Publisher: Oh, yes ... but I don't want to discourage anyone from trying to write a picture book. In fact, one of our best authors, Jayne Fisher, started writing when she was only nine years old. (Really?) Yes, she writes her own stories about the 'Garden Gang', a lively group of fruit and vegetable characters. She writes about colourful onions and tomatoes talking to each other! And she draws her own pictures in felt-tip pen.

Announcer: She must be quite talented.

Publisher: Oh, I'm sure there are lots of talented young people out there; they just haven't been discovered yet. I should mention that I'm always looking for appealing stories to be sent in to us. Most publishers of children's books are.

Announcer: What should any potential young writers do, then?

Publisher: First of all, the story must be easy to read. Most publishers prefer it to be typed double-space. It's very tiring to read through something messy. The standard size of a picture book is 32 pages, but the typed text can be anywhere from two to six pages. The rest is pictures.

Announcer: And how do you know what kind of pictures to include?

Publisher: After a story has been accepted, the usual procedure is for us to give it to an illustrator, or artist. Some of the writers might send in a 'dummy', a page-by-page sample of how they think the book might look with pictures, but that's not really necessary. They shouldn't forget to send in copies of their work – never the original – in case their work accidentally gets lost or damaged. And, of course, a self-addressed, stamped envelope so that we can return the work sent to us.

Announcer: Would a writer submitting material to another department follow the same procedure?

Publisher: Yes, he or she would post the manuscript ...

CAMBRIDGE

EXAMINATIONS, CERTIFICATES AND DIPLOMAS
ENGLISH AS A FOREIGN LANGUAGE

University of Cambridge
Local Examinations Syndicate
International Examinations

Examination Details	9999/01	99/D99
Examination Title	First Certificate in English	
Centre/Candidate No.	AA999/9999	
Candidate Name	A.N. EXAMPLE	

• Sign here if the details above are correct

• Tell the Supervisor now if the details above
  are not correct

☒

Candidate Answer Sheet: FCE Paper 1 Reading

Use a pencil

Mark ONE letter for each
question.

For example, if you think **B** is
the right answer to the
question, mark your answer
sheet like this:

0	A **B** C D

Change your answer like
this:

0	A B C D

1	A B C D E F G H I
2	A B C D E F G H I
3	A B C D E F G H I
4	A B C D E F G H I
5	A B C D E F G H I

6	A B C D E F G H I
7	A B C D E F G H I
8	A B C D E F G H I
9	A B C D E F G H I
10	A B C D E F G H I
11	A B C D E F G H I
12	A B C D E F G H I
13	A B C D E F G H I
14	A B C D E F G H I
15	A B C D E F G H I
16	A B C D E F G H I
17	A B C D E F G H I
18	A B C D E F G H I
19	A B C D E F G H I
20	A B C D E F G H I

21	A B C D E F G H I
22	A B C D E F G H I
23	A B C D E F G H I
24	A B C D E F G H I
25	A B C D E F G H I
26	A B C D E F G H I
27	A B C D E F G H I
28	A B C D E F G H I
29	A B C D E F G H I
30	A B C D E F G H I
31	A B C D E F G H I
32	A B C D E F G H I
33	A B C D E F G H I
34	A B C D E F G H I
35	A B C D E F G H I

FCE-1

DP999/99

CAMBRIDGE
EXAMINATIONS, CERTIFICATES AND DIPLOMAS
ENGLISH AS A FOREIGN LANGUAGE

University of Cambridge
Local Examinations Syndicate
International Examinations

Examination Details	9999/03	99/D99
Examination Title	First Certificate in English	
Centre/Candidate No.	AA999/9999	
Candidate Name	A.N. EXAMPLE	

• Sign here if the details above are correct

- -

• Tell the Supervisor now if the details above are not correct

Candidate Answer Sheet: FCE Paper 3 Use of English

Use a pencil

For **Part 1**: Mark ONE letter for each question.

For example, if you think **C** is the right answer to the question, mark your answer sheet like this:

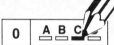

0	A	B	C	D

For **Parts 2, 3, 4** and **5**: Write your answers in the spaces next to the numbers like this:

0	*example*

Part 1				
1	A	B	C	D
2	A	B	C	D
3	A	B	C	D
4	A	B	C	D
5	A	B	C	D
6	A	B	C	D
7	A	B	C	D
8	A	B	C	D
9	A	B	C	D
10	A	B	C	D
11	A	B	C	D
12	A	B	C	D
13	A	B	C	D
14	A	B	C	D
15	A	B	C	D

Part 2		Do not write here
16		16
17		17
18		18
19		19
20		20
21		21
22		22
23		23
24		24
25		25
26		26
27		27
28		28
29		29
30		30

Turn over for Parts 3 - 5 →

Part 3	Do not write here
31	31 0 1 2
32	32 0 1 2
33	33 0 1 2
34	34 0 1 2
35	35 0 1 2
36	36 0 1 2
37	37 0 1 2
38	38 0 1 2
39	39 0 1 2
40	40 0 1 2

Part 4	Do not write here
41	41
42	42
43	43
44	44
45	45
46	46
47	47
48	48
49	49
50	50
51	51
52	52
53	53
54	54
55	55

Part 5	Do not write here
56	56
57	57
58	58
59	59
60	60
61	61
62	62
63	63
64	64
65	65

CAMBRIDGE

EXAMINATIONS, CERTIFICATES AND DIPLOMAS
ENGLISH AS A FOREIGN LANGUAGE

University of Cambridge
Local Examinations Syndicate
International Examinations

Examination Details	9999/04	99/D99
Examination Title	First Certificate in English	
Centre/Candidate No.	AA999/9999	
Candidate Name	A.N. EXAMPLE	

• Sign here if the details above are correct

- -

• Tell the Supervisor now if the details above
  are not correct

Candidate Answer Sheet: FCE Paper 4 Listening

Mark test version below

A	B	C	D	E
▭	▭	▭	▭	▭

Use a pencil

For **Parts 1** and **3**:
Mark ONE letter for
each question.

For example, if you
think **B** is the right
answer to the
question, mark your
answer sheet like this:

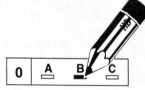

0	A	B	C
	▭	▬	▭

For **Parts 2** and **4**:
Write your answers in
the spaces next to the
numbers like this:

0	*example*

Part 1

1	A	B	C
2	A	B	C
3	A	B	C
4	A	B	C
5	A	B	C
6	A	B	C
7	A	B	C
8	A	B	C

Part 2

		Do not write here
9		▭ 9 ▭
10		▭ 10 ▭
11		▭ 11 ▭
12		▭ 12 ▭
13		▭ 13 ▭
14		▭ 14 ▭
15		▭ 15 ▭
16		▭ 16 ▭
17		▭ 17 ▭
18		▭ 18 ▭

Part 3

19	A	B	C	D	E	F
20	A	B	C	D	E	F
21	A	B	C	D	E	F
22	A	B	C	D	E	F
23	A	B	C	D	E	F

Part 4

		Do not write here
24		▭ 24 ▭
25		▭ 25 ▭
26		▭ 26 ▭
27		▭ 27 ▭
28		▭ 28 ▭
29		▭ 29 ▭
30		▭ 30 ▭

Changes to the FCE exam

	Old	New
Paper 1 Reading		
Title:	Reading Comprehension	Reading
Marks:	40	40
Time:	1 hour	1 hour 15 minutes
Number of texts:	Usually 3	Usually 4
Number of questions:	40	35
Type of questions	All multiple choice (Sections A and B)	Multiple matching (Parts 1 and 4), multiple choice (Part 2), gapped text (Part 3)
Type of answers:	Mainly dealing with specific detail	Often dealing with a more general understanding of gist and 'reading between the lines'
Type of texts:	First 2 (or 3) usually first- or third-person narrative or factual descriptive (place, process, trend), last text practical (rules, instructions)	Emphasis on useful texts: practical (ads, brochures, reports), fictional (narratives), personal (correspondence, messages), factual descriptive (articles)
Length of texts:	250–550 words each	350–700 words each
Level of vocabulary	All at FCE level	Some higher level words included, but items tested are always at FCE level
Paper 2 Writing		
Title:	Composition	Writing
Marks:	40	40
Time:	1 hour 30 minutes	1 hour 30 minutes
Number of tasks:	2 out of 5	2 out of 5
Type of questions:	Choice of letter, speech, description, narrative, discursive task or set book	Compulsory transactional letter plus choice of non-transactional letter, article, report, composition (descriptive, narrative, discursive) or set book
Choice of questions:	Any 2 out of 5	Part 1 (transactional letter) is compulsory, Part 2 is a choice of 1 out of 4
Number of words:	120–180	120–180

	Old	*New*
Precis/summary:	None	Now in Part 1, combining rubrics, text/pictures, notes
Set books – number of questions:	1	A choice of 1 out of 2 writing tasks, for a specific reader/purpose
Set books – number of books:	3	Bigger choice (5)

Paper 3 Use of English

Title:	Use of English	Use of English
Marks:	40	40
Time:	2 hours	1 hour 15 minutes
Number of parts:	5	5
Number of questions:	Varied (usually 48 plus precis)	65
Type of questions:		
Open cloze:	20 questions (question 1)	15 questions (Part 2)
Transformation:	Beginning of second sentence given (question 2)	Key word, beginning and end of second sentence given (Part 3)
Word formation:	Separate sentences (question 3)	A whole text (Part 5)
Sentence building:	Letter expansion, dialogue completion (question 4)	Replaced by multiple choice cloze (Part 1) (similar to former Reading Comprehension, Section A) and error correction (Part 4)
Precis/summary:	Section B	Now in Writing, Part 1
Type of answers:	Long answer	Short answer
Number of full texts:	One text (usually narrative) in the cloze (question 1)	Four texts (practical or fictional) (Parts 1, 2, 4, 5)

Paper 4 Listening

Title:	Listening Comprehension	Listening
Marks:	20 marks	40 marks
Time:	approx. 40 minutes	approx. 40 minutes
Number of questions:	Varied (up to 40)	30 questions

	Old	*New*
Type of questions:	Variety (true/false, label, match, multiple choice, gap filling, mark map, etc.)	4 set tasks (Part 1 multiple choice, Part 2 note taking/blank filling, Part 3 multiple matching, Part 4 selecting from two or three answers)
Type of answers:	Mainly dealing with specific details	Parts 1 and 3 deal with a more general understanding of gist, function, main points, mood, intention, roles, relationships, feelings
Type of texts:	Varied (usually long), played twice	Some long (3 minutes – Parts 2, 4) and short (30 seconds – Parts 1, 3), played twice

Paper 5 Speaking

Title:	Interview	Speaking
Marks:	40	40
Time:	15 minutes	15 minutes
Number of parts:	3 parts	4 parts
Type of questions:	Tasks not in context	Situationally based tasks
Type of answers:	Short and long answer	Short turns (Parts 1, 3, 4) and long turns (Part 2)
Theme:	All questions based on one theme	Parts 3 and 4 based on one theme
Warm-up:	Not graded	Graded (Part 1)
Photos:	Description of (3) photos (Section A)	Discussion of 2 sets of pictures in relation to students' attitudes and opinions (Part 2)
Communication activity:	Varied (role playing, opinion giving, problem solving, presenting points) (Section C)	Based on a visual stimulus (e.g. line drawing or picture) (Part 3)
Identify the passage:	Section B	Replaced by discussion of themes raised in Part 3 (Part 4)
Set book:	An option	Not an option
Number of candidates:	One (or more)	Two
Number of examiners:	One	Two – an interlocutor who interviews and an assessor who observes. Both award marks (the interlocutor on overall impression, the assessor on detail) and then jointly decide on a fair mark. Note that some approved circumstances may warrant a one candidate/one examiner ratio (check with the examination centre).

Test 1; Picture 1

Test 1; Picture 2

Test 1; Picture 3

Test 1; Picture 4

Test 2; Picture 1

Test 2; Picture 2

Test 2; Picture 3

Test 2; Picture 4

Test 3; Picture 1

Test 3; Picture 2

Test 3; Picture 3

Test 3; Picture 4

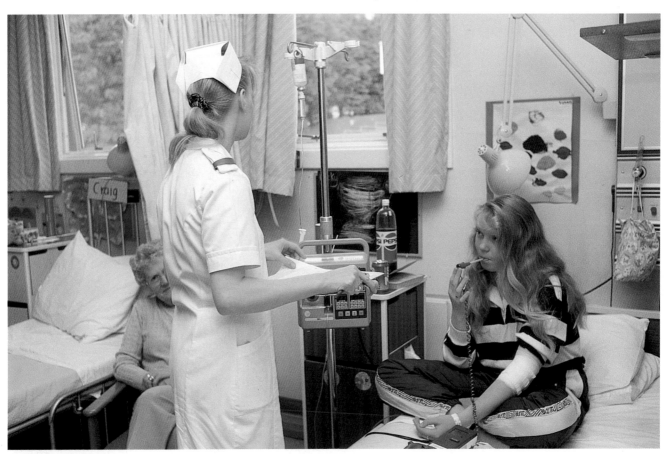

Test 4; Picture 1

Test 4; Picture 2

Test 4; Picture 3

Test 4; Picture 4

Test 5; Picture 1

Test 5; Picture 2

Test 5, Picture 3

Test 5; Picture 4

TEACHER'S NOTES AND ANSWER KEY

TEST 1

Paper 1 Reading

Teacher's notes
In this paper, 1 mark is given for each correct answer. This makes a total of 35 marks, which is mathematically adjusted to a mark of 40.

In general, correct answers paraphrase the text. The incorrect answers use incorrect facts or ideas loosely based on the text. Incorrect answers can: give opposite meanings, use the same words as the text, misinterpret the meaning of single words from the text, or give answers which seem acceptable. These distractors are listed in the key so that you can point them out to the students.

Symbols
opp., same, sing., accept.

Explanations
Opposite (opp.) means that this answer states the opposite of what has been stated in the text.
Same word(s) (same) means that this answer contains a word/phrase/sentence from the text.
Incorrect usage of a single word (sing.) means that this answer contains a word like a modal or quantifier which is incorrectly used.
Acceptability (accept.) means that this answer contains something that might be believable, according to what the text states or according to general knowledge.

Teaching suggestion: Students should tell you where they found each answer (the exact line), what it means in their own words, and how this connects with the correct answer. Then you can discuss why the other answers are wrong. The students will resist this process, but when they realise that they are answering more accurately, they will continue to approach the questions systematically.

PART 1

1 mark for each correct answer.

1 **F** *Levi's ... followed by Pepe and Wrangler*
2 **C** *Ever since Brando and Dean*
3 **B** *there's money in it*
4 **G** *satisfy those two great and differing human needs*
5 **A** *gone through several changes*
6 **H** *go from an idea ... slowly fade out of the shops*
7 **D** *say less about fashion than they do about you*

Total: 7 marks

PART 2

1 mark for each 'yes' answer.

8 **A** no: *the driver*
   B yes: *car*
   C no: *disappeared* (opp./neg.)
   D no: *car*

9 **A** no: *Thank God* (opp./neg.)
   B no: *Thank God*
   C yes: *Thank God that's all*
   D no: –

10 **A** no: *buildings around the square* (opp./neg.)
    B yes: *buildings around the square ... house*
    C no: *sped through the wet streets*
    D no: *in the direction of the dock* (same)

11 **A** no: *never killed ... did not want to* (opp./neg.)
    B no: *never killed* (sing.)
    C yes: *never killed* (sing.)
    D no: *never killed* (sing.)

12 **A** no: *You saved his life* (opp./neg)
    B yes: *You had better come ... You saved his life, I think*

C no: *ambulance* (accept.)
D no: *You saved his life*

13 **A** no: *He did not like it* (what happened on *this* job) (same)
    B yes: *He had done many unkind things ... but he had never been forced to ride ... with his victim. He did not like it* (he didn't like what happened on *this* job, implying he didn't mind the others)
    C no: *in the service of his country*
    D no: *unkind things*

14 **A** no: *the one that had hit Lars* (accept.)
    B no: *the other sailors ... Swedish* (same)
    C no: –
    D yes: *ride in an ambulance ... with his victim*

15 **A** no: *done many unkind things* (same)
    B no: *astonished ... not yet midnight* (same)
    C yes: *nothing to do but worry*
    D no: *his victim* (accept.)

Total: 8 marks

PART 3

1 mark for each correct answer.

16 **D** *Libraries usually have double doors* with *just one set of double doors*
17 **F** *Finding a library ... crossed the fancy wooden flooring* with *I entered*
18 **A** *I could see whom I was talking to ... he* with *His; I already knew what he looked like* with *had been shown in all the newspapers*
19 **E** *Sir George* with *he; was of medium height* with *he wore a sweater* (description)
20 **B** *this lot ... a sea of black and gold jumping gun dogs* with *The whole lot*
21 **C** *shouldn't sit with their backs to the door ... Sir George rose ... Grabbing collars ... Sir George returned* with *He reseated himself*

Total: 6 marks

PART 4

1 mark for each correct answer.

22 **E** *hunt it for ... sport*
23 **D** *Another problem is bamboo flowering*
24 **A** *In Chinese popular medicine ... this has made hunting even more popular*
25 **E** *populations have remained the same ... The population is large and increasing*
26 **D/F** *Accidental snaring in traps set for other animals*
27 **F/D** *occur by chance*
28 **B/F** *which live in the water*
29 **F/B** *marine ... oceans, estuaries and rivers*
30 **C/F** *meat*
31 **F/C** *in order to feed their families*
32 **A/D** *lives only in Asia*
33 **D/A** *all living in ... southwestern China*

1 mark for each 'yes' answer.

34 **A** yes: *fact sheet presents facts*
    B no: while somebody might be frightened by what's happening, it's not the aim (accept.)
    C no: not presenting anything amusing
    D no: while someone might want to contribute to WWF, no request for money is made (accept.)

35 **A** no: *hunted* – not for the hunters specifically, although they might read the literature (accept.)
    B no: *Commercial whalers have exploited* – not specifically for protesting in general, although they protest certain things that affect animals' rights (accept.)
    C yes: *WWF has spent SFr8 million on conservation in China* – the

whole thing is based on the animals and what is happening to them

   D no: *international* – not focusing on peace

Total: 14 marks

TOTAL PAPER: 35 marks

Paper 2 Writing

Teacher's notes
In this paper each writing task is given a mark out of 20 by examiners (who use an assessment scale). The two marks are then added together to give a mark out of 40.

The paper contains two parts. In Part 1 the question is compulsory. In Part 2 there is a choice of one out of four questions. In Part 1 the question is always a transactional (usually semi-formal) letter. In Part 2 the choice may include a non-transactional letter (usually informal), an article, a report, a composition (descriptive, narrative, discursive) and one question out of two on the set books.

Both writing tasks should be 120–180 words. Students should look closely at the instructions so that all parts of the question are answered in the number of words required.

Marks are given for the positive aspects of the composition such as range and variety of vocabulary and structure, accuracy and control (e.g. spelling, punctuation), use of cohesive devices, appropriate register, organisation of task, inclusion of all relevant points (especially Part 1) and effect on target reader.

Marks are deducted if instructions are not followed, if there are mistakes in the use of grammar, spelling and punctuation, if there is not a logical development of the topic, if it is difficult to understand and if it is not 120–180 words. If it is over 180 words, the extra words are read but not marked. If it is under 120 words, say 70 per cent of the correct length, the writing will be marked out of 70 per cent.

Writing tasks are graded within the following bands:

Band 5: Good range of structure and vocabulary. Minimal errors of structure, vocabulary, spelling and punctuation. All points covered with evidence of original output. Text suitably set out and ideas clearly linked. Appropriate and sustained register.
→ Very positive effect on target reader.

Band 4: Good range of structure and vocabulary but not always relevant. Errors only in more complicated vocabulary/structure, spelling and punctuation generally accurate. All points covered with sufficient detail. Text suitably set out and ideas clearly linked. Appropriate and sustained register.
→ Positive effect on target reader.

Band 3: Adequate range of structure and vocabulary. Some errors which do not impede communication. Points covered but some non-essential details omitted. Text suitably set out and ideas clearly linked; linking devices fairly simple. Register generally appropriate.
→ Satisfactory effect on target reader.

Band 2: Limited range of structure and vocabulary. Some errors obscure communication. Some omissions or large amount of irrelevant material. Text not clearly laid out, linking devices rarely used. Inconsistent register.
→ Message not clearly communicated to target reader.

Band 1: Very narrow range of structure and vocabulary. No systematic control of language. Important omissions and/or considerable irrelevance. Poor organisation of text, lack of linking. No awareness of register.
→ Very negative effect on target reader.

Band 0: Too little language for assessment (fewer than 50 words) or totally irrelevant or totally illegible.

The students should aim to do the two writing tasks answering the questions logically and clearly, using the language simply but correctly. They should aim for an above average mark so that they can be sure of a pass mark. They should avoid using difficult language if they are not sure of its meaning or its use. They should practise developing their answer logically covering each part of the question and rounding their writing off without leaving loose ends. Make sure they answer the question, remembering why they are writing and to whom.

TOTAL PAPER: 40 marks

PART 1

Teacher's notes
Make sure that the students refer to all parts of the question, i.e. the instructions, the picture(s)/text, any hand-written notes around the text and the notes.

Students should include
Instructions: sightseeing tour, lunchtime, different restaurants had advertisements, decided on English pub, two young children, no children's meals available, had to order full-course meal for them, left most of it.
Picture/text: Big Pizza House/Choosy Meal Express offer meals for children, children aren't welcome in Queen's Head.
Notes: not home cooking, not healthy balanced meals, no children's meals, possibly false advertising, wanted quicker service, but friendly.

Paper 3 Use of English

Teacher's notes
In this paper, 1 mark is given for each correct answer. This makes a total of 65 marks, which is mathematically adjusted to a mark of 40.

PART 1

Part 1 is a multiple choice cloze, Part 2 an open cloze, Part 3 a keyword transformation, Part 4 an error correction task and Part 5 a word formation task. In general, questions test for knowledge of grammar and vocabulary.

A text of between 180 and 200 words is given for Part 1, often describing a person, event or scene. Fifteen gaps must be filled chosen from a four-option word multiple choice answer. These gaps are numbered from **1** to **15**. The first gap is numbered **0** because it is the example. Always refer the students to the example before they begin to fill the gaps.

The structures around the gaps often given the students grammatical or contextual clues as to which word is missing. These structures are indicated below.

Note that *sth* stands for *something* and *sb* stands for *somebody*.

1 mark for each 'yes' answer.

1 **A** no: the story is *about* snakes
   B no: he jumped *off* the wall
   C yes: *of* (preposition): *a great deal of feeling*
   D no: he went *with* the children

2 **A** no: has *taken* part in many shows
   B yes: *given* (past participle – present perfect): *sth that he has given his life to*
   C no: has *seen* many snakes
   D no: has *spent* a lot of time collecting information

3 **A** no: *many* children
   B no: a *lot* of children
   C no: *much* information about crocodiles
   D yes: *large* (adjective): *a large number of children*

4 **A** no: he *surely* talks about crocodiles
   B no: he *probably* talks about crocodiles – not certain
   C no: he *undoubtedly* talks about crocodiles
   D yes: *even* (adverb – used for emphasis, showing surprise): *even crocodiles*

5 **A** no: a *usual* event
   B no: *proper* behaviour
   C yes: *important* (adjective): *an important part of the animal world*
   D no: a *specific* point

6 **A** no: he set *about* starting a rescue service
   B yes: *up* (particle – part of phrasal verb): *set up . . . a service*
   C no: he set *out* to give a talk
   D no: he set *off* on his talking tour

7 **A** yes: *help* (infinitive): *to help anyone . . . bitten by a snake*
   B no: *give* help to sb
   C no: *organise* a team to help
   D no: *provide* help

8 **A** yes: *lives* (verb – present simple): *lives in Sydney* (permanently)

B no: he *stays* in Sydney (temporarily)
C no: he *settles* in Sydney after travelling around other parts
D no: he *remains* until he begins his trip

9 **A** no: he *draws* pictures of the snakes' habitat
B no: he *shows* where the snakes live
C yes: *describes* (verb – present simple): *describes the snakes' habitat*
D no: he *tells* stories about snakes

10 **A** no: a book *for* children
B no: a book *of* pictures
C no: a book written *by* Jim Stopford
D yes: *on* (preposition): *on this subject*

11 **A** yes: *protected* (passive): *protected because they are dying out*
B no: children are *cared* for – they are looked after
C no: it cannot be *guaranteed* that sb may not be bitten by a snake
D no: Jim *favoured* setting up a rescue service

12 **A** no: *apart from* believing that snakes …
B yes: *also* (adverb – means 'in addition'): *also believes*
C no: Frank believes it. Jim, *too*, believes it.
D no: *besides* this, he also believes …

13 **A** no: he *departed* for his trip
B no: if snakes are left *undisturbed* they will not cause harm
C yes: *left* (passive): *are left alone*
D no: he *moved* to Sydney

14 **A** no: *While* Australia has … (incorrect meaning)
B no: *Despite* the fact that Australia has … (incorrect meaning)
C no: *Although* Australia has … (incorrect meaning)
D yes: *Since* (conjunction – add statement showing reason): *Since Australia has …*

15 **A** yes: *advised* (past participle – present perfect): *has always advised people to be careful*
B no: he *suggested* that people be careful
C no: he *claimed* that people should be careful
D no: he *explained* that people should be careful

Total: 15 marks

PART 2

Teacher's notes
A text of between 200 and 250 words is given for this question, often describing a person, event or scene. Fifteen gaps must be filled, each with **one word only**. These gaps are numbered from **16** to **30**. The first gap is numbered **0** because it is the example. Always refer the students to the example before they begin to fill the gaps. The missing word could be any type of word, e.g. noun, preposition, article.

The structures around the gaps often give the students grammatical or contextual clues as to which word is missing. These structures are indicated below.

1 mark for each correct answer.

16 *who* (Jules Verne + non-defining relative pronoun + clause)
17 *born* (past participle – simple past passive: *was born*)
18 *in* (preposition of time: *in 1828*)
19 *where* (Paris + adverb of place)
20 *his* (Verne + possessive adjective + *knowledge*)
21 *could/might* (modal – past – to show ability: *could use*)
22 *at* (time expression: *at first*)
23 *such* (determiner – adjective + *a success* + *that*)
24 *just* (adverb of degree: *just over*)
25 *One* (adventure stories + indefinite pronoun + phrase)
26 *story* (books + noun + *that* + clause)
27 *the* (definite article: *the world*)
28 *have* (auxiliary – present perfect: *have been made*)
29 *so* (conjunction – adds additional remark)
30 *become* (past participle – present perfect: *has … become*)

Total: 15 marks

PART 3

Teacher's notes
In this part, ten key word transformation sentences are given. The sentences are based on grammar and vocabulary covering three categories: phrasal verbs, verb structures and word sets (simple substitution and whole structural change). The students are required to substitute the key word with two to five other words to complete the response. It must be made clear to the students that they cannot change the given word or go over five words in order to complete the transformation. Always refer the students to the example at the beginning of the paper before they begin the exercise. Sometimes there may be two possible answers.

1 mark for each correct answer.

31 *put off* (*was postponed* to phrasal verb)
32 *apart from* (*except* to word set *apart from sb*)
33 *impossible to get/buy* (word set *to find sth impossible to do*)
34 *'d rather not* (*don't want to* to *would rather* + *not*)
35 *if/whether she wanted* (*Shall I* to word set *if/whether sb wanted sth done*)
36 *in order not to wake* (*so as to avoid waking* to word set *in order not to do sth*)
37 *might not have understood* (*didn't understand* to modal verb)
38 *made it difficult to concentrate* (word set *to make sth difficult to do*)
39 *isn't cool/cold enough* (*is too hot* to word set *is not cool enough to do sth*)
40 *must have heard* (*is certain to have heard* to modal verb)

Total: 10 marks

PART 4

Teacher's notes
A text of about 200 words is given for this question. It is usually narrative or informative. The lines of the text are numbered from **41** to **55**. The students are required either to tick the correct line or to identify the unnecessary word.

The first two lines numbered **0** and **00** are the examples. Always refer the students to the examples before they begin to do one exercise. The unnecessary word may be a verb, an adjective, an adverb, a pronoun, a link word, a preposition, an article, etc.

The students will have to read the whole sentence carefully in order to decide if a line is correct or if there is an unnecessary word in it. The other words in the sentence will help them to decide. Train the students to search for mistakes by looking more closely at the grammatical structure of a sentence. They will be able to recognise the errors by reading the text more carefully.

1 mark for each correct answer.

41 *she* (subject pronoun – referring to *My sister* – double subject)
42 *them* (object pronoun – referring to *training shoes* – double object)
43 √
44 *so* (adverb – incorrect when used with comparative *-er*)
45 √
46 *whole* (adjective – all of something: *the whole way* – contrast to *the rest of the way*: the remainder of something)
47 *that* (relative pronoun to connect a defining or non-defining clause)
48 *much* (adverb – incorrect position)
49 √
50 √
51 *at* (preposition – *achieve* is not followed by a preposition)
52 *feelings* (noun – these two nouns *excitement/feelings* do not go together)
53 *on* (preposition – *plan* is followed by an infinitive, *plan to continue*, or gerund, *plan on continuing*)
54 *being* (present participle – passive continuous – incorrect tense)
55 √

Total: 15 marks

PART 5

Teacher's notes
The structures around the gaps often give the students grammatical clues as to which word form is missing. Examples of these structures are given below in italics.

1 mark for each correct answer.

56 *importance* (adjective to noun – *The great importance*)
57 *attentive* (noun to adjective – *attentive manner*)
58 *consumers* (verb to noun – *Many consumers*)
59 *beneficial* (noun/verb to adjective – *can be beneficial*)
60 *unsuccessful* (adjective to adjective + prefix *un-* – *just another unsuccessful business project*)
61 *enjoyable* (verb to adjective – *an enjoyable way*)
62 *willingness* (adjective to noun – *This willingness*)
63 *quickly* (adjective to adverb – *developed quickly*)
64 *practical* (noun to adjective – *The practical side*)
65 *increasing* (verb to adjective – *an increasing number*)

Total: 10 marks

TOTAL PAPER: 65 marks

Paper 4 Listening

Teacher's notes
In this paper, 1 mark is given for each correct answer. This makes a total of 30 marks, which is mathematically adjusted to a mark of 40.

In general, correct answers paraphrase the taped text. The incorrect answers use incorrect facts or ideas loosely based on the taped text. Incorrect answers can: give opposite meanings, use the same words as the taped text, misinterpret the meaning of single words from the taped text, or give answers which seem acceptable. These distractors are listed in the key so that you can point them out to the students.

In the Listening Paper, identifying the correct answer can often depend on: intonation, stress, register and similar sounds. These are also noted for you in the key.

Symbols
opp., same, sing., accept., inton., stress, sounds, reg.

Explanations
Opposite (opp.) means that this answer states the opposite of what has been stated in the text.
Same word(s) (same) means that this answer contains a word/phrase/sentence from the text.
Incorrect usage of a single word (sing.) means that this answer contains a word like a modal or quantifier which is incorrectly used.
Acceptability (accept.) means that this answer contains something that might be believable, according to what the text states or according to general knowledge.
Intonation/tone of voice (inton.) means that this answer needs the listener to understand what somebody on the tape feels or thinks by listening to how his voice rises and falls.
Stress (stress) means that this answer needs the listener to understand what somebody on the tape feels or thinks by listening to the rhythm of his voice and the words he stresses.
Register (reg.) means that this answer needs the listener to understand what kind of situation is being presented by listening to certain language factors like formality and informality.
Similar sounds (sounds) means that this answer contains sounds or words which are easily confused with other sounds or words.

Teaching suggestion: Students should tell you exactly what the speaker said, what it means in their own words, and how this connects with the correct answer. Then you can discuss why the other answers are wrong. The students will resist this process, but when they realise that they are answering more accurately, they will continue to approach the questions systematically.

Exercise on intonation/tone of voice
A

Teacher's notes
After the students have done the exercise, continue to play the tape so they may hear the explanation of the answer.

Note that Part 1 is repeated on the tape, but you must rewind the tape to repeat Parts 2, 3 and 4.

PART 1

1 mark for each 'yes' answer.

1 A no: *I like doing homework* (laughs) (inton. – sarcastic)
   B yes: *I like doing homework*
   C no: *That's what you always say when I tell you to tidy up your room*

2 A no: *at my office* (same)
   B no: *Hyatt Hotel* (same)
   C yes: *Let's make it down in the cafeteria*

3 A no: *go to the café*
   B yes: *go to the café . . . half an hour*
   C no: *go to the café*

4 A yes: *cheeses are available at special low prices*
   B no: *Welcome* (same)
   C no: *– (accept.)*

5 A yes: *Mrs Townshend . . . Would you like to see the figures . . . Dave . . . coffee*
   B no: *Mrs Townshend . . . Would you like to see the figures . . . Dave . . . coffee* (reg.)
   C no: *Hold all of my calls while I'm taking this meeting*

6 A no: *we're going out Friday night* (same)
   B no: *Cindy . . . Joan* (accept.)
   C yes: *I want to break it off*

7 A no: *the girls* (same)
   B yes: *to tip the girls*
   C no: *to tip the girls* (opp.)

8 A yes: *came on screen*
   B no: *– (accept.)*
   C no: *dialogue was so good . . . write* (same)

Total: 8 marks

PART 2

1 mark for each correct answer.

9 hot/the right temperature: *Be sure that your oven has been heated to . . . 210 degrees centigrade*
10 small/individual dishes: *You can use small, individual soufflé dishes*
11 one large/tall dish: *or one, tall soufflé dish*
12 flour: *coat the buttered bottom and sides with flour*
13 from sticking (to the dish): *it won't stick to the dish*
14 constantly/all the time: *Then stir constantly*
15 stiff/they stand/they form peaks: *Beat the egg whites until stiff*
16 15 minutes/a quarter of an hour: *bake for 15 minutes*
17 doubles in size/gets twice as big: *double in size*
18 serve/eat (them) immediately/right away: *always serve them immediately*

Total: 10 marks

PART 3

1 mark for each correct answer.

19 C *ethnic . . . another world . . . oriental . . . lanterns . . . costumes . . . don't understand half the things on the menu . . . never use a knife and fork*
20 A *quick burger . . . chips . . . shake . . . young people . . . loud music*
21 D *fast . . . wine . . . not just one choice . . . Italian . . . pack it up*
22 F *good meal . . . followed by a superb performance . . . presenting 'China Town'*
23 B *staff wait . . . Light music accompanies . . . beef fillets . . . first-class service*

Total: 5 marks

PART 4

1 mark for each 'yes' answer.

24 A yes: *Oh, that explains it*
   B no: *Oh, that explains it* (inton. – sarcastic)
   C no: *Mum never mentioned anything last night about a picnic* (opp.)

25 A yes: *had another court case*
   B no: *court*
   C no: *With her favourite judge* (same)

26 A no: *no school ... Not for two more months*
   B yes: *no school ... Not for two more months*
   C no: *no school ... Not for two more months*

27 A no: *told you not to eat so many eggs* (opp.)
   B no: *told you not to eat so many eggs*
   C yes: *told you not to eat so many eggs*

28 A no: *Oh, I love crackers* (inton. – disappointed)
   B yes: *Oh, I love crackers*
   C no: *Oh, I love crackers* (inton. – disappointed)

29 A yes: *greengrocer ... carrots ... peas ... raw*
   B no: *We always have salami when we go on picnics ... None of that unhealthy stuff*
   C no: *boiled some chicken*

30 A no: *we shouldn't use foil very often* (sing.)
   B no: *we shouldn't use foil very often* (sing.)
   C yes: *we shouldn't use foil very often ... Only when we have to*

Total: 7 marks

TOTAL PAPER: 30 marks

Paper 5 Speaking

Teacher's notes
In this paper, marks are given for the positive aspects of the Speaking Paper such as: correct use of grammar, appropriate use of vocabulary, good pronunciation, appropriate level of fluency, suitable communication skills and proper task achievement. They are expected to take turns, hold the floor, negotiate meaning and initiate/respond appropriately. They must be able to give information, describe and compare, state and support an opinion, agree and disagree, speculate, and express certainty and uncertainty. This adds up to a total mark of 40.

In Part 1 students talk about themselves. In Part 2 they talk about sets of pictures. In Part 3 they work together to find an answer based on a visual stimulus (e.g. a photograph or line drawing). In Part 4 they talk about the subject brought up in Part 3. In general, questions test their ability to exchange information and opinions.

Topics to familiarise students with
This book has used topics from the list included in the Local Examinations Syndicate specifications for the revised FCE examination issued by the University of Cambridge. For your general information, your students should familiarise themselves with the following subjects: personal experiences, living conditions, jobs, education, pastimes, travel, shopping, eating/drinking, social relations, the media, the weather, environment, entertainment, health, services (e.g. the post office), places, language, music, fashion, animals, cinema, history, the arts, science/technology, transport, crime, sports and people. Note that the interviews are not on **one** theme all the way through. Only Parts 3 and 4 are thematically related.

PART 1

Teacher's notes
Encourage the students to get used to working in pairs. It might be useful to have them working with a different partner each time. It is also useful to have students acting as the examiners so that they can understand what the examiners are looking for. The 'examiners' can also award marks.

Answers are free, but make sure that students address the questions asked of them.

You might like to give the students some more practice on the themes:

1 Tell us three positive/negative adjectives that describe your neighbourhood. Are your neighbours friendly? Can you give an example?
2 Please describe your bedroom/kitchen/living-room. What's your favourite room? Why?

PART 2

Teacher's notes
Encourage the students to get used to: talking for approximately one minute each, co-operating with partners, drawing some kind of conclusion. Note that the 'describe the man in the photograph' kind of question has been replaced by questions which are more relevant to the students' own world.

Answers are free, but make sure that students address the questions asked of them.

PART 3

Teacher's notes
Encourage the students to work well with each other, once again drawing some kind of conclusion or 'agreeing to disagree' at the end. Note that this is good preparation for the CAE (Certificate in Advanced English).

There is no right answer but students should discuss some of the following: employment opportunities, the local economy, more amenities available, livelier atmosphere in the village, pollution, threat to natural environment, more tourists, congestion.

PART 4

Teacher's notes
Answers are free, but make sure that students address the questions asked of them.

TEST 2

Paper 1 Reading

PART 1

1 mark for each correct answer.

  1 E *numbness ... you don't know what to do*
  2 A *venting your anger on innocent members of your family*
  3 F *come to believe what has happened ... I've got to get on with it*
  4 G *feeling miserable ... is normal*
  5 C *Confide in your partner*
  6 H *planning to do something else that's constructive*
  7 D *a chance to rediscover other things in life*

Total: 7 marks

PART 2

1 mark for each 'yes' answer.

  8 A no: *absolute beginners to experts*
    B no: *dress must be neat*
    C no: *absolute beginners to experts*
    D yes: *dress must be neat*

  9 A no: *small fee for adults watching children* (opp.)
    B yes: *under 12's must be accompanied by an adult*
    C no: *over 14's on Friday and Saturday evenings*
    D no: *no newspapers, books, magazines, games, etc., permitted in Roller Cafe or Roller Bar*

10 A yes: *no smoking except in ... part of Roller Cafe*
    B no: *no smoking except in ... part of Roller Cafe*
    C no: *no smoking except in Roller Bar*
    D no: *no smoking except in Roller Bar and part of Roller Cafe*

11 A no: *Adult Night*
    B no: *Allskate*
    C yes: *Family Fun*
    D no: *over 14's*

12 A no: *Allskate ... 11.00*
    B no: *Allskate ... 11.00*
    C yes: *Fridays ... under 16's welcome until 11 pm ... out of there by 11 pm – don't make the manager have to throw you out ... older friends stay longer*
    D no: *Roller Mania ... 12.30* (no ages mentioned)

13 A no: *kitchen table* (same)
    B no: *in the car* (same)
    C yes: *don't make the manager have to throw you out*
    D no: *home* (same)

14 A no: *This is your last chance* (same)
  B no: *Make sure ... don't ... This is your last chance* (tone is angry, not pleased)
  C no: –
  D yes: *Make sure ... don't ... This is your last chance* (tone is angry, not pleased)

Total: 7 marks

PART 3

1 mark for each correct answer.

15 A *a roomy lift* with *the lift*
16 G *The suite itself* (description of rooms) with *The room* (further description)
17 B *in the main restaurant* with *There in the large foyer*
18 C *the management* with *Francois, the head waiter; did not like change* with *showed Harvey to his usual table*
19 E *he did not notice* with *all had an excellent view of Harvey; the four young men* with *Stephen, Robin, Jean-Pierre and James*
20 F *Not exactly what I expected* with *Put on a bit of weight since those photographs* (conversation)

Total: 6 marks

PART 4

1 mark for each correct answer.

21 F *library contains approximately 3000 volumes*
22 E *white water rafting company ... rivers*
23 A *Travel by the world's finest double-decker Supercoaches*
24 B *Services include ... child-care*
25 G *Escape the crowds ... private pools ... select hotels on secluded Caribbean islands ... escapists*
26 B/D *skiing*
27 D/B *cross-country skiing*
28 B/H *7 days skiing*
29 H/B *7 nights from £299*
30 A/B *Free child places*
31 B/A *Services include ... child-care*
32 C/D *3 Worldwide brochures: Walking ... treks ... rambles*
33 D/C *walking holidays all over the world*

1 mark for each 'yes' answer.

34 A no: not advertising one specific tour (accept.)
  B no: not outlining the schedule of one specific tour (accept.)
  C no: not offering general knowledge in geography
  D yes: in the classified advertisements section

35 A no: informative, but in order to sell (accept.)
  B yes: wants people to buy its product (holidays) e.g. *10 days from only £75*
  C no: not giving directions or instructions
  D no: supposed to be interesting, but not entertaining

Total: 15 marks

TOTAL PAPER: 35 marks

Paper 2 Writing

PART 1

Students should include
Instructions: write to yacht agency, interested in holiday on a yacht, need more information, give information about family.
Picture/text: need more information on activities, food and entertainment (suitability for children).
Notes: must be late July/early August, how many people on yacht, weather, length of cruise, price. The outcome of the family's decision will be based on the information asked for. This should be made clear in the letter.

TOTAL PAPER: 40 marks

Paper 3 Use of English

PART 1

1 mark for each 'yes' answer.

1 A no: there is one area *yet*
  B yes: *still* (adverb – used to emphasise the point): *still one area*
  C no: but *then* there is one area (to introduce some contrasting information)
  D no: there is *already* one area (incorrect meaning)

2 A no: the *development* of ski centres
  B no: in *conclusion*
  C no: as *proof* of this
  D yes: *result* (noun + preposition): *a result of this*

3 A yes: *built* (passive – simple past): *was built*
  B no: the opening ceremony was *prepared*
  C no: clubs were *formed*
  D no: centres were *created*

4 A no: the *biggest* size (opposite meaning)
  B no: the *longest* slope
  C yes: *smallest* (superlative adjective – to compare one with whole group): *the smallest size*
  D no: the *widest* size (incorrect meaning)

5 A no: the skiers *perform* certain numbers
  B no: the trainers *instruct* the skiers
  C yes: *operate* (verb – present simple): *centres operate like ... clubs*
  D no: the trainers *conduct* their lessons

6 A no: *otherwise* they cannot become members
  B no: *besides* being like golf clubs, they are also like squash clubs
  C no: *either* golf clubs or squash clubs
  D yes: *or* (conjunction – linking the two parts used as an example): *golf or squash clubs*

7 A yes: *range* (noun): *a full range of ... facilities*
  B no: a *row* of skiers
  C no: a *variety* of activities
  D no: a ski *area*

8 A no: *do* the work properly
  B yes: *use* (infinitive): *to use the ... centres*
  C no: *go* to the centres
  D no: *find* the centres (incorrect meaning)

9 A yes: *skied* (past participle – present perfect negative): *have never skied before*
  B no: *skated* on ice
  C no: *climbed* a mountain
  D no: *hiked* through the forest

10 A no: *with* doubt written all over her face
  B no: be *in* doubt about sth
  C yes: *without* (preposition – usually opposite of *with* before a noun phrase to show certainty): *without doubt*
  D no: the trainer gave her the benefit *of* the doubt

11 A no: *to* the dry-ski centre
  B no: go *under* an umbrella
  C no: go *round* an obstacle
  D yes: *over* (particle – part of phrasal verb): *go over the equipment*

12 A no: a *thorough* knowledge of sth
  B no: *minimum* requirements
  C no: *true* story
  D yes: *basic* (adjective): *basic skills*

13 A no: he *rarely* exercises
  B yes: *really* (adverb of degree – used for emphasis): *a really good way*
  C no: it is an *excellent* way
  D no: he *seldom* exercises

14 A yes: *regular* (adjective): *regular skiers*
  B no: *reliable* skiers (incorrect meaning)
  C no: a *continuous* number of lessons
  D no: *continual* rain

15 **A** no: has *made* a mistake
   B yes: *become* (past participle – present perfect): *has become a part of their entertainment*
   C no: has *developed* into a part of their entertainment
   D no: has *achieved* a new record

Total: 15 marks

PART 2

1 mark for each correct answer.

16 *was* (auxiliary – verb *to be* – past tense: *was to begin*)
17 *and* (conjunction: *had opened ... and had looked*)
18 *time* (noun phrase: *a long time*)
19 *finally* (adverb of time: *had finally chosen*)
20 *with/and* (preposition/conjunction: *skirt with/and ... blouse*)
21 *her* (*Sandra* + possessive adjective + *hair*)
22 *most* (adverb – superlative: *most modern style*)
23 *However* (conjunction – joins two contrasting statements)
24 *too* (adverb of degree: *too formally*)
25 *would* (modal – past tense with future meaning: *would be wearing*)
26 *into* (preposition of movement: *went back into the house*)
27 *changed* (verb – simple past: *changed into ... jeans*)
28 *which/that* (*shoes* + defining relative pronoun + clause)
29 *more* (adverb – comparative: *more comfortable*)
30 *herself* (*Sandra* + *enjoy* + reflexive pronoun)

Total: 15 marks

PART 3

1 mark for each correct answer.

31 *'d prefer to stop* (*would rather stop* to conditional verb)
32 *must go* (*he had to go* to word set *you must do sth*)
33 *haven't seen her since* (*last saw her* to word set *to have not seen sb since (time)*)
34 *bring her round* (*persuade her* to phrasal verb + object)
35 *their connection* (word set *a connection to sth*)
36 *have enough* (*can afford* to verb + determiner)
37 *in order to finish* (*so that they can finish* to word set *in order to do sth*)
38 *came across* (*found* to phrasal verb)
39 *did not speak politely to* (word set *to not speak politely to sb*)
40 *to avoid being* (*so that she would not be late* to word set *to avoid being sth*)

Total: 10 marks

PART 4

1 mark for each correct answer.

41 √
42 *been* (past participle – no such tense as *was been talking*)
43 *about* (preposition – used in questions: *How about the weather?*)
44 √
45 *it* (object pronoun – phrasal verb *take off* does not take an object when it means *aeroplanes leaving*)
46 *more* (adverb of degree – used in the comparative form)
47 *of* (preposition – needs a noun form after it, not a clause)
48 *being* (present participle – passive continuous – incorrect tense)
49 *he* (subject pronoun – referring to *Jim* – double subject)
50 √
51 *the* (definite article – not in prepositional phrase *on time*)
52 √
53 *not* (negative adverb – incorrect here with *Unless*)
54 *so* (adverb of degree – incorrect when used with comparative *-er*)
55 √

Total: 15 marks

PART 5

1 mark for each correct answer.

56 *performance* (verb to noun – *our performance*)
57 *competition* (verb to noun – *the ice-skating championship competition*)

58 *unbelievable* (adjective to adjective + prefix *un-* – *the unbelievable score*)
59 *length* (adjective to noun – irregular form, *-th* ending – *The length*)
60 *difficulty* (adjective to noun – *The difficulty*)
61 *musical* (noun to adjective – *the musical pieces*)
62 *famous* (noun to adjective – *becoming famous*)
63 *exciting* (verb to adjective – *the exciting days*)
64 *optimistic* (noun to adjective – *being young and optimistic*)
65 *popularity* (adjective to noun – *our popularity*)

Total: 10 marks

TOTAL PAPER: 65 marks

Paper 4 Listening

Exercise on stress
B

PART 1

1 mark for each 'yes' answer.

1 **A** no: *I don't want to go with* **him** *... it's a good film* (stress)
  B yes: *I don't want to go with* **him**
  C no: *Doesn't seem worth it*

2 **A** yes: *he'll show you our wonderful line of electrical products ... low-priced products*
  B no: *he'll show you our wonderful line of electrical products ... low-priced products*
  C no: *'Win a Trip with Distributor's Contest'*

3 **A** no: *dropped out*
  B no: *play his guitar ... pianos*
  C yes: *Now he owns his own business*

4 **A** no: *– (accept.)*
  B no: *that's way back down there* (opp.)
  C yes: *I'm having trouble finding Pendleton Street*

5 **A** no: *game ... ball*
  B yes: *game ... strikes ... pins ... ball*
  C no: *game ... team*

6 **A** no: *problems with the students* **and the parents** (stress)
  B yes: *problems with ...* **the parents. They're** *the real root of the problem*
  C no: *headmaster*

7 **A** no: *You've just gone out for a moment*
  B no: *make a big fuss* (same)
  C yes: *picture yourself at work*

8 **A** no: *so I can get something to eat*
  B yes: *short of cash ... so I can get something to eat*
  C no: *I'm a bit short of cash*

Total: 8 marks

PART 2

1 mark for each correct answer. Spelling mistakes do not matter.

9 technological: *the technological ... spies of the future*
10 industrial: *and industrial spies of the future*
11 (very) expensive: *She'd be expensive*
12 interesting/young: *just too boring ... someone that the young people can relate to*
13 attract/relate to the young people/teenagers: *someone that the young people can relate to*
14 all the others/other films: *it needs to be something rather different*
15 boats: *The chase will take place ... in boats*
16 on a (passing goods) train: *there is a fight on the train*
17 (small private) aeroplane: *He eventually escapes in a small private aeroplane*
18 rewritten/redone/written again: *Make those changes*

Total: 10 marks

PART 3

1 mark for each correct answer.

19 B *do a lot of talking ... like being with people ... persuade them ... Most people don't like spending, so ... make people trust you*
20 A *work long hours ... talk to people who are under a lot of stress ... studying and books ... don't prepare you for the challenges*
21 F *it's lifting and carrying ... being polite to the customers ... they don't even leave a tip*
22 C *talk ... preparation ... checking out the latest case developments ... not usually as exciting as it looks on TV ... have to look good ... a nice suit*
23 E *behind a desk ... explain how the whole system works so that they can find it themselves the next time*

Total: 5 marks

PART 4

1 mark for each correct answer.

24 yes: *An air bag has been installed*
25 yes: *mudflaps over the front and rear tyres*
26 no: *excellent cassette radio* (accept.)
27 yes: *the cover on the steering wheel ... that's pure leather*
28 no: *floor mats* (sounds)
29 yes: *And speaking of safety*
30 no: *our latest baby ... Madam, just look ... Come and touch it ... Sir, don't be shy* (uses humour) (reg./inton.)

Total: 7 marks

TOTAL PAPER: 30 marks

Paper 5 Speaking

PART 1

You might like to give the students some more practice on the themes:

1 Tell us about your family. Are you close to your brothers/sisters/ family members? Can you give us an example?
2 Can you describe a special religious/ethnic custom your family follows? Does your family have any special family customs you would like to share with us? Did you have more when you were younger?

PARTS 1, 2, 3 and 4

Teacher's notes
Answers are free, but make sure that students address the questions asked of them.

TEST 3

Paper 1 Reading

PART 1

1 mark for each correct answer.

1 G *protect the foot more from the cold*
2 D *introduced fashion by adding colour ornamentation, and different shapes*
3 A *only seven basic designs*
4 F *Because of her short stature, she wore shoes with 2- to 3-inch heels ... High heels became the rage of Europe*
5 B *left and right shoes gained a firm foothold*
6 H *This allowed mass production of footwear*
7 C *measurements applied separately to men's, women's, children's, and infants' shoes*

Total: 7 marks

PART 2

1 mark for each 'yes' answer.

8 A no: *From disarming a knife attacker to bringing round the victim* (opp.)
  B yes: *disarming a knife attacker ... bringing round the victim ... she is expected to perform as well as the boys*
  C no: *From disarming a knife attacker to bringing round the victim* (accept.)
  D no: –

9 A yes: *difficult ... I offer to drive ... But no-one else would ever ask me to drive* (implying that they respect her too much to do so, as they know **she** will offer in difficult situations)
  B no: –
  C no: *The driver always stays with the van* (same)
  D no: – (accept.)

10 A no: *several* (sing.)
  B no: *several* (sing.)
  C yes: *included having building blocks and bricks thrown at them in several protests and riots*
  D no: *several* (sing.)

11 A no: *their way of explaining* (same)
  B no: *men will react better* (same)
  C yes: *but that's usually their way of explaining why they've hit you* (implying that they're feeling guilty about hitting a woman)
  D no: –

12 A no: *he is dragged to a cell* (same)
  B no: – (accept.)
  C yes: *keeps swearing at her*
  D no: *sometimes a couple of men will react better to a woman telling them to calm down*

13 A no: *keeps swearing at her ... 'I'll see you in court', he shouts* (accept.)
  B no: –
  C no: – (accept.)
  D yes: *Porter looks on without emotion*

14 A yes: *At the station Porter books in her struggling prisoner ... It could be a busy night*
  B no: *To try to remedy this the unit was renamed 'support team' ... Being a woman makes little difference* (opp.)
  C no: *Porter says the violence is there* (same)
  D no: – (accept.)

Total: 7 marks

PART 3

1 mark for each correct answer.

15 D *a temporary job* with *offered him a full-time post*; *bakery* with *pie-packing*
16 B *I* with *I* (uses the first person); *job club* with *their facilities ... curriculum vitae ... apply for jobs*
17 F *I was financially OK* with *a golden handshake ... didn't ... spend it all*
18 A *a lot of choices* with *opportunities*; *at my new company* with *There may be opportunities*
19 E *I* with *my*; *I am over-qualified* with *But you've got to start somewhere*
20 H *employment agency, Brook Street* with *marketing executive of Brook Street*
21 C *people* with *People*; *no-one should take any refusals too much to heart* with *People should explore any opportunities* (advice)

Total: 7 marks

PART 4

1 mark for each correct answer.

22 A   *street theatre and dance from Columbia ... Trinidad*
23 F   *stone carvings*
24 C   *musical instruments ... on display*
25 A/I *Colombia ... Argentina ... Uruguay ... Brazil*
26 I/A *Brazil*

27 **D/B/A** *street theatre*
28 **B/A/D** *dance*
29 **A/D/B** *music*
30 **A** *music*
31 **C** *artists ... paintings* (there are instruments and paintings of musical scenes, but music is not played)
32 **C** *modern art*
33 **C** *modern art*
34 **B/A** *ballet ... choreographed by*
35 **A/B** *Musical adaptation ... Conducted by*

Total: 14 marks

TOTAL PAPER: 35 marks

Paper 2 Writing

PART 1

Students should include
Instructions: first hiking trip, wrote to hiking club for advice, which route and equipment is suitable.
Picture/text: Route 3 is a short route covering all points of their letter.
Suggested equipment – matches, rucksack, camera, first aid kit, binoculars, suntan oil, food (choices may vary – make sure students explain reasons for choices)
Notes: Route 3 is the best because all the points in the notes are covered.
- it's the shortest
- look at birds (it has bird park)
- take photos (it has bird park)
- barbecue for lunch (it has barbecue area)
- go swimming (1, 2 – no swimming)
Not the other routes because teenagers need to be more experienced (narrow paths) and the other routes do not include what they want to do.

TOTAL PAPER: 40 marks

Paper 3 Use of English

PART 1

1 mark for each 'yes' answer.

1 **A** yes: *feel* (verb – simple present): *feel that I have the training*
 B no: *regard* myself a good swimmer
 C no: *sense* danger
 D no: *propose* that we start a swimming club

2 **A** no: this *quite* difficult swim
 B no: *so* difficult a swim
 C no: this *rather* difficult swim
 D yes: *such* (determiner): *such a swim*

3 **A** no: *but* to do it (incorrect meaning)
 B yes: *and* (conjunction – joins two similar ideas) *Channel is ... the Mount Everest ... and to do it*
 C no: *as well as* to do sth else
 D no: *because* to do it (incorrect meaning)

4 **A** no: even greater *prize* (incorrect meaning)
 B no: will mean even more *work*
 C yes: *achievement* (noun): *an ... achievement for me*
 D no: even greater *duty* (incorrect meaning)

5 **A** no: have *moved* an obstacle
 B no: have *passed* by the Channel
 C yes: *crossed* (verb – past participle): *have crossed the Channel*
 D no: have *run* a race

6 **A** no: *forming* an opinion
 B no: *willing* to do it (incorrect meaning)
 C no: *agreeing* to do it (incorrect meaning)
 D yes: *hoping* (verb – present continuous): *am hoping to do it*

7 **A** no: *give* money to charity
 B yes: *raise* (infinitive): *to raise money*
 C no: *save* money in a bank
 D no: *contribute* money to a charity

8 **A** yes: *keen* (adjective + preposition): *keen on the charities*
 B no: *interested* in the charities
 C no: *thinking* about the charities
 D no: *in favour* of the charities

9 **A** no: swim *through* an opening
 B yes: *across* (preposition of movement): *swimming across the Channel*
 C no: *jump* over a hurdle
 D no: run *along* the road

10 **A** yes: *order* (noun – prepositional phrase): *in order to carry this out*
 B no: in *respect* of style
 C no: in *time* I will swim it
 D no: in *regard* to a subject

11 **A** no: *cut* this out (incorrect meaning)
 B no: *check* this out (incorrect meaning)
 C no: *clear* this out (incorrect meaning)
 D yes: *carry* (verb – phrasal verb): *carry this out*

12 **A** no: would *have* me spending thirty minutes ...
 B no: I would *spend* thirty minutes
 C no: would *amount* to thirty minutes ...
 D yes: *consist* (verb + preposition): *would consist of thirty minutes*

13 **A** no: *capable* of following my diet
 B yes: *conscious* (adjective + preposition): *conscious of my diet*
 C no: *enthusiastic* about following my diet
 D no: *accustomed* to following my diet

14 **A** yes: *be* (infinitive – simple future): *will be ready*
 B no: will *have* to be ready
 C no: will *do* what I can to get ready
 D no: will *try* to be ready

15 **A** no: has never been *given* (incorrect meaning)
 B no: has never been *made* (incorrect meaning)
 C yes: *done* (past participle – present perfect): *has never been done*
 D no: has never been *kept* (incorrect meaning)

Total: 15 marks

PART 2

1 mark for each correct answer.

16 *never* (frequency adverb: *had never been*)
17 *us* (*we* + above + object pronoun)
18 *this* (determiner – demonstrative adjective: *this storm*)
19 *my* (*I* + possessive adjective + *mouth*)
20 *towards* (preposition of movement: *ran ... towards the ... branch*)
21 *would* (modal – past: *would not be able*)
22 *to* (preposition of movement: *move ... to the side*)
23 *in* (preposition of time: *in time*) (note: *before he died*)
24 *who* (*Lord Brenton* + non-defining relative pronoun + clause)
25 *only* (adjective: *the only person*)
26 *so* (conjunction – joins two statements, one indicating purpose)
27 *was* (verb *to be* – simple past: *the house was ... like a ...*)
28 *tree* (noun: *a Christmas tree*)
29 *still* (adverb of time: *must still be*)
30 *the* (definite article: *the entrance of the ... house*)

Total: 15 marks

PART 3

1 mark for each correct answer.

31 *has been absent from* (*has not come to school* to word set *to be absent from sth*)
32 *a solution to* (word set *to find a solution to sth*)
33 *put me up* (*let me stay with you* to phrasal verb + object)
34 *suggested (that) he* (*advised him to* to verb + clause)
35 *to have my room* (word set *to have sth done*)
36 *seldom sees* (*doesn't often see* to verb + adverb)

37 *easy for me to* (word set *to be easy for sb to understand sth*)
38 *approve of us/our staying* (*like us to stay* to verb + gerund)
39 *works for IBM, doesn't* (*is employed* to *works*; *isn't she* to *doesn't she*)
40 *had difficulty in understanding* (*could not understand* to word set *to have difficulty in understanding sth*)

Total: 10 marks

PART 4

1 mark for each correct answer.

41 *it* (object pronoun – referring to *drought* – double subject)
42 *forward* (adverb – look forward *to* something happening)
43 *such* (determiner – needs a negative context like *it might not be such a good idea*)
44 *of* (preposition – incorrect with the verb *frighten* in this context)
45 *that* (relative pronoun – use it to begin a definite clause)
46 √
47 *of* (preposition – *because of* shows cause; *because* – conjunction – shows reason)
48 √
49 *some* (determiner – used in affirmative sentences)
50 √
51 *which* (relative pronoun – incorrect usage with conjunction *because*)
52 √
53 *from* (preposition – incorrect with preposition *besides*)
54 √
55 *have* (auxiliary – no such tense as *could have be saved*)

Total: 15 marks

PART 5

1 mark for each correct answer.

56 *alive* (verb/adjective to predicate adjective – *the panic ... comes alive*)
57 *suddenness* (adjective to noun – *its suddenness*)
58 *death* (adjective to noun – *the death*)
59 *survivors* (verb to noun – *some of the survivors*)
60 *patiently* (adjective to adverb – *sit patiently*)
61 *unconscious* (adjective to adjective + prefix *un-* – *I became unconscious*)
62 *weakness* (adjective to noun – *any weakness*)
63 *attention* (verb to noun – *another ship's attention*)
64 *hopeless* (noun/verb to adjective + suffix *-less* – *our situation would have been hopeless*)
65 *frightening* (noun to adjective – *this frightening experience*)

Total: 10 marks

TOTAL PAPER: 65 marks

Paper 4 Listening

Exercise on register
A

PART 1

1 mark for each 'yes' answer.

1 **A** no: *Betty ... would you mind giving Mary my report ... Yeah ... ask her to type it* (reg.)
    B no: *Sorry to ask you* (reg.)
    C yes: *Sorry to ask you – you've got your own stuff*

2 **A** no: *it's been a long time*
    B no: *that little trick*
    C yes: *that little trick you played on my mother*

3 **A** no: *the runway is blocked* (same)
    B no: *you may take down your hand luggage* (opp.)
    C yes: *Please stay in your seats*

4 **A** no: *a grammar book*

    B yes: *to do a grammar book*
    C no: *I met with the team ... designers*

5 **A** no: *besides our main guest star*
    B no: *great rock stars* (her son is)
    C yes: *we have another little surprise in store for you*

6 **A** no: *I'll get a ride home* (same)
    B yes: *but instead of coming home right away*
    C no: *Dad gave me some money* (opp.)

7 **A** no: *birds/cat/owl*
    B yes: *this one*
    C no: *It never hurts to learn a foreign language*

8 **A** yes: *when you used to play outside my house*
    B no: *homework*
    C no: *How's your mum?*

Total: 8 marks

PART 2

1 mark for each correct answer. Spelling mistakes do not matter.

9 Catherine: *Catherine*
10 Pool: *P – double O – L*
11 13 September 1993: *13 September 1993*
12 double/with a double bed: *A double, please*
13 1/one: *I'm alone*
14 17/seventeen: *17*
15 Saturday, Sunday: *then it'll be Saturday and Sunday*
16 £65/sixty-five pounds: *That will be £65 per night*
17 traditional English breakfast: *traditional English breakfast then*
18 no/none: *It's all right ... I'll be eating at about 8.00*

Total: 10 marks

PART 3

1 mark for each correct answer.

19 E *Couples ... South American ... or ... European origin*
20 B *soft shoe ... bar ... classical music ... choreographic pieces*
21 A *running shoes ... work rate ... exercises on mats ... quick dance music*
22 F *prepares women for the happy event ... to be prepared ... when the time comes*
23 C *move or dance to modern music ... parties*

Total: 5 marks

PART 4

1 mark for each correct answer.

24 false: *Good morning, ladies and gentlemen* (reg.)
25 true: *Tonight until Sunday evening*
26 false: *since his death in 1991*
27 true: *themes from nature*
28 true: *Oscar award-winning films*
29 true: *How the West Was Won, directed by Henry Hathaway, John Ford and George Marshall*
30 false: *there's an admission charge of 600 drachmas*

Total: 7 marks

TOTAL PAPER: 30 marks

Paper 5 Speaking

PART 1

You might like to give the students some more practice on the themes:

1 If you could have any hobby you wanted, what would you choose? Why? Do you play any team/individual sports? Why/ why not?

2 What's your favourite way to travel? Why? Would you like a job which involves a lot of travelling? Why/why not?

PARTS 1, 2 AND 4

Teacher's notes
Answers are free, but make sure that students address the questions asked of them.

PART 3

Teacher's notes
There is no 'right' answer, but the most logical one might be to try to make it down to Camp 2, which has provisions, until the storm lets up and they can get back to Camp 1, which has provisions and a radio. However, other answers are acceptable if the students can justify their choice.

TEST 4

Paper 1 Reading

PART 1

1 mark for each correct answer.

1 A *make your own freshly squeezed juice*
2 D *Blister packs ... cannot be recycled ... a comparable product without all the packaging*
3 B *individually wrapped restaurant portions ... Avoid them at restaurants*
4 F *Single-serving ... product of this type are wasteful ... Buy a larger pack*
5 E *buy eggs only in cardboard egg cartons*
6 G *Buy soft drinks in cans*

Total: 6 marks

PART 2

1 mark for each 'yes' answer.

7 A no: *The war was the most peaceful period of my life* (accept.)
   B yes: *The war was the most peaceful period of my life*
   C no: *The war was the most peaceful period of my life ... Life never seemed so simple and clear* (same)
   D no: *The war was the most peaceful period of my life* (opp.)

8 A no: *I called them Mrs Left and Mrs Right* (same)
   B no: *I put my feet out from under the clothes* (accept.)
   C yes: *I put my feet out from under the clothes ... and invented dramatic situations for them*
   D no: *she mostly contented herself with nodding agreement* (same)

9 A yes: *Mother and I could never agree about that*
   B no: *Mother and I could never agree about that* (sing.)
   C no: *Mother and I could never agree about that* (sing.)
   D no: *Mother and I could never agree about that* (sing.)

10 A yes: *Mother said ... how foolish she was ... she was too hard to please*
    B no: *Mother said we couldn't afford one* (accept.)
    C no: *foolish* (she might be intelligent, as an intelligent person can still be foolish) (accept.)
    D no: –

11 A no: *Santa Claus* (not stating that he really believed in him, it may only have been a game) (accept.)
    B no: *till Father came back from the war* (accept.)
    C no: *everyone knew they couldn't afford seventeen and six* (opp.)
    D yes: *Mother said we couldn't afford one ... seventeen and six ... probably a cheap baby*

12 A yes: *a deep valley ... houses up the opposite hillside, which were all still in shadow, while those at our side of the valley were all lit up*
    B no: *which were all still in shadow* (same)

C no: *a deep valley ... houses up the opposite hillside, which were all still in shadow, while those at our side of the valley were all lit up*
D no: *with long strange shadows that made them seem unfamiliar* (same)

13 A no: *I warmed up as I talked* (opp.)
    B no: *I warmed up as I talked*
    C no: *big bed* (opp.)
    D yes: *I warmed up as I talked*

14 A yes: *Life never seemed so ... full of possibilities ... as then* (now, he implies, life offers fewer possibilities)
    B no: *The war was the most peaceful period of my life* (then)(now we don't know how he feels)
    C no: *I fell asleep beside her* (then) (now we don't know how he feels) (accept.)
    D no: *Life never seemed so simple and clear ... as then* (now, he impies, life is more complicated)

Total: 8 marks

PART 3

1 mark for each correct answer.

15 D *How's school* with *convince your Mom and Dad to bring you here; Gigi* with *your* (addressing her)
16 H *Whyte Ridge* with *Speaking of Whyte Ridge*
17 A *We* with *we; Mom's* with *brought her back here*
18 F *Nick's back is slowly getting better* with *It was very painful; Nick* with *he*
19 C *our house. Everything* with *throughout* (description)
20 G *Got to go* (closing)
21 B *had a girl* with *And Pattie is pregnant; girl* with *third* (baby)

Total: 7 marks

PART 4

1 mark for each correct answer.

22 B *starting or adding to the family ... bigger family*
23 F *put those dreams to good use*
24 J *romantically involved ... the time is right for you to be brave*
25 G/I *concentrate on business deals*
26 I/G *And at how profitable it will be!*
27 E *passionate nature ... emotions ... Put the brake on ... Do not get upset*
28 C *remember to say 'thank you'*
29 K *you also want something more permanent*
30 H/A *Neglecting to do something now may prove disastrous in the years to come*
31 A/H *A family crisis can be stopped if you unexpectedly change your mind*
32 D *look to your childhood for the answers*
33 I *project ... the time has come for you to finish it*

1 mark for each 'yes' answer.

34 A no: there is no 'news' reported
    B no: nothing is being advertised
    C yes: this is typical of a horoscope column in a magazine for the general public
    D no: there is no information given that is taught in schools

35 A no: not specifically for people with problems, but to everyone (accept.)
    B yes: information (predictions) is given, e.g. *things will fall into place*
    C no: some of the people are advised to be careful, but that's not the main aim (accept.)
    D no: nothing mentioned about whether he accepts letters (accept.)

Total: 14 marks

TOTAL PAPER: 35 marks

Paper 2 Writing

PART 1

Students should include
Instructions: thank Mr Hammel for his response regarding the interview.
Picture/text: address different points in the letter concerning the interview, referring to date (same as talk), time (9.30 pm), place (suggest one), list of questions (mention it).
Notes: refer to what will be in the article (general description of talk and some specific points: his reason for coming, other clubs involved in the movement), ask if he can bring photos, inform him photos will be taken at the interview.

TOTAL PAPER: 40 marks

Paper 3 Use of English

PART 1

1 mark for each 'yes' answer.

1. A yes: *However* (conjunction – to make a contrast): *Nowadays ... However, in the past*
   B no: *In spite of* this (incorrect meaning)
   C no: *Because* of this (incorrect meaning)
   D no: *Despite* this (incorrect meaning)

2. A no: could easily be *glimpsed* (incorrect meaning)
   B yes: *noticed* (past participle – passive): *could easily be noticed*
   C no: could easily be *understood* (incorrect meaning)
   D no: could easily be *made* (incorrect meaning)

3. A no: had *bought* cookers
   B no: cookers *put* in
   C no: cookers *connected* to the power source
   D yes: *installed* (verb – simple past): *cookers installed*

4. A no: *baked* the bread
   B no: *stirred* the soup
   C no: *boiled* the water
   D yes: *cooked* (verb – simple past): *still cooked*

5. A no: *raise* her hands
   B no: difficulties *arise*
   C yes: *rise* (infinitive): *to rise at five*
   D no: had to *get* up at five

6. A yes: *handy* (adjective): *a candle ... kept handy*
   B no: was *far* away (opposite meaning)
   C no: was *obvious* to her
   D no: was *reachable*

7. A yes: *by* (preposition): *by the side of the ... door*
   B no: *next* to the side
   C no: *close* to the side
   D no: *outside* the house

8. A no: in *so far as* being able to make the tea
   B yes: *order* (part of expression): *in order to make sth*
   C no: in *view* of the changes
   D no: in *case* someone was thirsty

9. A no: the day was *ended*
   B yes: *done* (past participle – passive): *was done*
   C no: the wood was *used up*
   D no: an ambition is *fulfilled*

10. A no: *often* feed the animals (incorrect meaning)
    B no: *sometimes* feed the animals (incorrect meaning)
    C yes: *always* (frequency adverb): *she made sure she always fed the animals*
    D no: *seldom* feed the animals (incorrect meaning)

11. A no: *sat at* the table
    B no: put the meat *in* the pot
    C no: go *without* food
    D yes: *on* (preposition): *fed the animals on the left-overs*

12. A no: get *down* to work
    B no: get *away* with murder
    C no: get *along* with a person
    D yes: *on* (particle – part of phrasal verb): *got on with breakfast*

13. A no: the plates would be *cleaned* before being washed
    B no: the plates would be *removed* from the table
    C yes: *washed* (past participle): *the plates would be washed*
    D no: shoes are *polished*

14. A no: this *time* of day
    B yes: *process* (noun): *This process of lighting the cooker*
    C no: a *procession* moved down the hill
    D no: this *progress* made the housewives happy

15. A yes: *place* (noun – used in an expression): *in place of*
    B no: an *exchange* of money
    C no: in *favour* of a political party
    D no: in the *position* of mayor

Total: 15 marks

PART 2

1 mark for each correct answer.

16. *with* (preposition: *help with*)
17. *done/finished/completed/started/carried out* (verb – passive: *be done*)
18. *which* (Stonehenge + non-defining relative pronoun + clause)
19. *on* (preposition of date: *on a midsummer day*)
20. *out* (particle – part of phrasal verb: *laid out*)
21. *each* (determiner – distributive adjective: *each pillar*)
22. *middle/centre* (noun: *In the middle of*)
23. *always/sometimes/often* (adverb of frequency: *have always wondered*)
24. *those* (determiner – demonstrative adjective: *those ... stones*)
25. *an* (indefinite article: *an area*)
26. *about/explaining* (preposition: *theories ... about*)
27. *One* (many theories + adjective + *theory*)
28. *space* (outer + noun)
29. *and* (conjunction – joins two equal statements)
30. *brought/carried/moved* (past participle – present perfect passive: *have been brought*)

Total: 15 marks

PART 3

1 mark for each correct answer.

31. *is an expert on* (word set *to be an expert on sth*)
32. *are under age* (are not old enough to word set *to be under age*)
33. *I hadn't lent* (I regret + I gave to clause – conditional)
34. *was so boring* (such a boring movie to word set *it was so boring*)
35. *are supposed to be* (People say + are to passive verb)
36. *out of the question* (word set *it's out of the question*)
37. *get on with* (continue to phrasal verb – 2 particles)
38. *not as fast as* (word set *to be not as fast as sb at doing sth*)
39. *can't/cannot decide on* (can't make up my mind to verb + preposition)
40. *on your own* (by yourself to word set *on your own*)

Total: 10 marks

PART 4

1 mark for each correct answer.

41. √
42. *been* (past participle – past perfect passive – incorrect tense)
43. *of* (preposition – we make a study *of* sth)
44. √
45. *was* (auxiliary – past passive – incorrect tense)
46. *just* (adverb – used with a perfect tense)
47. *a* (article – used to show a specific student's life, not in general)
48. *there* (adverb of place – incorrect use)
49. *with* (preposition – we learn *with* someone)
50. *deal* (noun – would need to be *a great deal of help*)
51. √
52. √
53. *the* (definite article – incorrect with prepositional phrase *on foot*)
54. *much* (adverb of degree – incorrect to use with *well*)
55. √

Total: 15 marks

PART 5

1 mark for each correct answer.

56 *lovely* (noun/verb to adjective – *a lovely place*)
57 *variety* (verb to noun – *the great variety*)
58 *dissatisfied* (verb to adjective + prefix *dis-* – *No one can be dissatisfied*)
59 *quickly* (adjective to adverb – *quickly growing*)
60 *foreigners* (adjective to noun – *many foreigners*)
61 *living* (verb/adjective to adjective – *the living conditions*)
62 *entertainment* (verb to noun – *all types of entertainment*)
63 *historical* (noun to adjective – *historical buildings*)
64 *peaceful* (noun to adjective – *peaceful atmosphere*)
65 *sightseer* (noun to compound noun – *a sightseer*)

Total: 10 marks

TOTAL PAPER: 65 marks

Paper 4 Listening

Exercise on similar sounds
B

PART 1

1 mark for each 'yes' answer.

1 **A** yes: *sheep*
   B no: *sheep* (not ship) (sounds)
   C no: *sheep* (not asleep) (sounds)

2 **A** no: *also giving a professional presentation*
   B no: *a commercial and a professional*
   C yes: *if you call me*

3 **A** no: *at first we thought we'd make it at our house*
   B yes: *we booked St Michael's hall*
   C no: *To the left of the park* (same)

4 **A** yes: *Try putting your coin in there ... There's your ticket*
   B no: *Having trouble?*
   C no: *coin* (same)

5 **A** no: *you're away all the time on business*
   B no: *clubs* (same)
   C yes: *I miss the children ... It's still not too late to have another*

6 **A** yes: *I didn't want it so short*
   B no: – (accept.)
   C no: *But that's the way you, you told me to do it* (inton.)

7 **A** yes: *factory ... now trapped inside ... Out here*
   B no: *factory ... Out here*
   C no: –

8 **A** no: *read* (same)
   B no: *history* (same)
   C yes: *we shall read about the features of each ... These continents*

Total: 8 marks

PART 2

1 mark for each correct answer. Spelling mistakes do not matter.

9   enter/go into/use each other's/the wrong washrooms: *At no time may boys enter the girls' washrooms, or the other way around*
10 clean/tidy: *keep the toilets and showers clean*
11 accompanied by/with a member of staff/teacher: *stay out of here unless accompanied by a member of staff*
12 use/enter/go in: *don't use the teachers' washrooms or toilets*
13 emergencies/help/questions/problems: *assistant helpers ... if there is an emergency, please speak to them*
14 8.00 am/in the morning to 8.00 pm/in the evening: *Swimming is allowed between 8.00 am and 8.00 pm*
15 (too much/a lot of) noise: *try not to make too much noise*
16 four/4 hours (of lessons): *You will all have four hours of lessons*

17 sporting activities/sports: *The rest of the day will be filled with sporting activities and excursions*
18 a mess/it dirty/messy: *don't leave a mess*

Total: 10 marks

PART 3

1 mark for each correct answer.

19 **E** *they forgot our wake-up calls ... missed breakfast*
20 **A** *no sign of the coach ... discovered it*
21 **F** *got the addresses of the other people*
22 **C** *museum ... it didn't open until late afternoon ... too late*
23 **B** *the whole day with nothing to do*

Total: 5 marks

PART 4

1 mark for each correct answer.

24 **H** *Hi there ... I'm not going to sit here waiting* (intonation – cheerful, impatient, upset)
25 **C** *James, this is Trevor*
26 **C** *I'll just run a security check on her first*
27 **T** *you two go on. I can stay and do up the rest of this lot*
28 **T** *Look, there's no, there's no reason for you to stay longer. I can uh, easily ...*
29 **H** *Darling, if this takes much longer, I'll have to go alone*
30 **H** *I'm not going to sit here waiting*

Total: 7 marks

TOTAL PAPER: 30 marks

Paper 5 Speaking

PART 1

You might like to give the students some more practice on the themes:

1 What do you think you'll be doing ten years from now? Are you optimistic or pessimistic? Do you want to change the direction in which you are heading? Why/why not?
2 Did you learn English through private lessons or in a classroom? Have you been pleased with your lessons? Why/why not?

PARTS 1, 2 and 4

Teacher's notes
Answers are free, but make sure that students address the questions asked of them.

PART 3

Teacher's notes
The most obvious solution is that Room A should be the cafeteria (it has large windows so that people can view the planes arriving/taking off) and Room B should have the luggage carousels (it's near the gates where people will be coming off the plane). However, if the students come up with a different solution, and can give sound reasons for their choice, the answer will be acceptable.

TEST 5

Paper 1 Reading

PART 1

1 mark for each correct answer.

1 **H** *theatres around the country*
2 **C** *This week's offers ... producers ... Theatre Weekend ... ballet matinee*
3 **E** *to book seats*
4 **B** *Send a cheque ... made payable to The Theatre Club*
5 **F** *New Year's Day ... Christmas ... Santa*
6 **D** *learn at first hand the producer's role*
7 **G** *chocolate ... sweets ... hot chocolate ... Cadbury World*

Total: 7 marks

PART 2

1 mark for each 'yes' answer.

8 **A** yes: *the last of the lights had gone out* (implying that the people in the house had gone to sleep)
   B no: *the car would be facing the right way* (same)
   C no: *nylon ropes and the torch were on the passenger seat beside him*
   D no: *The moon was full*

9 **A** yes: *so that the car would be facing the right way for when he left ... the quicker he could leave the easier it would be*
   B no: *problem* (same)
   C no: *He stopped the car just past the entrance to the driveway* (same)
   D no: *Just after midnight the last of the lights had gone out* (same)

10 **A** no: *–* (neither one) (accept.)
   B no: *determinedly* (but not disappointed) (accept.)
   C no: *–* (neither one) (accept.)
   D yes: *Treading slowly and determinedly* (both)

11 **A** no: *the low dry-stone wall* (same)
   B no: *The moon* (same)
   C yes: *making the house look almost as if it were all lit up*
   D no: *the slope* (same)

12 **A** no: *slowly and determinedly* (opp.)
   B yes: *slowly and determinedly*
   C no: *towards the house* (not away from it)
   D no: *slowly and determinedly* (opp.)

13 **A** no: *despite his keeping well against the wall* (opp./neg.)
   B yes: *but nobody stirred*
   C no: *–*
   D no: *but nobody stirred*

14 **A** no: *The kind that decorators use* (same)
   B no: *was locked*
   C yes: *he opened the door slowly. There was a smell of stale smoke*
   D no: *projection screen ... slide projector ... sound projector* (accept.)

15 **A** no: *–* (he wasn't 'caught')
   B no: *he guessed it was not used as a bedroom ... papers and books ... slide projector and a 16mm sound projector* (accept.)
   C yes: *gun ... he guessed it was not used as a bedroom ... papers and books ... slide projector and a 16mm sound projector*
   D no: *–*

Total: 8 marks

PART 3

1 mark for each correct answer.

16 **B** *Let's ... Our* with *we've ... we; Most bats are gentle and kindly* with *But unless we've been introduced ... how can we love them*
17 **F** *cavemen* with *the ancient civilisations; Their first reactions ... fear ... respect* with *were sympathetic ... respected*

18 **A** *'chiroptera'* with *This means* (definition)
19 **D** *of the more than 1,000 kinds of bats on our planet, only one, the vampire bat* with *just one out of more than one thousand; sucks blood* with *are completely vegetarian*
20 **C** *great communities of bats* with *they; In the evenings and nights* with *Then*
21 **G** *Bats* with *them; our planet* with *we*

Total: 6 marks

PART 4

1 mark for each correct answer.

22 **A** *mining company ... gold*
23 **E** *telephony, data communications and mobile telephony*
24 **G** *is owned by ... and by key executives of the bank*
25 **A** *operating gold mines located in North and South America*
26 **D** *diverse products contribute to the health and well-being of all age groups*
27 **B/H** *oil and gas company*
28 **H/B** *oil and gas reserves*
29 **C/G** *bank offers corporate financial services*
30 **G/C** *bank focuses on asset management*
31 **B/F** *has about 12,000 employees*
32 **F/B** *employing over 56,000 people worldwide*
33 **D/F** *pharmaceutical company ... products contribute to the health and well-being of all age groups*
34 **F/D** *treatment of disease ... development of new drugs*

1 mark for the 'yes' answer.

35 **A** no: this might be the ultimate goal, but the specific purpose of this text is for people to order reports (accept.)
   B no: not asking for CVs or personnel
   C yes: *Choose which of the following reports you wish sent to you*
   D no: not advertising products

Total: 14 marks

TOTAL PAPER: 35 marks

Paper 2 Writing

PART 1

Students should include
Instructions: write to cinema manager, went to cinema with family, problems in watching the film, safety hazards, disappointed.
Picture/text: forced to sit up front and at side and couldn't see, boxes blocking left exit, right exit locked (what would have happened in a fire?), exit lights were distracting.
Notes: overcrowded cinema, poor soundtrack, poor colour in film, sounds of staff in snack bar, leads you to the decision that you would think carefully before visiting the cinema again.

TOTAL PAPER: 40 marks

Paper 3 Use of English

PART 1

1 mark for each 'yes' answer.

1 **A** yes: *leave* (infinitive): *a place where ... never want to leave*
   B no: *to go* (opposite meaning)
   C no: *to depart from somewhere/for somewhere*
   D no: *to set off* (opposite meaning)

2 **A** no: *the boy is nearly outside the park*
   B no: *the boy is almost outside the park*
   C yes: *just* (adjective – used for emphasis): *just outside Paris*
   D no: *recently built outside Paris*

3 **A** no: *composed of different areas*
   B yes: *created* (verb – simple past): *especially created to provide the best*

C no: *consisted* of different parts
D no: *placed* outside Paris

4 A no: the *rights* of guests (incorrect meaning)
   B yes: *demands* (noun): *demands of its new guests*
   C no: the guests' comfort was taken into *consideration*
   D no: they had a lot of *dealings* with the guests

5 A no: food is *shared* out among the guests
   B no: food is *distributed* among the guests
   C no: the park is *calculated* to be very profitable
   D yes: *divided* (verb – present passive): *is divided into five areas*

6 A no: *Whereas* the guests … (incorrect meaning)
   B no: *Unless* the guests … (incorrect meaning)
   C yes: *As if* (conjunction – for comparison): *As if in a film*
   D no: *Wherever* the guests … (incorrect meaning)

7 A no: the *staff* take the guests along
   B yes: *guests* (noun): *the guests are taken along*
   C no: the *members* of the club are taken along
   D no: *teams* of workers take the guests along

8 A yes: *full* (adjective): *full of excitement*
   B no: *crowded* with people
   C no: *complete* with excitement
   D no: *packed* with excitement

9 A yes: *look* (phrasal verb): *look into the future*
   B no: *go* into the future (impossible)
   C no: *run* into someone you know
   D no: *turn* into world travellers

10 A no: the trees have been *dug* up from the ground
    B yes: *planted* (verb – present perfect): *The trees that have been planted*
    C no: the trees have *grown* in the park
    D no: things should not be *stuck* on the trees

11 A no: in *answer* to a question
    B no: in *reply* to the letter
    C no: in *debt* to someone
    D yes: *addition* (noun – prepositional phrase): *In addition to these six hotels*

12 A no: a *supply* of sporting equipment
    B yes: *shortage* (noun): *no shortage of … opportunities*
    C no: a large *amount* of excitement
    D no: a large *quantity* of food

13 A no: *expect* to find
    B no: *hope* to achieve your dreams
    C yes: *wish* (verb – present participle): *you may wish to follow*
    D no: *order* someone to follow

14 A no: *contacted* by phone
    B no: easily *arrived* at by road
    C yes: *reached* (verb – present passive): *easily reached by road or rail*
    D no: *entered* through a large gate

15 A yes: *relaxed* (verb – past participle): *you will be relaxed enough to enjoy*
    B no: the guests walked in an *unhurried* manner
    C no: it will be *easy* enough to enjoy the park
    D no: you will be too *lazy* to enjoy the park

Total: 15 marks

PART 2

1 mark for each correct answer.

16 *one/them* (carnival processions + pronoun)
17 *along/up/down/through* (preposition of movement: *along the street*)
18 *a* (indefinite article: *a wonderful time*)
19 *come* (past participle – past perfect: *had come*)
20 *no* (adverb – before comparative: *no longer*)
21 *faces* (masks + noun)
22 *not* (adverb – after modal verb – negative meaning: *could not believe*)
23 *was* (auxiliary – verb *to be* – past progressive: *was smiling*)
24 *but* (conjunction – joins two contrasting statements)
25 *so* (adverb of degree: *so much*)

26 *on* (particle – part of phrasal verb: *kept on*)
27 *heard/saw* (clause *he did not hear me at first* + verb – simple past)
28 *him* (*brother* + *to* + object pronoun)
29 *procession/parade* (noun + *over*)
30 *in* (prepositional phrase: *in agreement*)

Total: 15 marks

PART 3

1 mark for each correct answer.

31 *takes pleasure in* (*really likes* to word set *to take pleasure in sth*)
32 *don't need much/needn't take much/don't have to take much* (word set *not to need much luggage*)
33 *may not have received* (*Perhaps + hasn't received* to modal verb)
34 *take care of* (phrasal verb *look after* to *take care of*)
35 *could not decide* (*was not certain* to negative modal verb)
36 *to prevent the dog (from)* (word set *to do sth* to *prevent sb from doing sth else*)
37 *objected to paying* (*did not like to pay* to verb + preposition + gerund)
38 *such a nice day* (*The day was so nice* to word set *such a nice day*)
39 *saw everyone except* (word set *to see everybody except sb*)
40 *drop in on* (*visit* to phrasal verb – 2 particles)

Total: 10 marks

PART 4

1 mark for each correct answer.

41 *have* (auxiliary – no such tense as *could have ask*)
42 *a* (indefinite article – not used before *someone*)
43 *that* (conjunction – incorrect with an infinitive after a reporting verb *agreed to help us*)
44 √
45 √
46 *them* (object pronoun – incorrect when used with the noun *materials* in the object part of the sentence)
47 √
48 *our* (possessive pronoun – incorrect when used with word set *a game of football*)
49 √
50 *had* (auxiliary – past perfect tense – incorrect verb tense: *sat/ordered/looked*)
51 *he* (subject pronoun – referring to *man* – double subject)
52 √
53 *of* (preposition – possessive – incorrect when used with word set *a few hours*)
54 *be* (infinitive – no such tense as *to be finish*)
55 *it* (object pronoun – phrasal verb *make up for* does not take an object when completed by phrase *lost time*)

Total: 15 marks

PART 5

1 mark for each correct answer.

56 *heavily* (adjective to adverb – *had been raining heavily*)
57 *careful* (noun/verb to adjective – *very careful*)
58 *judgement* (verb/noun to noun – *their good judgement*)
59 *setback* (noun to compound noun – *the setback*)
60 *unbearable* (adjective to adjective + prefix *un-* – *things were unbearable*)
61 *optimistic* (noun to adjective – *they had to be optimistic*)
62 *leader* (verb to noun – *Their leader*)
63 *importance* (adjective to noun – *The importance*)
64 *harden* (adjective to verb – *to harden*)
65 *dangerous* (noun to adjective – *how dangerous*)

Total: 10 marks

TOTAL PAPER: 65 marks

Paper 4 Listening

Teacher's notes
In Test 5, the tape includes a fuller beginning and ending, like the Cambridge First Certificate Examination. At the end of the test, let students fill in the answer sheet (at the back of the book) as instructed.

PART 1

1 mark for each 'yes' answer.

1 **A** no: – (accept.)
   B yes: *would you mind ... opening the boot*
   C no: *you can go now*

2 **A** no: *Want to look your very best ...*
   B no: *industry's technology leader ... state-of-the-art* (but it's not the purpose)
   C yes: **Suretan** *is ... At leading beauty salons everywhere*

3 **A** yes: *Well, it* **sounds** *good*
   B no: *Well, it* **sounds** *good* (stress)
   C no: *Well, it* **sounds** *good* (stress)

4 **A** no: *have you?* (question tags, not a final rise) (inton.)
   B yes: *have you?* (question tags, final fall)
   C no: *have you?* (question tags, final fall) (inton.)

5 **A** no: *watch* (not wash) (sounds)
   B yes: *watch ... eat foods that are full of iron*
   C no: *watch* (not walk) (sounds)

6 **A** no: *but the players are ... we're running around that field the whole game*
   B no: *we're running around that field the whole game*
   C yes: *we're running around that field the whole game ... And nobody likes us*

7 **A** no: *Monday to Wednesday*
   B yes: *Thursday to Saturday*
   C no: *Sunday*

8 **A** yes: *Mr Worthington ... Carl ... Sorry to bother you at home ... sir*
   B no: *Mr Worthington ... sir* (reg.)
   C no: *Mr Worthington ... sir* (reg.)

Total: 8 marks

PART 2

1 mark for each correct answer. Spelling mistakes do not matter.

9 adults: *they will then have weight problems in adult life*
10 get overweight/eat too much (in the first place)/overeat: *they really shouldn't have let them get overweight in the first place*
11 pleasant/relaxed/a time to chat/talk/discuss: *mealtime is a pleasant, relaxed time when you can chat*
12 slowly: *If the child eats slowly, he'll have the time to start feeling full*
13 wait: *let him or her wait before giving a second helping*
14 stop (eating): *Babies know when they're full and they just stop eating*

15 (also) overweight (too): *If both parents are overweight the risk goes up to 80 per cent*
16 times/hours/intervals: *thinner children eat snacks and meals according to a more regular timetable ... four o'clock*
17 chocolate/sweet: *you have to give him the occasional chocolate as well*
18 embarrass them/make them ashamed: *never to embarrass them in front of other people*

Total: 10 marks

PART 3

1 mark for each correct answer.

19 **D** *their photographer will call you*
20 **F** *set up a photo shoot with you ... Leave a message on my machine*
21 **B** *you haven't bothered to phone us for two weeks*
22 **E** *Don't you think the time is right ... Jack*
23 **A** *we're going out at eight tonight*

Total: 5 marks

PART 4

1 mark for each correct answer.

24 false: *Light Publishers* (sounds)
25 true: *Mr Parker* instead of *Mitch* (reg.)
26 false: *Well, that's what everybody* **thinks** (stress)
27 false: *started writing when she was only nine years old*
28 true: *I'm always looking for appealing stories to be sent in to us*
29 false: *Some ... writers might send in a 'dummy'* (sing.)
30 false: *a candle with a flame in front of an open window*

Total: 7 marks

TOTAL PAPER: 30 marks

Paper 5 Speaking

PARTS 1, 2 and 4

Teacher's notes
Answers are free, but make sure that students address the questions asked of them.

PART 3

Teacher's notes
Area A could be the cooking/eating area (it is close to the house and the electrical sockets) and Area B could be the swimming pool (it's near the well). However, it could be argued that it would be a better choice to put the swimming pool in Area A (farther from the low fence and possible danger of nursery school children seeing it and climbing in). Both answers are valid, as long as students can give sound reasons for their choice.